Cloud Computing: Principles, Design and Applications

Cloud Computing: Principles, Design and Applications

David Fisher

www.statesacademicpress.com

Published by States Academic Press,
109 South 5th Street,
Brooklyn, NY 11249, USA

ISBN: 978-1-63989-115-3

Cataloging-in-Publication Data

Cloud computing : principles, design and applications / David Fisher.
p. cm.
Includes bibliographical references and index.
ISBN 978-1-63989-115-3
1. Cloud computing. 2. Electronic data processing--Distributed processing. 3. Web services.
I. Fisher, David.
QA76.585 .C56 2022
004.678 2--dc23

For information on all States Academic Press publications
visit our website at www.statesacademicpress.com

Contents

Preface VII

Chapter 1   **Understanding Cloud Computing** 1

     i.   Characteristics of Cloud 12

     ii.   Evolution of Cloud 19

     iii.   Cloud Computing Technologies 20

     iv.   Social Cloud Computing 48

     v.   Cloud Architecture 50

     vi.   Cloud Model 55

Chapter 2   **Cloud Deployment and Service Models** 57

     i.   Cloud Deployment Models 57

     ii.   Cloud Service Models 81

Chapter 3   **Cloud Storage** 90

     i.   Object Storage 94

     ii.   File Hosting Service 102

     iii.   Cloud Storage Gateway 106

     iv.   Cloud E-commerce 140

     v.   Cooperative Storage Cloud 143

Chapter 4   **Distributed Systems and Computing** 146

     i.   Distributed Systems 146

     ii.   Distributed Computing 148

     iii.   Communication in Distributed Computing 154

     iv.   Interprocess Communication in Distributed Systems 176

Chapter 5   **Parallel Computing** 178

     i.   Ocean Current Simulation 211

     ii.   Bit-level Parallelism 225

iii.   Instruction-level Parallelism 225

iv.   Task Parallelism 228

Permissions

Index

Preface

The delivery of various computing services such as servers, databases, storage and analytics in the absence of any direct active management by the user is known as cloud computing. These are usually provided by large centers which are situated over multiple locations. Some of the important characteristics of cloud computing are agility, device and location independence, performance, productivity, and security. Deployment models refer to the environmental parameters affecting the location and ownership of the infrastructure. A few of the various deployment models are private cloud, public cloud, community cloud and distributed cloud. Cloud computing finds extensive application in the fields of data analysis, audio-video streaming, embedded intelligence, application testing, etc. This book is a compilation of chapters that discuss the most vital concepts in the field of cloud computing. While understanding the long-term perspectives of the topics, it makes an effort in highlighting their impact as a modern tool for the growth of the discipline. This book is a complete source of knowledge on the present status of this important field.

A detailed account of the significant topics covered in this book is provided below:

Chapter 1- The delivery of computing services such as servers, storage, software, networking, databases over the Internet is termed as cloud computing. This is an introductory chapter which will introduce briefly all the significant aspects of cloud computing such as characteristics of cloud, evolution of cloud, cloud computing technologies, etc.

Chapter 2- The type of access to a cloud is defined through cloud deployment models. A few types of cloud deployment models are public cloud, private cloud, hybrid cloud and community cloud. This chapter closely examines the key concepts of these cloud deployment models as well as cloud service models to provide an extensive understanding of the subject.

Chapter 3- The digital data in cloud computing is physically stored in multiple servers which are managed and owned by hosting companies. It involves keeping the data safe and accessible. The topics elaborated in this chapter will help in gaining a better perspective about the different aspects of data storage in cloud computing such as object storage and cooperative storage cloud.

Chapter 4- Distributed systems refer to the systems which have multiple components situated on different machines which are in communication with each other and coordinate their actions in such a manner that it appears as a single coherent system to the end user. This chapter discusses in detail the different aspects of distributed systems and computing.

Chapter 5- The process of breaking down larger problems into smaller operations which can be worked upon simultaneously by multiple processors is known as parallel computing. Some of the major types of parallelism are bit-level parallelism, instruction-level parallelism and task parallelism. This chapter has been carefully written to provide an easy understanding of these facets of parallel computing.

It gives me an immense pleasure to thank our entire team for their efforts. Finally in the end, I would like to thank my family and colleagues who have been a great source of inspiration and support.

David Fisher

Understanding Cloud Computing

The delivery of computing services such as servers, storage, software, networking, databases over the Internet is termed as cloud computing. This is an introductory chapter which will introduce briefly all the significant aspects of cloud computing such as characteristics of cloud, evolution of cloud, cloud computing technologies, etc.

Cloud computing is the delivery of different services through the Internet. These resources include tools and applications like data storage, servers, databases, networking, and software. Rather than keeping files on a proprietary hard drive or local storage device, cloud-based storage makes it possible to save them to a remote database. As long as an electronic device has access to the web, it has access to the data and the software programs to run it.

Cloud computing is a popular option for people and businesses for a number of reasons including cost savings, increased productivity, speed and efficiency, performance, and security. Cloud computing is named as such because the information being accessed is found remotely in the cloud or a virtual space. Companies that provide cloud services enable users to store files and applications on remote servers and then access all the data via the Internet. This means the user is not required to be in a specific place to gain access to it, allowing the user to work remotely.

Cloud computing takes all the heavy lifting involved in crunching and processing data away from the device you carry around or sit and work at. It also moves all of that work to huge computer clusters far away in cyberspace. The Internet becomes the cloud and voilà, your data, work, and applications are available from any device with which you can connect to the Internet, anywhere in the world. Cloud computing can be both public and private. Public cloud services provide their services over the Internet for a fee. Private cloud services, on the other hand, only provide services to a certain number of people. These services are a system of networks that supply hosted services. There is also a hybrid option, which combines elements of both the public and private services.

The beginning of this journey started in 1940 and this phase went on for about 15 years till the first change came in 1956. This phase of 15 years is termed as the First Generation of computing devices. The computers in this era used vacuum tubes for circuitry and magnetic drums for memory. They were very large in size, often taking up entire rooms. They were also very expensive to operate needing a great deal of electricity and generating a lot of heat often causing malfunctions. First generation computers relied on machine language. This is a binary language that is understood by computers. At a point in time only one problem could be solved by these computers. Punched cards and paper tapes were used for inputs while outputs would be printed on papers. Not only were these hard to operate, they were also not very reliable. Two examples of computers of the First Generation are UNIVAC and ENIAC.

The Second Generation of computing devices started in around 1956when transistors replaced the vacuum tubes. While the transistors were invented in 1947, its use in computers came in around 10 years later and started the next generation of computing devices. With transistors, the size of the computers became smaller and the computers became cheaper too. Not only binary or machine language was replaced by symbolic language and the operating system was improved making the machines faster during this generation, high-level language appeared with the early versions of FORTRAN and COBOL. This generation also saw the first computers that stored instructions in their memory.

Around 1964, when transistors became smaller and could be placed on silicon chips in the form of integrated circuits, the Second Generation gave way to the Third Generation of computing devices. In this generation, computers became more efficient, input and output devices like the keyboard and monitor appeared and communication with the operating system was made possible. The ability of multi programming, i.e., running different applications at the same time, marks an important achievement of this era. This era also made computers available for the mass audience due to two factors: size and price, both of which became lesser.

Around 1971 came the age of microprocessor, with the ability to put a large number of integrated circuits on one chip. Intel 4004 chip marked the beginning of this era that could fit in all the components of a computer in a chip. With this, the concept of home computers appeared. Graphical User Interface (GUI) along with mouse and other handheld devices became part of the computer in this era termed as the Fourth Generation. Many new features were added in this generation and modern computers of today continue to have all these features developed in the Fourth Generation.

Around 1990, development of computing devices was augmented with the appearance of Artificial Intelligence and parallel processing. This age had the aim of using Natural Language Processing and providing the comfort of interacting with the computers using natural languages. This is the current era, which is still developing and is termed as the Fifth Generation.

Evolution of Internet and Internet-Connected Devices

With the advent of computing devices, other areas such as networking, the Internet and computing paradigms also have seen major evolutions. However, these cannot be demarked as clearly as the computing devices. Advances in the concepts of networking made way for the unprecedented growth of the Internet and internet connected devices. With so much of advancement all around, the requirement today is to provide concurrent computing services to billions of the Internet users. This can be made possible in two ways. The first is that we use supercomputers to provide such services, which is expensive and hard to implement at the required level since this calls for a large number of supercomputers. The second option is to use large datacenters with clusters of commodity computers that can replicate the power of supercomputers at a feasible level. The computing world, by and large, used the second option and since it is financially not so challenging, we saw an unprecedented growth in the internet-connected devices. It is predicted that this number is going to grow more in future. The world is witnessing an unprecedented growth in the number of internet-connected devices in the last two decades. We also observe in this figure that while in the five years between 2015 and 2020 the world population is to going to grow from 7.2 to 7.6 billion; both the internet-connected devices and the internet-connected devices per person are going to become almost double. This comparison perhaps provides a perspective to the rate of growth of the Internet and the devices connected to it.

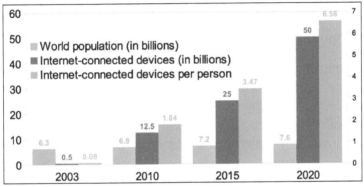

Internet-Connected Devices.

Along with the increase in the number of Internet users and devices, the mechanism of Internet usages also has gone through a major evolution. While initially users were happy by merely publishing and obtaining available information, the phenomenal growth in the Internet usage gave rise to greater interaction leading to the need of intelligent and machine-based automatic discovery mechanisms. Large number users in the Internet also meant the use of different terms to indicate same concept and hence the advent of semantic computing came forth. Currently, with the popularity of social networking and data analytics, new challenges have appeared in the horizon and the corresponding development has to match these growth as well in the form of deep web.

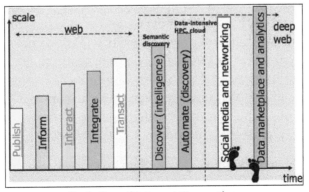

Evolution of Internet Computing.

Evolution of Computing Paradigms

Along with all computing devices and the Internet usage, computing paradigms also developed keeping pace with these advancements. While initially computing was perceived to be centralized, other advanced mechanisms came about. Overall, the computing paradigms can be categorized as follows:

- Centralized Computing.

- Parallel Computing.

- Cluster Computing.

- Distributed Computing.

- Cloud Computing.

In centralized computing paradigm, all computer resources such as processors, memory, storage etc. are typically located in one physical system and controlled centrally. Resources are shared and used by various processes under one operating system. While such systems can offer high security and integrity and low maintenance with high reliability, they suffer from scalability, inflexibility and lack of usability problems.

Parallel computing paradigm refers to the mechanism of a computer system, which makes it capable of running computations parallelly. Typically processors share a central memory and communicate through the shared memory in a tightly coupled manner. Alternatively, they can be loosely coupled having distributed memory. Communication in this case, can be via message passing. Cluster computing paradigm refers to a cluster of connected computers. It is a type of parallel or distributed processing system, consisting of a collection of interconnected stand-alone computers cooperatively working together representing a single, integrated computing resource.

Distributed computing paradigm consists of a collection of independent computers, each having its own memory and other capabilities cooperating with each other to solve a problem. The participating computers communicate with each other through message passing and the group appears to be a single coherent system to the users. While cluster is a collection of tightly coupled independent computers, often kept in the same room, that work in cooperation with each other to achieve a goal with the help of specialized software, distributed computing has no such restrictions. In a distributed paradigm, geographically dispersed independent computers can communicate using message passing in a loosely coupled environment. What is common in both is the ability to achieve the power of a supercomputer by harnessing the power of a large number of workstations. In reality, cluster computing is a special case of distributed computing.

Last but not the least is cloud computing paradigm, which is a specialized distributed environment. It is an internet-based paradigm, with shared resources that is capable of providing services on-demand. Cloud helps achieve the concept of utility computing in which computing services is offered as an utility in a similar manner as any other utility services such as electricity. Even though cloud is a special kind of distributed computing environment, it is interesting to track down the path through which it came about. Web hosting is the mechanism of providing space in the World Wide Web to host one's server(s). Users could be Application Service Providers (ASP-s) who offered applications as service delivered to a rather smaller number of users. However, such service offerings suffered from the problem of scalability, which was mitigated by the use of virtualization. This made this model more effective and financially viable and gave rise to the concept of offering software services to a larger number of users giving birth to Software as a Service (SaaS). Eventually SaaS grew in popularity due to the ease of use, giving rise to what is today known as cloud, where not only software, but also platform and infrastructure are offered as a service, called Platform as a Service (PaaS) and Infrastructure as a Service (IaaS) respectively. In the current cloud technology, however, it is possible to provide anything and everything as a service, which gave rise to the term Anything-as-a-Service (XaaS) being widely used.

Gartner's Hype Cycle

With the continuously changing backdrop of computing, it is important to track the trends and make relevant predictions that would help the industry, researchers as well as the users stay abreast of the advancements coming in the near and far future. In this respect, a very dependable opinion and forecast is provided by the company Gartner. They provide insight with respect to all aspects of information technology. Among other methods of prediction, Gartner uses a graphical presentation called "The Hype Cycle" to represent the maturity, adoption and social application of new and emerging technologies. As goes without saying, the journey of cloud from a fledgling SaaS to full-fledged technology also attracted a lot of the predictions and opinions. Industry experts as well as researchers expressed their opinions about the possible future of cloud, as they thought applicable. To understand the pointers provided by Gartner, and to match it with reality, first let us understand the Hype Cycle by Gartner and widely used by the IT industry. Figure below shows the basic structure of Hype Cycle.

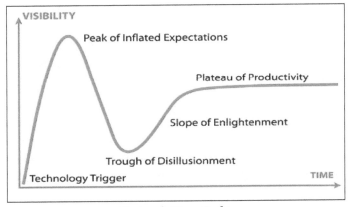

Gartner's Hype Cycle.

The Cycle is divided in five phases, the first one being the Technology Trigger. A technology is positioned in this phase when a new and potential technology comes into the horizon. A technology here indicates that there exists some proof-of-concept and the technology has generated significant interest. While no usable products are expected from a new technology in this phase, there must be enough promise from it. The next phase if Peak of Inflated Expectations. While a powerful appearance of a technology produces sufficient interests among the industry users, it is highly possible that the concept may fail. This happens especially if the technology generates a very high expectation it may not be able to meet and hence fails completely. Every emerging technology goes through this test of expectation and has to survive to emerge in the next phase.

Trough of Disillusionment is the third phase when through experiments and implementations, users taste an initial disappointed about the technology. At this phase, the producers of the technology get the verdict, whether the technology would survive or be removed. Investments continue only if the surviving providers who continued to believe in the new technology can improve their products to the satisfaction of the users who have tried adopting the technology initially. A survivor through the Trough of Disillusionment phase would emerge in the Slope of Enlightenment. In this phase, the technology is believed to be good ready to be adopted by many and hence more funding is channelized. New products as well as new support appear in the market, although the adoption is not yet complete since the more cautious companies still stay out.

The last and final phase is the Plateau of Productivity. This phase witnesses adoption of the technology at all level. Products mature and providers that pass through the assessment of the matured users continue to flourish. This phase indicates that the technology has matured and is going to be used widely as applicable. Special symbols mark the number of years predicted for an emerging technology to reach maturity and market adoption. The hollow circles indicate technologies that are predicted to be adopted by the industry in two years, the gray circles in two to five years, the solid circles in five to 10 years, and the triangles denote those that would require more than 10 years. The crossed circles represent technologies that are predicted to become obsolete before they reach the plateau.

Gartner publishes many articles, graphs, charts and other documents every now and then for the information and knowledge of the users and practitioners of various technologies. Hype Cycle for Emerging Technologies is published every year by Gartner indicating the current position of all upcoming technologies and Gartner's prediction about their future adoption by the IT world. All new and emerging technologies appear in the Hype Cycle based on two perspectives: their position in a specific phase of the Hype Cycle indicate the relevance of the technology and the accompanying indicator describes the number of years the technology would still take to be adopted in the mainstream, if at all. With this knowledge about the Hype Cycle, let us now turn to cloud computing and see how it faired as an emerging technology. Cloud computing first appeared in the Hype Cycle for Emerging Technologies in the year of 2008. Cloud computing (inside yellow box) was in phase 1 with a promise of coming into the mainstream in 2-5 years indicated by the gray circle.

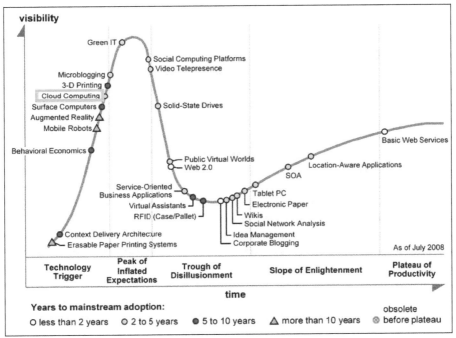

Hype Cycle for Emerging Technologies, 2008.

The next two years saw cloud computing in the Peak of Inflated Expectations. However, it started its downward journey through the next four years.

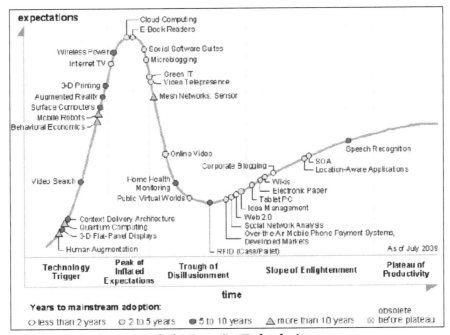

Hype Cycle for Emerging Technologies, 2009.

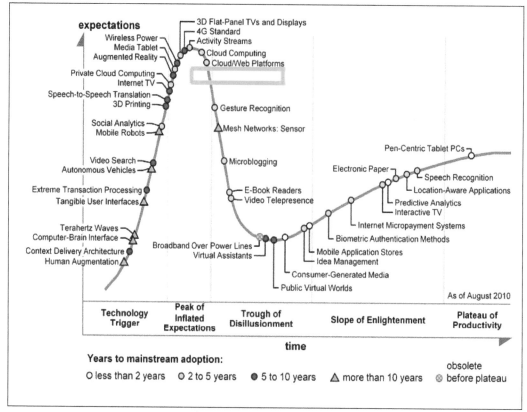

Hype Cycle for Emerging Technologies, 2010.

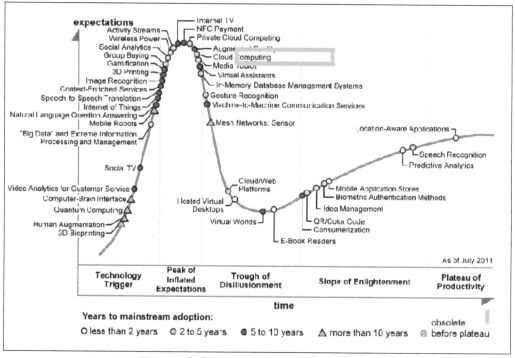

Hype Cycle for Emerging Technologies, 2011.

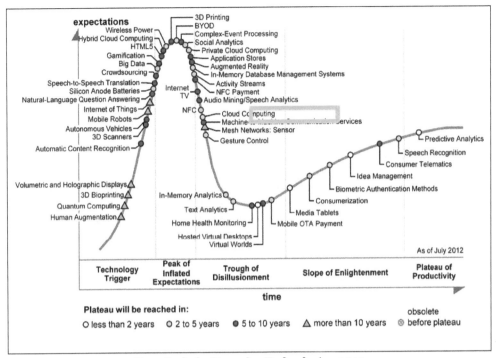

Hype Cycle for Emerging Technologies, 2012.

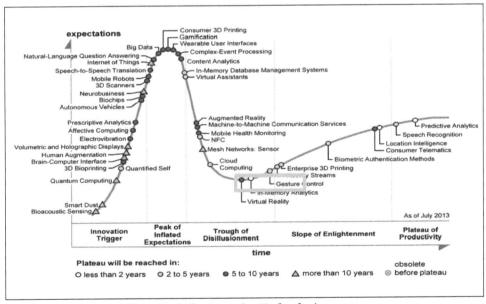

Hype Cycle for Emerging Technologies, 2013.

Even in the year of 2014, the prospect of cloud computing still is that it will take another 2-5 years to mature completely and be adopted in the mainstream. In all these years, there are many technologies that appeared in the Hype Cycle and disappeared, while cloud computing has remained and is still growing. This can also be observed from the multiple large organizations that have offered products in cloud.

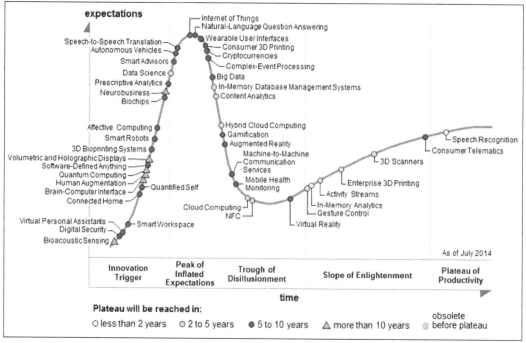

Hype Cycle for Emerging Technologies, 2014.

Types of Cloud Services

Regardless of the kind of service, cloud computing services provide users with a series of functions including:

- Email.

- Storage, backup, and data retrieval.

- Creating and testing apps.

- Analyzing data.

- Audio and video streaming.

- Delivering software on demand.

Cloud computing is still a fairly new service but is being used by a number of different organizations from big corporations to small businesses, nonprofits to government agencies, and even individual consumers.

Deployment Models

There are various types of clouds, each of which is different from the other. Public clouds provide their services on servers and storage on the Internet. These are operated by third-party companies, who handle and control all the hardware, software, and the general infrastructure. Clients access services through accounts that can be accessed by just about anyone.

Private clouds are reserved for specific clientele, usually one business or organization. The firm's data service center may host the cloud computing service. Many private cloud computing services are provided on a private network.

Hybrid clouds are, as the name implies, a combination of both public and private services. This type of model allows the user more flexibility and helps optimize the user's infrastructure and security.

Types of Cloud Computing

Cloud computing is not a single piece of technology like a microchip or a cellphone. Rather, it's a system primarily comprised of three services: software-as-a-service (SaaS), infrastructure-as-a-service (IaaS), and platform-as-a-service (PaaS).

- Software-as-a-service (SaaS) involves the licensure of a software application to customers. Licenses are typically provided through a pay-as-you-go model or on-demand. This type of system can be found in Microsoft Office's 365.

- Infrastructure-as-a-service (IaaS) involves a method for delivering everything from operating systems to servers and storage through IP-based connectivity as part of an on-demand service. Clients can avoid the need to purchase software or servers, and instead procure these resources in an outsourced, on-demand service. Popular examples of the IaaS system include IBM Cloud and Microsoft Azure.

- Platform-as-a-service (PaaS) is considered the most complex of the three layers of cloud-based computing. PaaS shares some similarities with SaaS, the primary difference being that instead of delivering software online; it is actually a platform for creating software that is delivered via the Internet. This model includes platforms like Salesforce.com and Heroku.

Advantages and Disadvantages

Advantages of Cloud Computing

- Easy implementation: Cloud hosting allows business to retain the same applications and business processes without having to deal with the backend technicalities. Readily manageable by the Internet, a cloud infrastructure can be accessed by enterprises easily and quickly.

- Accessibility: Access your data anywhere, anytime. An Internet cloud infrastructure maximizes enterprise productivity and efficiency by ensuring your application is always accessible. This allows for easy collaboration and sharing among users in multiple locations.

- No hardware required: Since everything will be hosted in the cloud, a physical storage center is no longer needed. However, a backup could be worth looking into in the event of a disaster that could leave your company's productivity stagnant.

- Cost per head: Overhead technology costs are kept at a minimum with cloud hosting services, enabling businesses to use the extra time and resources for improving the company infrastructure.

- Flexibility for growth: The cloud is easily scalable so companies can add or subtract resources based on their needs. As companies grow, their system will grow with them.

- Efficient recovery: Cloud computing delivers faster and more accurate retrievals of applications and data. With less downtime, it is the most efficient recovery plan.

Disadvantages of Cloud Computing

- No longer in control: When moving services to the cloud, you are handing over your data and information. For companies who have an in-house IT staff, they will be unable to handle issues on their own. However, Stratosphere Networks has a 24/7 live help desk that can rectify any problems immediately.

- May not get all the features: Not all cloud services are the same. Some cloud providers tend to offer limited versions and enable the most popular features only, so you may not receive every feature or customization you want. Before signing up, make sure you know what your cloud service provider offers.

- Doesn't mean you should do away with servers: You may have fewer servers to handle which means less for your IT staff to handle, but that doesn't mean you can let go of all your servers and staff. While it may seem costly to have data centers and a cloud infrastructure, redundancy is key for backup and recovery.

- No Redundancy: A cloud server is not redundant nor is it backed up. As technology may fail here and there, avoid getting burned by purchasing a redundancy plan. Although it is an extra cost, in most cases it will be well worth it. Bandwidth issues. For ideal performance, clients have to plan accordingly and not pack large amounts of servers and storage devices into a small set of data centers.

Characteristics of Cloud

Cloud being massive in scale, its infrastructure also is expected to be large. Indeed, as a distributed system, one would expect cloud to be essentially distributed in nature. Thus we identify the first point of cloud infrastructure being distributed across geographical regions. The data centers that house the essential components of cloud are built in different regions for various reasons and hence they are distributed. The second point of infrastructure is about virtualization. The infrastructure is distributed implies that whatever service is being provided to a user may be located in any of the multiple data centers used by the service provider. The users should be able to acquire the services from any remote location wherever they are and this perhaps is the most important characteristic of cloud computing. This is why cloud computing is part of distributed system.

The success of cloud lies in an underlying technology called virtualization. Many of the essential characteristics of cloud come from the fact that the resources are virtualized. Typically, the data centers are virtualized to maximize resource sharing and hence resource utilization, thereby rendering the whole environment profitable for both service providers as well as service consumers. The effect of virtualization is also that we do not expose the actual location or the details of the underlying hardware to the user. A layer of indirection on top of the hardware implements virtualization and this allows flexible use of the underlying resources.

The third point of infrastructure is the autonomous system. It is obvious that the large scale and the flawless resource provisioning that is expected of cloud cannot be achieved using manual control. Thus cloud is an autonomous environment. The point is that without human intervention the system should be able to continue on its own and the mechanisms of the systems are such that while each one can independently work, collaboration is also possible. This implies that such autonomous systems should be able to work independently as well as together to achieve a better goal than a single autonomous system.

The NIST Essential Attributes

The five essential attributes of a cloud computing environment according to the NIST are as follows:

- On Demand Self Service.

- Broad Network Access.

- Resource Pooling.

- Rapid Elasticity.

- Measured Service.

On Demand Self Service

Cloud services are available on-demand and essentially used on a "pay-as-you go" model or on the basis of subscription. Thus, user pays for the services that are consumed just like paying for electricity. However, with the advent and proliferation of different modes of deployment, usage of cloud may also be free or may be compensated via other means, like advertisements on websites.

The other important part of this characteristic is self-service. By self-service, we mean that a consumer can unilaterally acquire resources without any human intervention from either side. These resources include computing capabilities, server time as well as storage over the network. This is highly advantageous, as the user does not have to go through a lengthy procedure to access resources. Instead, a simple and automated request mechanism to a service provider's portal allows a customer to acquire and use the necessary amount of computing, storage, software, process, or other resources and services.

Broad Network Access

All the capabilities and resources hosted by a service provider's cloud network are available to the users. They are accessed through mechanisms developed and standardized by the service provider through heterogeneous client platforms including PCs, mobile phones, tablets etc. accessed over the Internet. This provides a very important characteristic and actually catapults the cloud advantage. During the mainframe era, resources were expensive and scarce. To reduce the usage and hence save expense, various criteria such as some priority or the importance of the work would be used. However, with advents of technologies and more competition, the resources are more easily available. Further, the access to the network has improved with greater bandwidth being available making the environment more scalable. In the cloud computing era, it has become imperative that the network be unrestrained by the use of broad access.

Resource Pooling

The essence of cloud computing is perhaps the fact that there is a pool of shared resources. It is not possible to improve scalability unless there is an improvement on the resource pooling. If resources like computing, networks, and even storage are not put to service in a pool, a service provider may have to operate across multiple independent resources with few or no interconnections to cater to the customers' requests, thereby losing the primary benefit provided in cloud. Therefore, resource pooling helps the providers to combine in a pool all the resources and be able to satisfy the needs of many consumers in such a way that the consumer is not able to understand or control over the location from where the resources are being served.

However, even in this situation, users are able to specify if they need some location specific service such as country, state or even data centers. Also the pooled resources help provide service using a multi-tenant model, with different physical and virtual resources dynamically assigned and reassigned according to consumer demand. The concept of multi-tenancy directly stems from this characteristic.

Multi Tenant Environment

In such a situation, adjacent resources may be used by multiple customers at the same time in a sharable manner. This model extends to the sharing of both software as well as hardware resources. In a cloud environment, resources are dynamically assigned and reassigned according to consumer requirements. It drives cost efficiency and improves utilization. However, this sharing also leads to an inherent increase in operational expenditures, although the additional expenditure gets compensated by the benefits thereof. Let us understand this using a practical example.

Let us consider an apartment building versus an independent house. An apartment building has certain resources (like the staircase, common passage ways, swimming pool, gymnasium etc.), which are not 'owned' by any one resident, but are shared among all the residents. As a result, the facilities are utilized to the maximum possible extent, more so than they would be in a private house. However, as a byproduct of this increased utilization, maintenance costs also rises.

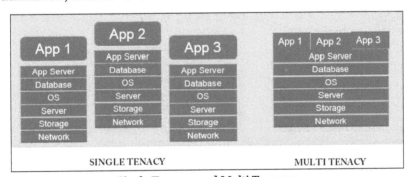

Single Tenancy and Multi Tenancy.

The figure displays the architecture of typical single and multitenant systems. Single tenancy gives each customer a dedicated software track. Configuration, monitoring, upgrades, security updates, patches, tuning and disaster recovery are all focused on servicing one user at a time. On the other hand, in a multi-tenant environment, all applications run in a single logical environment. Obviously, it is faster, more secure, more available, automatically upgraded and maintained.

Rapid Elasticity

This characteristic ensures that capabilities of the data centers of the provider be elastically provisioned and released, perhaps automatically, to scale rapidly outward and inward as per the demand. This means that user should feel that any resource could be appropriated in any quantity at any time. The requirement of resources to be elastic stems from a need to provide resources to users at improved speeds at the same time reducing associated costs. A cloud based architecture should be able to provision any amount of resources at a fast rate so as to appear unlimited and instantaneous to the consumer. This leads to the illusion of infinite computing resources in cloud.

Measured Service

While resource pooling is a key aspect of cloud computing from the implementation perspective, measured service is a key aspect of cloud from the financial perspective. Measured service implies that usage of the pooled resources is monitored and reported, providing a mechanism to capture the amount of consumption and hence their associated costs. In a way, the usage of resources is controlled by leveraging a metering capability on them. This is helpful from the perspective of both the service providers as well as the consumers. This monitoring, controlling and reporting of resource usage provides a transparency for both the provider as well as the consumer. This model reflects the pay-per-use system that is employed typically in electricity and other day-to-day utility services.

Gartner's Core Attributes

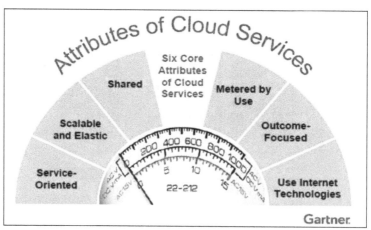

Gartner's Core Attributes of Cloud Services.

While the above are the characteristics as per NIST, Gartner, an American IT research and advisory company providing technology related insights, envision cloud services to have six core attributes. These are:

- Service Oriented: In a cloud environment, the implementation details are hidden from the customers using well defined service interfaces. This also enables a completely automated response by the provider to the consumer of the service. Service orientation is also implemented in the sense that the consumer gets what is needed from the provider. Services are not created as per the technological development rather these technologies are tailored to meet the demands of the consumers making service to be supreme in the world of cloud.

- Scalable and Elastic: Cloud resources and services must be created in such a way that these can easily be scaled up or down to meet the requirements of the customers. While scalability is a feature of the underlying infrastructure and software platforms, elasticity is a trait of a shared resource pool. With scalability comes the option of upward scaling where new services may be added on demand and downward scaling whereby resources/services may be removed as needed. The cloud computing environment thus enables scaling in both directions in an automated fashion.

- Shared: Cloud resources are shared by multiple users of the service, in order to achieve maximum efficiency. The details of the sharing are usually unknown to the consumers, so each feels as if she is getting exclusive access to the entire set of resources. This model of having a common pool of virtualized and shared resources enables maximal utilization of all available resources, allowing resources to serve different purposes for different users simultaneously.

- Metered by Use: Usage metrics are applied to track the usage of services by customers. The service provider is expected to possess a usage accounting model to measure and keep track of the amount of services used by consumers each time resources are consumed. Based on this information, various pricing plans and models can be created and offered to the user. Any unit can be used to measure the usage, for example it can be the number of hours of execution, or it can be the amount of data that is transferred or any other metric. In certain cases, it can even be free.

- Outcome Focused: As the term suggests, the usage of resources in a cloud environment must be oriented towards result or the outcome of the usage. This means that the resources are aimed at providing maximal utility to the users, tailored to suit their needs.

- Usage of Internet Technologies: Cloud services are delivered using Internet protocols, formats and identifiers such as URLs, HTTP, IP and representational state transfer web-oriented architecture. Thus Internet connectivity and usage is a prerequisite of cloud use.

Negative Side of Cloud

While cloud eliminates the need for up-front financial commitment, is based on a pay-as-you-go approach and has attracted new users for existing applications as well as new applications through the technological breakthroughs that have made cloud computing feasible, there are still major obstacles for this new technology such as:

- Availability of Service: While consumers are supposed to completely depend on cloud for all their needs, what happens when the service provider cannot deliver? Can a large company such as General Motors move its complete IT needs to the cloud and have assurances that its activity will not be negatively affected by cloud overload, power outage or any other problem? A partial answer to this question is provided by service-level agreements (SLAs). These are agreements between two parties, a service consumer and the corresponding service provider that should be implemented and respected by both the parties. While for the time being it is sufficient to know that SLAs may be an answer to provide some guarantee to a user, we will discuss the various implementation issues of SLAs at length later. However, even though SLAs, it is impossible for a service provider to guarantee 100% availability of its services at all time. A temporary fix of this negative economical implication is overprovisioning by the service provider, that is, the service provider should acquire enough resources to satisfy the largest projected demand and must have enough back up facility. However, neither of the solutions, SLA and over-provisioning, is devoid of problems.

- Vendor Lock-In: Once a customer stores her data and runs the applications in a cloud solution provided by a specific service provider, it is hard to move to another service provider, mainly due to the lack of standardization among various service providers. Typically the format or the method of data storage, computation execution, results presentation are proprietary and not be same or even similar amongst various service providers making the migration from one provider to the next a difficult, even an impossible, task. The standardization efforts at National Institute of Standards and Technology (NIST) attempt to address this problem.

- Data Confidentiality and Auditability: The data of the client are out of the control of the client and under complete control of the service provider either the data is stored in the cloud, which is a server away from the client's premise or data has to be supplied during computation being executed in a cloud server. This is indeed a serious problem that has led to the development of a private cloud that we are going to discuss next. However, this is a serious problem in cloud being accepted completely by the industry.

- Data Transfer Bottlenecks: Cloud communication is Internet based and many applications are data-intensive. Hence a basic need is to transfer large amount of data for different purpose. However, transferring data over the Internet may be very slow. For example, transferring 1 TB of data on a 1 Mbps network takes approximately 10 days making large data transfer a costly affair. A solution therefore is found in incorporating the strategy of storing the data as close as possible to the site where it is needed. Very high-speed networks will alleviate this problem permanently in the future.

Evolution of Cloud

The evolution of sharing on the Cloud went through: networking, network sharing, information sharing, resources sharing, and services sharing. The first stage of the Cloud was around networking, the TCP/IP abstraction. Multiple regional networks, linking computers, were built at universities and national laboratories. Their inter-networking with TCP/IP led to network sharing and the emergence of the Internet and its worldwide adoption. The second stage of the Cloud was around documents, the WWW data abstraction. The HTML format, the HTTP protocol, and the Mosaic browser were adopted by universities for document exchange and then worldwide for information sharing. Then, grid computing emerged with the creation of standards and software for remote resources sharing and collaboration, exclusively utilized for highly scalable High Performance Computing (HPC) jobs. The newest stage of the Cloud, cloud computing, has emerged to provide services sharing by abstracting infrastructure complexities of servers, applications, data, and heterogeneous platforms.

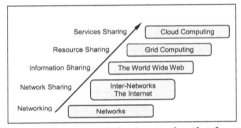

The Evolution of Sharing on the Cloud.

According to the U.S. Government's National Institute of Standards and Technology (NIST), cloud computing is a "model for enabling convenient, on-demand network access to a shared pool of configurable computing resources (e.g., networks, servers, storage, applications, and services) that can be rapidly provisioned and released with minimal management effort or service provider interaction". The origin of the term comes from the early days of the Internet where the network was depicted as a cloud. Cloud computing is an Internet-based delivery model for Information Technology (IT) services that enhances collaboration, agility, scalability, and availability.

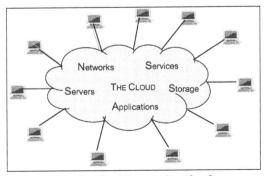

The Standard Enterprise Cloud.

The optimized and efficient computing is provided through a virtualized technology infrastructure, which is maintained and secured for the users. Cloud computing services are offered on a pay-as-you-go basis and assure considerable reduction in hardware and software investment costs, as well as in carbon footprints and energy costs. Currently, cloud computing is more attractive for Web infrastructure, collaboration, development and testing, high performance computing applications, but still less attractive for database and transaction processing, and regulated applications.

Cloud Computing Technologies

Virtualization

Virtualization is a concept used to create a virtual environment on a real physical environment. Thus created virtual environment is virtually segmented and isolated system with the same characteristics as that of real system. The segmented virtual components act as if these are independent systems themselves.

With the virtualization technology, any physical or logical components in an operating environment can be virtualized. The following is a list of components that can be virtualized:

- Network interface card and its functionalities.
- Hardware:
    ○ Processor and its functionalities.
    ○ Memory and its functionalities.
    ○ Storage and its functionalities.
- Software:
    ○ Operating System: Kernel space and User space, Desktop.
    ○ Database, Application.

Types of Virtualization

Based on the components that are virtualized and the functionalities offered by the virtualized components, the virtualization concept is categorized into multiple hierarchies. The topmost in this list is the machine.

- Machine-level virtualization:
    ○ Processor virtualization.

- ○ Memory virtualization.
- Network virtualization.
- Storage virtualization.
- Desktop virtualization.
- Other types.

Of the different types of virtualization, the most important is the machine-level virtualization, which is being discussed next. Other important types are network virtualization, which virtualizes the underlying network interface to LAN and storage virtualization that virtualizes the underlying storage components such as primary storage (hard disk) and secondary storage (such as SAN or NAS).

Machine-Level Virtualization

The first and foremost type of virtualization is machine-level virtualization also called the hardware virtualization. Generally, virtualization environment is often referred to as machine level virtualization. In this approach, the underlying hardware components of an operational system (Processor, Memory) is segmented, isolated and operating systems are deployed on top of the isolated segments to make independent operational environments. Each of the segments is called as virtual machine. We see the traditional computer in figure where an operating system that is specifically compiled for the underlying hardware architecture is present. Contrast this with a virtualized environment as shown in figure where user applications are running on top of their own operating systems, also called the guest OSs, in a virtualized environment. A software layer called the virtual machine monitor or VMM or Hypervisor virtualizes the host machine into different virtual machines (VM) and these can run on the same hardware. The VMs are not dependent on the host OS.

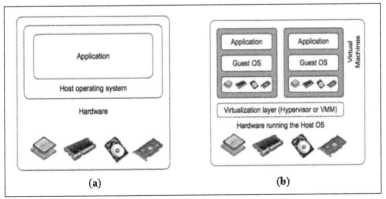

Machine Level Virtualization.

However, this is one way of virtualizing. The virtualization layer can be implemented at various operational levels in a machine, thereby creating different abstraction layers.

Common virtualization layers include the instruction set architecture (ISA) level, hardware level, operating system level, library support level, and application level.

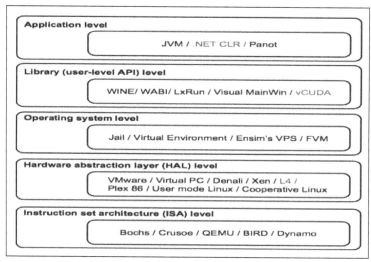

Virtualization at Different Implementation Levels.

Application Level Virtualization

In application level virtualization, the end user application is virtualized and executed as its corresponding virtual machines. A generic application will be implemented with 3-tier architecture such as:

- Database layer running on a database engine or database server.

- Application layer running on Application server.

- Web layer running on Web server.

In application level virtualization, all the three services are virtualized and made to work as individual virtual machines. Multiple virtualized web server, application server and database server will be running as independent units on a single application server, web server and database server. These parallel execution services forms application virtual machine which constitutes of virtualized web service, virtualized application service, virtualized database service. Each independent user is provided access to application VM where the functionalities of web server, application server and database server can be customized by corresponding users. This feature is called multi-tenancy, where same service is virtualized and functionalities are customized independently for multiple users.

This methodology is also called as process-level virtualization since the web server, application server and database server is virtualized into individual process and every process is executed in parallel independent of one another. Java Virtual Machine is an example. This virtualization is applicable to the application and database implemented with web service compatibility.

Library-Level Virtualization

Certain Application Programming Interfaces (APIs) of the user-level libraries are commonly used by many applications and databases. These API are good candidates for virtualization. API hooks are used controlling the communication between applications and the rest of a system. WINE is a tool that has implemented this mechanism and can support Windows applications on Unix machines. vCUDA is another example.

OS Level Virtualization

Operating system comprises of Kernel space and user space. In operating system level virtualization, an abstraction layer between the traditional OS and user applications is introduced. This layer virtualizes the operating system user space components thereby abstracting it from user applications. This individual virtualized space is called container. Multiple containers are executed in parallel on single operating system kernel with each container customized according to its users. The containers show the behavior of real servers. Jail is an example, which is a FreeBSD-based system. It helps partition a computer into mini-systems. These minisystems are called jails.

HAL Level Virtualization

Hardware abstraction layer or HAL is a set of routines in that behave the same way as the underlying platform, such that programs can access the hardware directly. Virtualization at the HAL-level generates a virtual hardware environment for a VM. This virtualization is applied on the bare machine. A computer's resources such as processors, memory, and I/O devices are virtualized so that many users can share the same hardware. In the 60s, IBM's VM/370 implemented the idea first. Recently, Xen, VMware and a host of other hypervisors use this approach.

ISA Level Virtualization

ISA is the instruction Set Architecture that represents hardware architecture. Virtualization is the core technology that offers cloud services. At the Instruction Set Architecture level, virtualization is performed by emulating a given ISA by the ISA of the host machine. Emulation process is the backbone for virtualization. In simple terms, emulation is the process, which enables one system to behave as another system. QEMU and Dynamo are examples of this category.

Network Virtualization

Network virtualization is the process of virtualizing the overall network employed for establishing the cloud environment and its components, primarily the network interface card that is directly attached to the servers. In an advanced network virtualization the hardware and software network resources along with its corresponding functionalities are virtualized, implemented using software and combined into a single, software-based administrative entity. The network underwent virtualization called Virtual networks which may be Local area network or Wide area network. The advanced network virtualization functionality and its method of operation are termed as Software defined networks or SDN.

Storage Virtualization

Storage virtualization is the process to virtualize the storage components. The storage system can be of various categories such as the local storage directly attached to the servers (hard disk) or secondary extended storage such as Storage Area Network. In the cloud perspective, the computation units and storage units are virtualized and controlled as independent entity. Storage virtualization process isolates the storage units according to the desired user capacity and creates the virtualized storage space as mountable volumes. These volumes are identified by certain identification numbers and are mounted to the virtual machines.

Storage virtualization decouples the physical organization of the storage from its logical representation. The users accessing their own data in cloud either directly or through virtual machines are not aware of the specific location of their data. A logical path is provided to their data volumes and the path will be mounted to their VMs or to their devices through which the users will get access to their storage volumes and to the data. Multiple storage facilities can be represented by a single standard file system.

Other Virtualizations

There are other virtualization techniques depending on the level of implementation:

- Desktop Virtualization: Desktop Virtualization is the technique, which virtualizes the user space of Operating system whereas the kernel space of the operating is same. This method makes multiple desktops of operating system to be running simultaneously on the same system with single operating system. Each desktop instance is allocated to different users and the users in turn will access their corresponding desktop through remote desktop connectivity. The applications and files stored by corresponding users will be hidden from other users sharing the same hardware and OS.

- I/O Virtualization: I/O Virtualization is the process of managing the Input and output of the instructions to the virtualized environment. Emulation is a key factor for implementing I/O Virtualization. This technique emulates the underlying devices to Guest OS for flow of input and output in both directions. The instruction/data/signals from the devices such as network, graphic devices, audio devices, display devices are managed by its corresponding device drivers. These instructions/data from device drivers are then passed on to Input/Output stack. The device emulator fetches the instruction from the stack and emulates the instruction according to the guest OS running in the guest operating system. The emulated instructions are passed on to the Guest drivers that reach the Guest OS. This procedure is followed in reverse direction also. The base drivers, I/O Stack and device emulators forms the virtualization stack and the Guest drivers, Operating system forms the guest VM.

Hardware Virtualization

While there are various ways to virtualize a computer, the most popular way of virtualizing a machine is by the way of deploying a virtualization layer. The idea of virtualization originated in 1960 and with gradual improvements virtualization today has become an integral part of Cloud computing. In 1972, IBM introduced virtual machine operating system. The current version is called a Virtual Machine Monitor (VMM) or Hypervisor. VMM runs on the physical machine. The typical layering of hardware, OS and application is modified in a virtualized environment.

The modified virtualized environment can be either a three or a four layers environment depending on the type of hypervisor being used. Virtual Machine Monitor (VMM) or Hypervisor is the piece of software that provides the abstraction of a virtual machine. This is responsible for the entire virtualization process. We will use the two terms VMM and hypervisor interchangeably. The operating system running on top of the Hypervisor in virtual machine catering to the needs of the application is the guest OS and the OS that sits on top of the hardware is called the host OS.

Virtual Machine Monitor

VMM is the software that plays a major role and is responsible for the entire virtualization process. Virtualization software or Hypervisor is categorized into two different types:

- Type 1 hypervisor.

- Type 2 hypervisor.

Type 1 Hypervisor

Type 1 hypervisor has three layers. The lowermost layer is the hardware layer and networking layer comprises CPU, storage and network components. On top of this is the operating system layer. The next layer is the virtualization layer where the hypervisor resides and virtualizes the underlying resources. On top of the virtualization layer reside the guest environments, which are the virtual machines. The architecture is depicted in figure.

The hypervisor is installed on bare metal, i.e., directly on a hardware environment in contrast to the four-layer architecture and hence this hypervisor is also called as bare metal hypervisor. The guest environment contains the guest OSs that are installed on top of the hypervisor. Guest OSs run in less privileged mode. The privilege level of guest OS is emulated by the Virtual Machine Monitor or Hypervisor.

Type 1 Virtualization Architecture.

Type 2 Hypervisor

Type 1 hypervisor is difficult to use and implement, hence the other type called Type 2 hypervisor is employed. In type 2 hypervisor there are four layers, as depicted in the figure. Here also the lowermost layer is the hardware layer. On top of this is the operating system layer. Next layer is the virtualization layer with the guest environment on top. Here the hypervisor is installed on top of a host operating system. This is also called hosted environment.

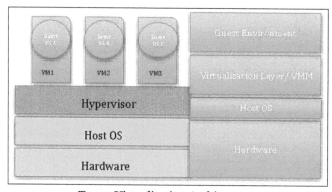

Type 2 Virtualization Architecture.

The Hypervisor utilizes the functionalities available on host OS to control and manage resources desired by each of the virtual machines. These can support broadest range of underlying host hardware configurations.

Hybrid Hypervisor

While the hosted/Type 2 hypervisor is easier than bare metal/Type 1 hypervisor, the efficiency of virtualization in Type 2 is not available in Type 1 since the hypervisor works like an application. Hence, it is desirable that some part of the VMM must be in direct control of the hardware. This is achieved by creating a hybrid model hypervisor as shown in figure.

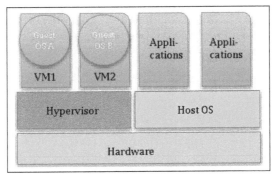

Hybrid Hypervisor.

The VMM here shares the hardware with a host operating system. This is done through mechanisms commonly provided to extend the functionality of an operating system such as kernel extensions and device drivers. Applications that run on top of the VMM are run in the VM environment. The hybrid system supports multiple virtual machines. On the other hand, there are applications that can be run on the normal system on top of the operating system itself. This system is referred to as a dual mode hosted VM system.

Virtual Machines (VMs)

The virtual machine (VM) is the core component formed as a result of virtualization. The basic cloud services such as IaaS (Infrastructure-as-a-Service) and PaaS (platform-as-a-Service) are delivered to the end users as virtual machines. Like the rest of the system, the guest environment in the virtualized system, or the virtual machines, also follow a layered approach, where the bottom layer within the virtual machines is the virtual hardware and layer on top of the virtual hardware is the operating system layer. On top of the operating system layer resides the user applications.

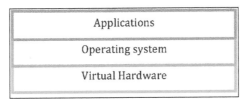

Layers of a Virtual Machine.

VM Taxonomy

From the perspective of the scope, we can divide the virtual machines into two major categories:

- Process VM.

- System VM.

Process VM

These VMs are platforms created by operating system specifically for the process. These VMs are created when the application is initiated and they are destroyed when the application finishes execution. These VM support binaries compiled on different instruction set. For example Java Virtual Machine.

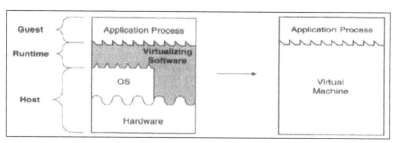

The virtualizing software in the process VM environment translates one instruction from one platform to another platform. With the help of this, programs developed for variety of operating system or with different instruction set architecture can be executed. These VMs terminates automatically once the process terminates.

System VM

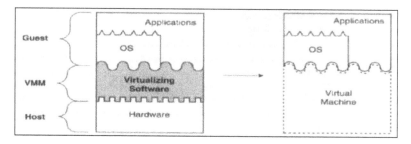

System VM is the VM that is generally created for virtualizing the underlying hardware and networking resources. These VMs provide a complete operational environment, comprising guest operating system, user process, networking components, input output environment, graphical display components and so on. These VMs are tied to the system and not any specific process and will be running as long as the host hardware is running or user terminates the VMs.

These VMs have their own guest operating systems, which are made bootable from OS template called images. These support multiple images simultaneously. Each image runs its own OS and is associated with specific application programs at any point in time. Each guest OS controls and manages its own virtualized hardware resources. The hardware environment is shared among the VMs running simultaneously. Virtual Machine Monitor manages the allocation of, and access to, the hardware resources of the host platform.

Operations on VM

There are four basic operations that can be defined as the primitive operations of a VM as follows:

- VM Multiplexing.

- VM Suspension.

- VM Provision.

- VM Migration.

VM Multiplexing

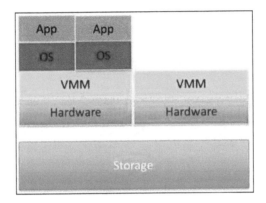

The word multiplexing here indicates the ability of using multiple instances. In a non-virtualized environment, while multiple applications may be run on top of a given hardware/machine, there are severe restrictions in the number and types of the applications. In a virtualized environment, these applications are deployed in VMs and hence restrictions regarding the number of VMs that can be launched, the type of application that can be run in the VMs, the amount or share of the hardware that can be consumed by these applications become irrelevant. Hence this is called VM multiplexing.

VM Suspension

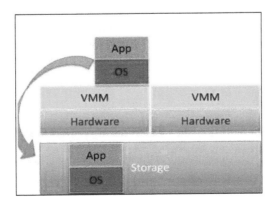

VM Suspension is the process of moving the virtual machines to a paused state from running state. Any running or waiting VMs may be suspended from the current state and moved to storage. The VMs reside in storage until revoked back to execution.

VM Provisioning

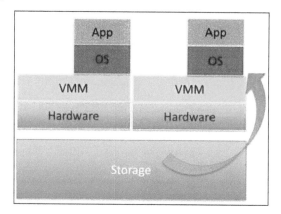

When needed, a suspended VM can be brought back to the execution environment and be scheduled on the same hardware or on a different hardware.

VM Migration

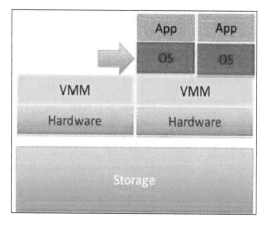

The VMs can be migrated directly from one server to another server either as live migration without shutting down the virtual machines or as cold migration by shutting down the VMs and migrating the VM and rebooting the VM at destination.

Benefits of Virtual Machines

We can intuitively understand the benefits of using VMs and hence using virtualization. Some of these benefits are:

- Virtual machine is a way of consolidation of servers. Various hardware can be brought together and these hardware can be better utilized by deploying and executing multiple VMs. Thanks to the various operations that can be performed on the VMs, the different hardware can be utilized to their fullest.

- The point above directly makes optimal utilization of server and storage resources possible, which otherwise would not be possible.

- With guest OSs running inside the VMs, a VM environment looks the same as a normal OS environment provided to an application running in a non-virtualized machine.

- Perhaps one of the most important advantages of virtualization is the ability of the VMs to run applications in different OS environment using the same hardware.

- Higher levels of security are possible since the VMs run applications in isolated environment.

- High level of availability is possible since, in case of the failure of a certain server, migration can be applied to seamlessly move the VMs from the failed machine to another machine.

- Since servers can be added and removed without affecting the running VMs, a virtualized environment supports scalability and portability.

- It is easy to backup all the data, which promotes faster recovery as a result.

Emulation

Emulation is the process where the virtualizing software mimics that portion of hardware, which is provided to the guest operating system in the virtual machine. The presented emulated hardware is independent of the underlying physical hardware. Emulation provides VM portability and wide range of hardware compatibility, which means the possibility of executing any virtual machine on any hardware, as the guest operating system interacts only with the emulated hardware.

In an emulated environment, both the application and guest operating system in virtual machines run in the user mode of base operating system. In simple terms, the behavior of the hardware is produced by a software program. Emulation process involves only those hardware components so that user or virtual machines does not understand the underlying environment. Only CPU & memory are sufficient for basic level of emulation.

Typically, emulation is implemented using interpretation. The emulator component takes each and every instruction of user mode and translates to equivalent instruction suitable according to the underlying hardware. This process is also termed as interpretation. This means that the guest OS remains completely unaware of the virtualization. Also, in interpretation, each and every instruction issued by a VM is trapped in the VMM and interpreted for execution in the hardware. Computationally it is a very expensive method. However, in some cases, it is needed to use an interpretation technique. However, due to the huge disadvantage of performance, emulation using interpretation is hardly used in virtualization.

Trap and Emulate

Trap and emulate is a technique that takes the basic of the emulation but improves performance by using interpretation selectively. Both the user applications and guest operating system of virtual machines run in the user mode and the hypervisor runs in the privileged mode. However, here the application runs the instructions natively on the hardware. Only when a privileged instruction is to be executed in virtual user mode, a trap to the virtual kernel mode occurs. This causes a trap to the VMM in turn. The hypervisor gains control of the execution. All the special instructions that need to be managed, are managed by the VMM and not by the guest OS.

When hypervisor traps, it executes the necessary equivalent operations in the underlying instruction set architecture and returns control to guest in user mode. User mode code in guest runs at normal speed. There is no change from running in non-virtualized environment. But kernel mode privileged codes run slower due to trap-and-emulate. The mechanism works fine, except that the CPU is slower in kernel mode. Unfortunately, it becomes a performance issue when there are several guests and each guest needs to trap to VMM for all privileged mode instructions.

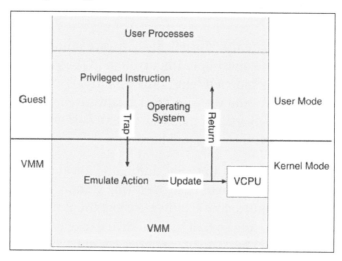

The privileged instruction from the guest operating system is trapped by the hypervisor and emulated. This emulated instruction is then passed on to the kernel. On return the privileged instruction from the kernel is emulated and returned to the user mode where the operating system of virtual machine is running.

There are issues prevailing in Trap and Emulate methodology. Not all ISAs can be emulated using trap-and-emulate method. Those that do not follow Popek-Goldberg theorem cannot be emulated. Sensitive instructions are not Privileged instructions. Let us consider the example of Intel x86 popf instruction. The CPU flags are loaded from the contents of stack. In privileged mode, all flags are replaced whereas in user mode only some flags are replaced, hence no trap is generated.

Let us take the example of the popf instruction. This instruction loads a set of flags from the stack into a register and can be executed in both the user mode and privileged mode. When executed in privileged mode, popf loads all flags, which include a mix of ALU flags and system flags. In this mode, both the set of flags get modified, as per requirement, since the OS has the permission to make necessary changes in the system flags. However, when the same popf gets executed in user mode, the processor simply does not allow modification of the system flags even if the situation demands it. But, no error or exception is generated due to this. This is what is meant by 'going totally unnoticed' by the underlying OS.

This works fine in a non-virtualized environment. Now, let us see why this would cause a problem in a virtualized environment using a trap and emulate kind of mechanism. The guest user mode runs the popf instruction without altering the system flags and this is just a normal action. What happens when the guest OS executes the popf instruction? It is 'expected' to modify the system flags as per requirement. But since this itself is running in the user mode, it will not be allowed to modify the system flags. However, a question here is that the same is applicable for all other privileged instructions in this scenario yet there were no problems with them. The explanation to this question is as follows: Since, in all other privileged instructions when the guest OS attempts to execute a privileged instruction, the processor will detect this 'unnatural' behaviour and will wake up the VMM. However, since processor is supposed to allow the execution of popf in user mode as well, it will not raise the VMM when the guest OS attempts to execute the instruction. It just does not allow the guest OS to modify the system flags since it is expecting the guest OS to 'behave' like an application and not as an OS. As a result, the outcome of this execution is not the same as the expected outcome of this instruction.

Binary Translation

The issue of popf and other such instructions that occur in the trap and emulate method can be taken care of if the VMM gets more proactive. This additional activity of VMM is the Binary Translation. Although the concept of binary translation is simple, the complexity lies in implementation of binary translation. If guest vCPU is in user mode, guest can run instructions natively, whereas if guest vCPU is in kernel mode, VMM checks every instruction (and does not wait for a trap). Non-sensitive instructions run normally but sensitive instructions are translated appropriately. Performance of this method is worse than trap-and-emulate since all codes of the guest kernel is inspected by the VMM. However, many optimizations have been proposed.

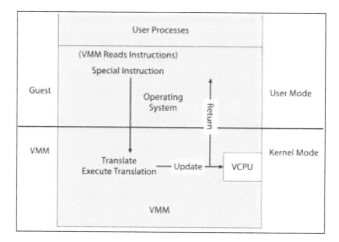

One such available optimization for improving the performance is caching. In caching technique, a block of instructions are translated once and stored in cache. When guest executes the code with sensitive instructions, the cached translation is first checked. If instruction is available in cache as translated instruction, then no more translation is necessary. Translation takes place otherwise. This improves the efficiency of Binary Translation.

CPU Virtualization

It is time to see what the cloud industry has actually used to virtualize various hardware environments. As expected, the industry responded to the need of virtualization and came up with multiple solutions, some of which took advantage of the methods, yet others came up with unconventional solutions. Over all, there are four methods in CPU virtualization:

- Emulation with Interpretation.

- Full virtualization with dynamic binary translation.

- Para virtualization.

- Hardware-assisted virtualization.

Emulation with Interpretation

This is the virtualization at the ISA level as we have discussed in our earlier discussion on the implementation of hardware virtualization. Although they are called virtualization, this mechanism is largely used when a program that is written for one ISA needs to run on a different ISA. For example, one may need to run an android application written for Android platform in a Windows-based machine. An appropriate emulator may be run on a Windows box. Some of the very popular platforms available are Bochs and QEMU. Of these two, QEMU, besides being an emulator, even has a virtualizer, which attempts to bypass the emulator and run some of the x86 codes natively.

Full Virtualization with Dynamic Binary Translation

The requirement in a virtualized environment is to run an existing operating system along with applications in an isolated virtual machine. We should be able to run many such VMs in such a way that these do not affect each other's performance running on the same hardware. In an x86 architecture, the guest OSs and VMs are not executed in ring 0. There are two issues out of this action. The first is that these guest OSs should be supervised by a host OS running in ring 0. Hence VMM is run in ring 0. Where do we run the guest OS? These must run deprivileged in either ring 1 or 2. Typically the application is run in ring 3 and guest OS in ring 1. This methodology is termed as full virtualization.

However, deprivileging an OS comes with an associated cost. Since the guest operating systems are written for execution on top of the hardware (ring 0), many instructions may be unsafe or even potentially harmful to be run in user mode. Simple traps for all these 'sensitive' instructions may not work. To ensure safety of the virtualized environment, all those instructions that can cause problems must be intercepted and rewritten, if required. Hence complete binary translation of the kernel code of the guest OSs is required to ensure the safety of the processor and the machine while allowing the user code to run natively on the hardware. Further, a guest OS could easily determine that it is not running at privilege level 0. Since this is not desirable, the VMM must take an appropriate action. Another problem of deprivileging the OS is that, as normal OS, the guest OS program expects to enjoy unrestrained access to the full memory but as a mere application, running in a higher ring, it cannot enjoy the same privilege. Hence the VMM must make way for ensuring that this is taken care of.

This method is called the full virtualization with binary translation. In this virtualization one or more guest operating systems of virtual machines share hardware resources from the host system. The presence of the hypervisor beneath is not known to the guests. However, the issue that restricts full virtualization with binary translation is the performance. Translation takes time and translating all the kernel codes of the guest OS is expensive in terms of performance. This problem is resolved by using dynamic binary translation.

In dynamic binary translation, a block of code is used. These blocks may or may not have critical instructions. For each block, dynamic BT translates critical instructions, if any, into some privilege instructions, which will trap to VMM for further emulation. Full virtualization technology uses and exploits dynamic binary translation. The execution of instructions in full virtualization using dynamic binary translation is explained in the figure.

The virtual machine monitor or hypervisor executes in ring 0, guest OS in ring 1 and application in ring 3. The black arrow shows the direct execution of user request on the hardware. The orange line shows the binary translation of the OS code. The VMM translates the guest OS's instructions from ring 1 and passes to hardware for execution.

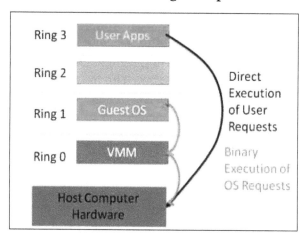

Although this methodology provides performance, there are shortcomings in this methodology. Binary translation does not work for certain cases where the guest OS may be using self-modifying or self-referencing codes. Real-time systems also cannot be virtualized since such systems cannot tolerate the delays caused by the translation.

Paravirtualization

The problem of full virtualization is that the guest OS is unaware of the fact that it has been diprivileged and hence its behaviour continues to be the same. In para virtualization, the guest OS is modified or patched for virtualization. Hypervisor sits as the base OS or in ring 0 in case of x86 and guest OS resides on top of VMM. Here, since the Guest OS is aware that it is running above VMM rather than on top of the physical machine, many problems of full virtualization are taken care of. The modified kernel of the guest OS is able to communicate with the underlying hypervisor via special calls. These special calls are provided by specific APIs depending on the hypervisor employed. These special calls are equivalent to system calls generated by an application to a non-virtualized OS. Xen Hypervisor is an example that uses para virtualization technology.

The Guest OS is modified and thus run kernel-level operations at Ring 1. The guest OS is now fully aware of how to process both privileged and sensitive instructions. Hence the necessity for translation of instructions is not present any more. Guest OS uses a specialized call, called "hypercall" to talk to the VMM. VMM executes the privileged instructions. Thus VMM is responsible for handling the virtualization requests and putting them to the hardware.

Paravirtualization mode in the figure shows the hypercalls using orange lines, while the grey line shows the native execution of the user process as usual. Hypercalls are passed onto the hypervisor in the virtualization layer and VMM passes the calls to hardware after processing. The issue here is the fact that the guest OS must be modified. This causes problems in OS maintainability and supportability. Also, since the guest OS and hypervisor are tightly coupled, compatibility problem arises. Each time the hypervisor is updated, guest OS must also be recompiled.

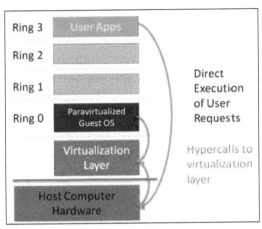

Hardware-Assisted Virtualization

Legacy processors are not designed for virtualization. The methods that may be applied for implementing virtualization, each has its own problems. However, if the processors are made virtualization-aware, the VMM design will be more efficient and simple. Many issues can be easily taken care of with such a processor.

This is the reason why hardware vendors rapidly embraced virtualization and developed new features to simplify virtualization techniques. The two giants in the hardware arena, Intel and AMD came up with came up with designs of new CPU execution mode that allows VMM to run in a new root mode below ring 0. This is the way to handle the privileged mode. In this new design, both privileged and sensitive calls automatically trap to the hypervisor. Hence, in this new design, there remains no need for either binary translation or paravirtualization. Now, the latest x86's meet Popek & Goldberg requirements, hence they can be virtualized without any complexities. Examples of this new design are Intel VT-x and AMD-V.

Intel VT-x have two modes of operations: VMX root and VMX non-root. While "VMX root" mode operation executes the hypervisor/VMM in the ring 0, "VMX non-root" mode operation executes the guest OS, also in ring 0, thereby removing the need to de-privilege the guest OS. Both the modes support all privilege rings and are identical. Unmodified guest OS runs in ring 0 in non-root mode and traps instructions to root mode. The privileged and sensitive calls automatically trap to the hypervisor. VMM controls the execution of the guest OS. While it is possible to run unmodified guest OS in the above set up thereby allowing execution of legacy/unmodified operating system, the challenge in hardware assisted virtualization is that an unmodified OS cannot take the advantage of virtualization. The OS is unaware of whether it is running in a virtualized environment or conventional environment. Partial implementation of paravirtualization may solve this problem.

Utility Computing

Utility computing plays a significant role in business models and gives a unique service provider to the customer IT services according to pay per use methods. The few IT services are provided to customer storage, software applications, and computing power. So for any questions and advice required for deployment in the business model, the service providers provide the unit divisions to the company. As the term "Utility" refers to basic amenities like electricity, water, gas, the basic software requirements for a business model are provided by utility computing.

Working of Utility Computing

Utility computing is the same as virtualization because the cumulative amount of web storage space along with calculating power is available to the resources is much the larger amount when compared to the one time-sharing computer. The backend servers are available in multiple amounts which are used to do this kind of possible web server. The concerned web servers are applied in the cluster forms which are developed and then given to lease to end-users. The technique of using one unit computation on the multi web server is known as distributed computing. The working of utility computing is easy and simple. The company pays to other companies for its usage of computing services. It includes usage of a particular computer application or some confidential access to computer processing power, rental of hardware components, and data storage space. It is based on the client requirements and the things which can be offered by utility computing. Utility computing is also offered as a package or bundle of resources.

Components of Utility Computing

The few components that included in the package of utility computing is computer hardware component, software applications, internet access, and cloud systems.

- The computer hardware such as monitors, input devices, servers, CPU and network cables.

- The browsing software and web servers provide internet access.

- The software applications that execute the huge amount of computer mandatory programs such as communication tools, mailbox, report generation, CRM and other project and process-oriented applications and everything that lies in between the client, company and the end-users. The experts from the industries call this process as software as a service.

- Enabling the confidential access to a few processes of a supercomputer. Because few enterprises have substantial computational requirements. The status of the financial company keeps on changing rapidly concerning the updating cycle of the stock market. The normal computers take maximum processing time to retrieve or process the data whereas the supercomputer takes only minimum time to process and execute the information and complete the task as quickly as possible.

- The usage of the grid computing system runs on unique software is known as middleware. It finds the ideal processing power of CPU and enables an application executing on another computer to retrieve the benefits of it. The bunk of a larger computational system is divided into smaller chunks which makes the user access easily.

- Cloud storage is the offsite data storage that provides reasons for companies to store and handle the data. If the company has to process higher dimensional data, but it doesn't have the space to hold such huge data. so it looks for any third party to save the data offsite. An off-site backup is a smart way to protect the data in terms of catastrophe. Or in case of fire accident to any organization, if the data is stored in some other location it will be helpful to retrieve and use the data.

The price of utility computing varies upon the usage of the company and its requested service. The company charges the client depending on the service they use instead of giving it as a flat fee. The more the client uses the services, the more they should pay. Few companies opt for the packing of services at a reduced rate.

Use Case of Utility Computing

The application of utility computing is popular and diverse in many areas from petty shops to large scale industries. The men tailor shop can update his business by providing many web services and online sales and delivery and he can also customize a mobile app for customers to track their orders. The transportation company in Russia deployed a new system to make instant ticket reservations for passengers. The holiday packages and gifts are offered by IBM to manage the traffic surge at thanksgiving time are managed by utility computing and it reached a grand success in that year by enabling the pay as you go policy.

Properties of Utility Computing

The important properties of utility computing are its scalability, demand pricing, standardized utility computing services, utility computing on virtualization and automation.

- Scalability is an important metric that should be ensured in utility computing to provide sufficient IT resources available at any time. If the demand gets extended, the response time and quality should not get impacted.

- Demand pricing is scheduled effectively to pay for both hardware and software components as per the usage.

- The catalog is produced with standardized services with different service level agreements to the customers. So the consumer has no influence on the behind technology on the computer platform.

- The web services and other resources are shared by the pool of machines which is used in automation and virtualization technologies. It segregates the network into many logical resources instead of the available physical resources. An application is allotted with no specific predefined servers or storage space of any severs with more memory or free server runtime from the resource pool. The deployment and installation of a new server can be done easily and repetitive tasks and jobs can be automated according to SLA.

Utility computing is a bundle of advantage and treats to any type of business because of their variety of services and the pay per use policy. So it is most welcomed in the market and gathered huge attention which can be used and remove according to the demand.

Web Services

A service is a discrete functionality, usually a business activity capable of independent operation, in collaboration with other such services. Web service is the implementation of services using the web technology. Service Orientation is the process of exploring or thinking in terms of services, the service-based development of applications and the outcomes of service implementation.

Service Oriented Architecture (SOA) is architecture for establishing service orientation. SOA specifies the procedure where collection of services communicates with each other using standard protocols, exchanging data or information or providing service interaction. In simple terms, this collection of multiple heterogeneous services under service oriented architecture forms another service or forms an application to serve a business purpose.

SOA is an architectural framework that enables a series of web services to deliver desired functionalities. SOA is a logical way of designing a software system to provide services to end-users or to applications or to other services distributed in a network through standard, published and discoverable interfaces.

Characteristics of SOA Services

The services under SOA framework are as follows:

- Reusable: The services can be reused by multiple process or services depending on their coarse of granularity.

- Autonomous units of business functionality: Each service acts as an independent entity to deliver its desired business functionality.

- Contract-based: The interface and policies are strictly described by standard specification.

- Loosely coupled: Any change in the service implementation does not affect the interface.

- Platform independent: Since SOA supports the transport and interface requirements, the service consumer and SOA service can be on any platform.

- Discoverable and location independent: The service can relocate without disturbing the consuming system as the service are located through a registry and accessed through Universal Resource Locators.

- Standards-based: The services are built, consumed, and described using various standards such as Web Services Definition Language (WSDL) providing information about the service, and a packaging mechanism called Simple Object Access Protocol (SOAP).

Services

A service is a repeatable process typically related to business functionality with a logical representation producing desired result, implemented with standard definitions. To exhibit the desired functionality, the service can act as an individual entity or can interact with other services. The interaction procedure and communication of one process with other process to act as a single process is transparent to the users. An example of service scenario is conducting online courses, online examination and publication of result where multiple services interact with each other to exhibit desired business functionality as a single process. Service interactions can be:

- Man-to-Man: This interaction defines user to user interaction. For example, going to a shop to buy an item and make appropriate payment.

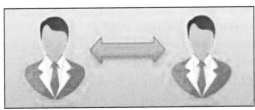

Man-to-Man Interaction.

- Man-to-Machine: This interaction method defines the interaction between an end user with that of the computer or embedded machines employed for specific purpose. Examples for this interaction include user interacting with ATM machines to withdraw cash.

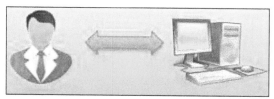

Man-to-Machine Interaction.

- Machine-to-Machine: This defines the interaction of one service from one machine to the service of another machine automatically in distributed manner. This service interaction is generally offered by web services. Example for Machine-to-Machine interaction includes smart phone service synchronizing with Google services.

Machine-to-Machine Interaction.

Web services are the open standard implementation of services through web-based interface mostly for machine-to-machine or service-to-service interaction. These services can be local or distributed, or web-based in nature. Web services are built on top of open standards such as TCP/IP, HTTP, Java, HTML, and XML. The applications programmed in different languages and deployed on various running platforms can use the web services to exchange information or data among themselves over any network including the Internet similar to the inter-process communication in a single computer. This interoperability among platforms is facilitated by the use of open standards.

Web services are self-describing, self-contained software modules, capable of solving problems, on behalf of users or applications. Web Services handle transactions on a distributed infrastructure communicating over public or private networks. Hence, web service is an application component that communicates via open protocols such as HTTP, SMTP etc. It processes eXtensible Markup Language based (XML-based) messages using Simple Object Access Protocol (SOAP). The messages are described using XML Schema. The endpoint description is provided using Web Services Description Language (WSDL) and can be discovered using Universal Description, Discovery, and Integration (UDDI). Web services implementation standards are as follows:

- Discovery: UDDI.

- Description: WSDL.

- Schema: XML.

- Messaging protocol: SOAP.

Characteristics of Web Services

The characteristics of Web services are as follows:

- XML is used by web services at data representation and data transportation layers. The binding of services with platform or network is eliminated by the usage of XML.

- Web services are loosely coupled. If the interface of web service changes, the ability of the service to interact with other service or with users does not change.

- Web services specify a way of defining coarse-grained services, which can access the exact business logic while executing the services.

- Web services can be either synchronous or asynchronous. The binding of the service with the client accessing the service is defined through a synchronous service. In synchronous service implementation, the client will wait for the existing invoked service to complete its operation before proceeding. But, the asynchronous service implementation does not wait but retrieves the result of the service at a later stage.

- Web services are based on RPC calls.

- XML supports complex documents along with data. Business interaction is facilitated by the support of transparent exchange of documents.

Interaction Using Web Services

The interaction of a web service based application with other web service based applications occurs in a structured manner.

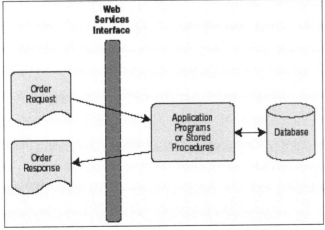

Application to Application Interaction Using Web Service.

A typical 3 tier application consists of web servers at the top layer, the middle layer being the application layer containing business logic with the bottom layer as the database layer. The application layer can interact with the legacy applications. The top layer is the web server layer that interacts with the web servers of other applications through the firewall, which is securing the entire layers of the application. The web server of one application interacts with the web server of the other application over the Internet.

Goals of Web Services

The goals of web services are as follows:

- To enable distributed applications to be dynamically assembled according to changing business needs.

- To allow customization based on devices such as PCs, Workstations, Laptops, mobile phones, PDAs and other forms of network connectivity.

- To allow users access while enabling wide utilization of any given piece of business logic.

Examples of Web Services

Web services can take any of the following forms for establishing the business process as follows:

- A self-contained business task like funds withdrawal or funds deposit service in a bank account.

- A full-fledged business process like automated purchase of office supplies.

- An application like life insurance application, demand forecasts and stock replenishment.

- A service-enabled resource like providing access to a particular back-end database containing patient medical records.

Types of Web Services

The implementation of web services is basically categorized into two types. These are:

- Service-Oriented Web Services using SOAP standards: This implementation focuses mainly on services, where one service offers multiple functionalities. The generic programming is based on JAX-WS, which is a JAVA-API for XML-based Web Services, mainly using WSDL/SOAP.

- Resource-Oriented Web Services using RESTful standards: This implementation focuses mainly on resources. Resources are defined as any directly accessible and distinguishable distributed component available on the network. The standard followed for establishing the services is RESTful Web Services. The generic programming is based on JAX-RS, which is JAVA-API for RESTful Web Services, using only HTTP.

The Web services implements two data formats such as XML and JSON.

- Data Formats: The possible data formats used are XML and JSON. XML is designed to describe data. XML tags are not predefined. Users define their own tags. XML is the perfect choice for enabling cross-platform data communication in web services. The other alternative data format is JSON, which stands for JavaScript Object Notation. This is the syntax for storing and exchanging data. It is a lightweight data interchange format which is language independence, "self-describing" and easy to understand and is an easier-to-use alternative to XML.

Web Services Architecture

The architecture of the web service consists of three major components:

- Registry where the web services are described.

- Requester.

- Provider.

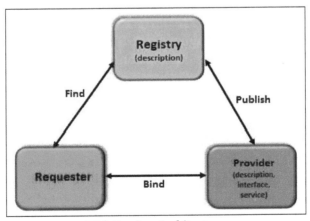

Web Services Architecture.

The Provider

Providers are the components that offer the service. Provider owns the Web service with complete control and implements the business logic. The service provider is responsible for publishing the Web services it provides in a service registry hosted by a service discovery agency. The description involves describing the business, service, and technical information of the Web service, and registering that information with the Web services registry in the format prescribed by the discovery agency.

The Requester

Requester is the client who is in need of the web service may be a human or another web service. The Web services requestor searches the service registry for the desired Web services. This means first to discover the Web services description in a registry provided by a discovery agency and then using the information in the description to bind to the service.

The Registry

Registry is a searchable directory where service descriptions can be published and searched. Service requestors find service descriptions in the registry and obtain binding information for services. This information is sufficient for the service requestor to contact, or bind to, the service provider and thus make use of the services it provides. The Web services discovery agency is responsible for providing the infrastructure required to enable the three operations in the Web services architecture: publishing the Web services by the Web services provider, searching for Web services by Web services requestors, and invoking the Web services.

Components of Web Services Implementation

The components of web service implementation are:

- Web Service Description Language (WSDL): WSDL is an XML technology providing standard for interface description. This provides rules for binding service consumer and provider. This standardizes how a web service represents the input and output parameters of an invocation externally. The function's structure include the nature of the invocation (in only, in/out, etc.); the service's protocol binding and allows different clients to understand other web services.

- Simple Object Application Protocol (SOAP): SOAP is a lightweight protocol used to exchange structured messages and provides a standard packaging structure for transporting XML documents over a variety of standard Internet technologies. SOAP defines encoding and binding standards. This provides a simple structure for doing RPC: by providing document exchange using standard transport mechanism.

- UDDI: Universal Description, Discovery, and Integration (UDDI) provide a worldwide supporting registry of web services. The available web services can be discovered using searching by: Names; Identifiers; Categories; Specifications implemented by the web service. UDDI provides a structure for representing businesses; business relationships; web services; specification metadata and Web service access points.

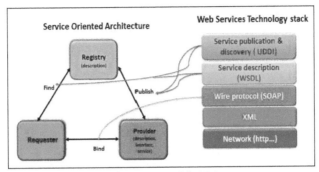

Web Services with SOA.

The services are described using WSDL. The service provider publishes the services and its specification in the registry through UDDI and WSDL. The requester finds the service from the registry using service publication and discovery using UDDI specification. The requester binds with the provider through SOAP.

Representation of Services in Web Service

The services in web service are represented by three components: URI, URL and URN.

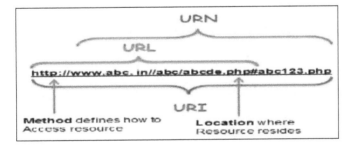

- Uniform Resource Identifier (URI) is an identifier for some resource that can be further classified as a locator, a name, or both. For example, http: is a URI scheme.

- Uniform Resource Locator (URL) gives specific information as to obtain the resource, refers to the subset of URIs that identifies a resource and provides a means of locating the resource.

- Uniform Resource Name (URN) is a subset of URIs that includes a name within a given space, but no location, intended to serve as persistent, location-independent identifier and allows simple mapping of namespaces into a single URN namespace.

SOA and Cloud Computing

Cloud Computing delivers the underlying resources as services. The services are represented in Service Oriented Architecture or SOA. In an advanced stage of implementation of business requirements, both the service consumer and service provider can be placed in a cloud environment and the provider expose the services as cloud enabled services which can realize the cloud functionalities.

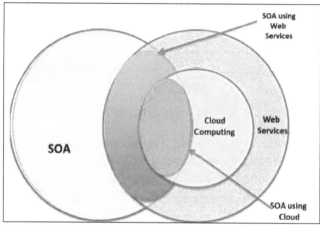

SOA and Cloud Overlapping.

Social Cloud Computing

Cloud environments typically provide low level abstractions of computation or storage. Computation and Storage Clouds are complementary and act as building blocks from which high level service Clouds and mash-ups can be created. Storage Clouds are often used to extend the capabilities of storage-limited devices such as phones and desktops, and provide transparent access to data from anywhere. There are a large number of commercial Cloud providers such as Amazon EC2/S3, Google App Engine, Microsoft Azure and also many smaller scale open Clouds like Nimbus and Eucalyptus. These Clouds provide access to scalable virtualized resources (computation, storage, applications) through pre-dominantly posted price mechanisms.

A Social Cloud, therefore, is a scalable computing model in which virtualized resources contributed by users are dynamically provisioned amongst a group of friends. Compensation for use is optional as users may wish to share resources without payment, and rather utilize a reciprocal credit (or barter) based model. In both cases guarantees are offered through customized SLAs. In a sense, this model is similar to a Volunteer computing approach, in that friends share resources amongst each other for little to no gain. However, unlike Volunteer models there is inherent accountability through existing friend relationships. There are a number of advantages gained by leveraging Social networking platforms, in particular we gain access to huge user communities, can exploit existing user management functionality, and rely on pre-established trust formed through user relationships.

There are multiple instances of Social network and Cloud computing integration. However, most examples use Cloud platforms to host Social networks or create scalable applications within the Social network. For example, Facebook users can build scalable Cloud based applications hosted by Amazon Web Services. Social networking as a means of dynamic user management, authentication and user experience. Automated Service Provisioning ENvironment (ASPEN) takes an enterprise approach to integrating Web 2.0, Social networking and Cloud Computing by exposing applications hosted by Cloud providers to user communities in Facebook. There are similar efforts in the Grid community to leverage Social networking concepts, communities, and mechanisms. PolarGrid is one such example which extracts Social data using the OpenSocial interface and relies on OpenID for identification.

Different Social networking functions are then incorporated in an application specific portal. An alternative approach involves building a Social network around a specific application domain such as MyExperiment for biologists and nanoHub for the nanoscience community. MyExperiment provides a virtual research environment where collaborators can share research and execute scientific workflows remotely. nanoHub allows users to share data as well as transparently execute applications on distributed resource providers such as TeraGrid. These platforms highlight the types of collaborative scientific scenarios possible in Social networks, however they are not generic as they are focused on the communities they serve and lack the sizable user bases of Social networking platforms. Additionally, administrators need to create and manage proprietary social infrastructures and users require credentials for each network they participate in (unless they use OpenID). The same functionality can be realized using a Social Cloud deployed in an existing Social network. For example Social Storage Clouds can be used to store/share data and information (for example academic papers, scientific workflows, datasets, and analysis) within a community.

Volunteer computing is a distributed computing model in which users donate computing resources to a specific (academic) project. The first volunteer project was the Great Internet Mersenne Prime Search in 1996; however the term gained much exposure through the SETI@Home and Folding@home projects in the late 90's. These projects showed the enormous computing power available through collaborative systems. One of the most relevant Volunteer computing efforts is Storage@Home which is used to back up and share huge data sets arising from scientific research. The focus of volunteer computing has since shifted towards generic middleware providing a distributed infrastructure independent of the type of computation, for example the Berkeley Open Infrastructure for Network Computing (BOINC). Most Volunteer platforms do not define SLAs, typically users are anonymous and are not accountable for their actions (they are rewarded with different incentives however). In a Social Cloud context this does not suffice as users need to have some level of accountability. A more realistic model for this type of open sharing is a credit based system in which users earn credits by contributing resources and then spend these credits when using other resources. This type of policy is used in systems such as PlanetLab.

Social Cloud Architecture

The Social Cloud architecture presented is designed as a Facebook application, to make use of this widely used platform, development environment and API. In a Social Cloud, services can be mapped to particular users through Facebook identification, allowing for the definition of unique policies regarding the interactions between users. For example, a user could limit trading with close friends only, users in the same country/network/group, all friends, or even friends of friends. A specialized banking component manages the transfer of credits between users while also storing information relating to current reservations. A high level architecture of a Social Cloud is shown in figure.

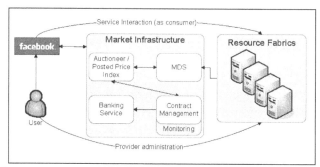

Social Cloud Architecture: Users register Cloud services and friends are then able to provision and use these resources through the Social Cloud Facebook application. Allocation is conducted by the underlying market infrastructure(s).

Cloud Architecture

Cloud Architecture refers to the various components in terms of databases, software capabilities, applications, etc. engineered to leverage the power of cloud resources to solve business problems. Cloud architecture defines the components as well as the relationships between them. In the world of cloud computing, all the requirements used to fulfill the promise of cloud can be organized in a layered architecture. The architecture must depict the basic cloud stack and all the actors involved in cloud computing.

There is a cloud stack, which is the main block. This is flanked by the various actors either responsible to support the stack in some way or to consume the services provided by the stack.

Actors in Cloud Computing

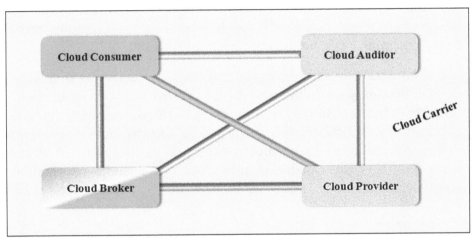

Cloud Service Provider

"A cloud provider is a person, organization or an entity responsible for making a service available to interested parties". It is the responsibility of the provider to acquire and manage the complete infrastructure starting from the procurement and installation of the required infrastructure, the necessary cloud software that provides the services, and making arrangement to deliver the appropriate services to the Cloud Consumers through network access. The various activities are described below:

- Activity 1 - Manages the cloud stack: The first part of managing the stack is the procurement and installation of the hardware and software needed and arranging these appropriately in one or more data centers, after deciding the location, size and the number of data centers. This is a continuous process since there will be newer versions of the software used, machines needed to be maintained/replaced, new technology coming in etc.

- Activity 2 - Makes services available: This includes service deployment and service orchestration. In the deployment part, a service is made available to the consumers based on the type of service and the type of cloud for which it is being deployed. For example, in case the service is being deployed for a public cloud, it will be made available at a cost and hence the arrangements must be done accordingly. On the other hand, if it is for a private cloud, the arrangements will vary since; a private cloud doesn't normally offer a pay-as-you-go model. Hence it is the job of the service provider to ensure that methodologies in making a service available have been adopted as is appropriate.

- Activity 3 - Service management: Many functions are required including business support, provisioning and configuration of the services, ensuring that appropriate portability and interoperability are provided so that the services are consumed properly. Another major part of service management is the availability of service orchestration. As given by NIST, "Service Orchestration refers to the composition of system components to support the Cloud Providers activities in arrangement, coordination and management of computing resources in order to provide cloud services to Cloud Consumers".

- Activity 4 - Security and privacy: At this point in time, there is still not a well-defined boundary to decide who has to provide the security of the data and processes of the consumers when present in cloud. However, that the service provider plays a major role in providing security goes without question. Privacy, on the other hand, must be the sole responsibility of the providers since only they are capable of protecting the personal information of the consumers in the cloud.

Cloud Consumer

As defined by NIST, "The cloud consumer is the principal stakeholder for the cloud computing service. A cloud consumer represents a person or organization that maintains a business relationship with, and uses the service from a cloud provider". The major activities of the consumer are to look up for services to see if a service matching her own requirement is available in the list of services provided by the service provider. Typically, a service provider would make a catalog of services available for the probable consumer to browse, and, if found, the consumer will proceed to the next stage. For the consumer, the next stage after deciding the required service is to request the appropriate service as per the interface made available by the service provider.

Accordingly, a service contract along with the necessary Service Level Agreements (SLAs) will be set up between the two parties and on agreement of all the necessary terms and conditions regarding the price and other items, the consumer will start using the service. According to the amount of usage, the cloud consumer will be charged keeping in mind the SLA that has been drawn before such consumption. SLA may cover terms regarding other aspects such as the limitations of the service by the provider, the QoS(quality of service) expected, kind of security provided, the expected performance and failures thereof etc. A cloud consumer may choose one cloud provider over another offering the same service for a better pricing and other favorable conditions.

Cloud Auditor

From the time of conception of cloud, the question that arises is whether my data is safe with the cloud and how does an independent consumer decide that there is no leakage of sensitive data stored in the cloud to the business rival. A cloud auditor is one tool that can solve the problem, given sufficient power and trust of both the producers and the consumers. The auditor must have the power to perform an independent examination of cloud service controls and would be able to express an opinion. If a cloud provider makes promises about the standards being followed, an auditor can verify conformance to standards through review of objective evidence. Evaluation of the services provided by a cloud provider can be done by an auditor for security measures, conformance to the promised privacy practices, etc. Two major activities are the security audit and the privacy audit. In security audit, the auditor would be able to check and decide conformance to agreement in terms of confidentiality, integrity and availability of the data and the overall system as is implemented by the service provider and as is expected by the consumer according to the SLA drawn between these two parties. A privacy audit is more relevant to the Federal agencies that need to check that confidentiality, integrity, and availability of an individual's personal information are not being compromised and are maintained with high integrity at every stage of development and operation.

Cloud Broker

With the advent of the cloud technology, computing in cloud is becoming more and more complex for a consumer to just rent and consume a service. To this end, a cloud broker can help. In the presence of a broker, services may be requested through a broker by a client, rather than requesting a service for herself. Typically a broker is expected to manage the use, performance and delivery of cloud services. They are also expected to negotiate between cloud providers and cloud consumers. Cloud broker implements three important activities, viz., service intermediation, service aggregation and service arbitrage. In intermediation, a cloud broker provides certain value-added services to cloud consumers such as performance reporting, enhanced security etc. They essentially extend the services provided by the provider for the convenience and requirements of the consumer. When a certain provider does not have all the required services needed by the consumer, it is the broker who can aggregate different services by different providers to create a new service to the benefit of the consumer. This is service aggregation. In service arbitrage also a broker does service aggregation except that broker has freedom in choosing and flexibly selecting different services from multiple agencies.

Cloud Carrier

The job of providing connectivity and transport of cloud services between cloud consumers and cloud providers is performed by the cloud carrier. In cloud, different access devices are used and integrating these is the task of the carrier. The success of service delivery depends on the contract that may be drawn in the form of an SLA between the service provider and a carrier. Cloud provider will set up such SLAs based on its own SLA with the consumer, ensuring the level of security and other assurance required by the consumer.

Cloud Stack

The heart of the architecture is the cloud stack, which is realized as a layered arrangement as shown in figure below. Hardware resources are at the lowest layer, middleware at the middle layer and software is at the top most layer.

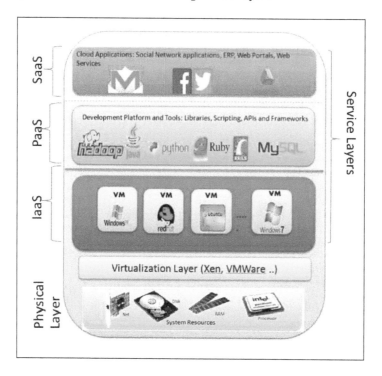

The lowest layer is the Physical Layer that comprises of a number of data centers, which in turn consists of thousands of nodes grouped together. This layer is built using networks and clusters of computing and storage nodes. This layer is responsible for communication between the hardware devices and the operating system i.e., the management of the distributed resources.

Above the physical hardware layer is the Virtualization Layer, which is the key enabling technology behind cloud computing. It is an abstract layer over which a pool of virtual resources called virtual machines (VM) are created from the underneath physical resources. In this layer, the hypervisor or virtual machine monitor (VMM) exposes the distributed infrastructure as a set of virtual machines. The hardware resources like CPU, memory are finely partitioned as per the needs of the users or the applications.

Cloud Model

The Cloud model is composed of five essential characteristics, three service models, and four deployment models as illustrated in figure. The essential cloud characteristics are on-demand self-service, broad network access, resource pooling, rapid elasticity, and measured service. Computing capabilities, such as server time and network storage, can be unilaterally provisioned or de-provisioned as needed and automatically. They are available over the Internet and accessible through heterogeneous client platforms, such as laptops and mobile phones. The computing resources are pooled and dynamically assigned and reassigned to serve multiple consumers. The capabilities appear to be unlimited, as they can be rapidly and elastically provisioned to quickly scale out and rapidly released to quickly scale in. The resource use is automatically controlled and optimized by leveraged metering capabilities.

The cloud service models are Software as a Service (SaaS), Platform as a Service (PaaS), and Infrastructure as a Service (IaaS). SaaS allows use of applications that run on the cloud infrastructure and are accessible from various client devices. PaaS allows creation of applications with supported programming languages and tools, and their deployment onto the cloud infrastructure. IaaS allows to provision processing, storage, networks, and other fundamental computing resources to deploy and run software, including operating systems and applications.

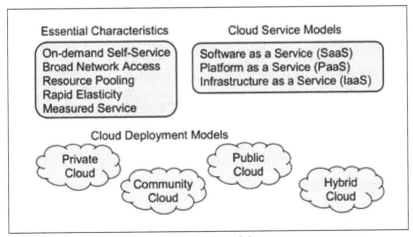

The Cloud Model.

With SaaS, the users do not manage or control even the individual application capabilities. With PaaS they have control over the deployed applications and the hosting environment configurations. With IaaS, users do not manage or control the underlying cloud infrastructure, but they have control over the operating systems, deployed applications, storage, and limited control on networking components.

The cloud deployment models are private, community, public, and hybrid. Private clouds are operated for individual organizations. Community clouds are operated for organizations with shared interests. Public clouds are available to the general public or large industry groups.

Hybrid clouds comprise unique clouds, bound by technology that enables interoperability amongst the clouds. The relative efficiencies of the different cloud computing models can be determined by measuring and analyzing the following set of cloud computing infrastructure metrics:

- Hardware costs: Measured by determining the virtualized environment needed to consolidate a traditional infrastructure of independent servers. The consolidation goal is to increase the efficiency by reducing the overall infrastructure costs through elimination of redundant and under-utilized servers.

- Software costs: The dominant costs are determined by the suite of virtualization software and service management software. The virtualization software provides the intelligence for server consolidation and improving system utilization by executing different workloads on a single server. The service management software facilitates efficient workflows, administration and management of multiple workloads, and automated service provisioning.

- Real-time provisioning costs: Measured by determining the elapsed time for deploying new systems, upgrading existing systems, or migrating to a new consolidated cloud computing platform. Realtime provisioning is usually accomplished via automated tools that may also be integrated into the service management system.

- System administration costs: Realized by measuring the efficiency of managing virtual servers. Cloud computing models have more virtual servers and comparably few physical servers. In addition, in today's environment, virtual servers are more complex to administer than physical ones. Effective system administration in the cloud computing model would require a paradigm shift from the traditional centralized approach to a fully distributed approach neatly integrated into virtual servers.

References

- Cloud-computing: investopedia.com, Retrieved 02, March 2020

- Advantages-and-disadvantages-of-cloud: stratospherenetworks.com, Retrieved 30, July 2020

- What-is-utility-computing: educba.com, Retrieved 22, April 2020

- Social-Cloud-Cloud-Computing-in-Social-Networks-221399959: researchgate.net, Retrieved 14, August 2020

Cloud Deployment and Service Models

The type of access to a cloud is defined through cloud deployment models. A few types of cloud deployment models are public cloud, private cloud, hybrid cloud and community cloud. This chapter closely examines the key concepts of these cloud deployment models as well as cloud service models to provide an extensive understanding of the subject.

Cloud Deployment Models

A cloud deployment model is defined according to where the infrastructure for the deployment resides and who has control over that infrastructure. Deciding which deployment model you will go with is one of the most important cloud deployment decisions you will make. It indicates how the cloud services are made available to users. Each cloud deployment model satisfies different organizational needs, so it's important that you choose a model that will satisfy the needs of your organization. Perhaps even more important is the fact that each cloud deployment model has a different value proposition and different costs associated with it.

Public Cloud

A public cloud is a platform that uses the standard cloud computing model to make resources such as virtual machines, applications or storage available to users remotely. Public cloud services may be free or offered through a variety of subscription or on-demand pricing schemes, including a pay-per-usage model. The main benefits of the public cloud are as follows:

- A reduced need for organizations to invest in and maintain their own on-premises IT resources.

- Scalability to meet workload and user demands.

- Fewer wasted resources because customers only pay for what they use.

Public cloud is an alternative application development approach to traditional on-premises IT architectures. In the basic public cloud computing model, a third-party provider hosts scalable, on-demand IT resources and delivers them to users over a network connection, either over the public internet or a dedicated network. The public cloud model encompasses many different technologies, capabilities and features. At its core, however, a public cloud consists of the following key characteristics:

- On-demand computing and self-service provisioning.
- Resource pooling.
- Scalability and rapid elasticity.
- Pay-per use pricing.
- Measured service.
- Resiliency and availability.
- Security.
- Broad network access.

The public cloud provider supplies the infrastructure needed to host and deploy workloads in the cloud. It also offers tools and services to help customers manage cloud applications, such as data storage, security and monitoring.

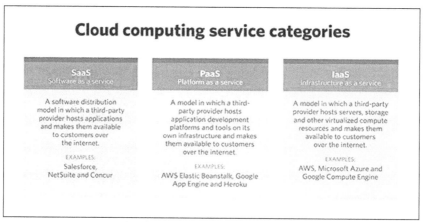

Cloud computing service categories.

When selecting a provider, organizations can opt for a large, general-use provider such as AWS, Microsoft Azure or Google Cloud Platform (GCP) or a smaller provider. General cloud providers offer broad availability and integration options and are desirable for multipurpose cloud needs. Niche providers offer more customization.

Migration

Myriad factors drive businesses to migrate from on-premises facilities to the public cloud. For example, some organizations require support for more diverse workload types that data centers can't provide. Cost considerations, less overhead maintenance and redundancy are other common reasons.

After choosing a provider, the IT team must select a cloud migration method to move data into the provider's cloud. Offline migration requires IT teams to copy local data onto a portable device and physically transfer that hardware to the cloud provider. Online data migration occurs via network connection over the public internet or a cloud provider's networking service. When the amount of data to transfer is significant, offline migration is typically faster and less expensive. Online migration is a good fit for organizations that won't move high volumes of data.

Organizations also onboard existing on-premises applications into the cloud, and there are a few approaches to consider. A lift-and-shift method moves the application to the cloud as is, without any redesign. This approach is fast, but is prone to complications the application may not perform properly within cloud architecture and may cost more than if it remained on premises. Alternatively, IT teams can refactor on-premises applications ahead of the migration. Refactoring takes more time and planning, but this method ensures that the application will function effectively in the cloud. Another option is to rebuild entirely as a cloud-native application.

Public Cloud Architecture

A public cloud is a fully virtualized environment that relies on high-bandwidth network connectivity to transmit data. Providers have a multi-tenant architecture that enables users or tenants to run workloads on shared infrastructure and use the same computing resources. A tenant's data in the public cloud is logically separated and remains isolated from the data of other tenants.

Providers operate cloud services in logically isolated locations within public cloud regions. These locations, called availability zones, typically consist of two or more connected highly available physical data centers.

Organizations select availability zones based on compliance and proximity to end users. Cloud resources can be replicated across multiple availability zones for redundancy and protection against outages. Public cloud architecture can be further categorized by service model. These are the three most common service models:

- Infrastructure as a service (IaaS), in which a third-party provider hosts infrastructure components, such as servers and storage, as well as a virtualization layer. The IaaS provider offers virtualized computing resources, such as VMs, over the internet or through dedicated connections.

- Platform as a service (PaaS), in which a third-party provider delivers hardware and software tools usually those needed for application development, including operating systems to its users as a service.

- Software as a service (SaaS), in which a third-party provider hosts applications and makes them available to customers over the internet.

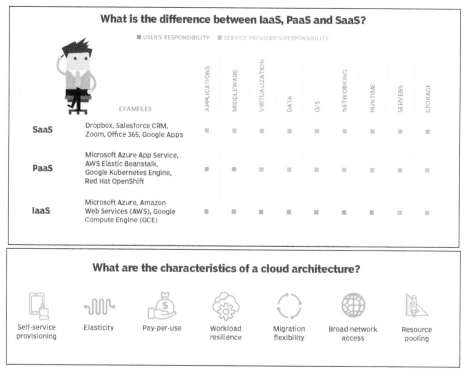

Understand the basics of cloud computing.

The service model determines how much control the user has over certain aspects of the cloud. For example, in IaaS deployments, cloud customers create virtual machines, install operating systems and manage cloud networking configurations. But in PaaS and SaaS models, the cloud networking architecture is fully managed by the provider.

In addition to the three main service models, a function-as-a-service model further abstracts cloud infrastructure and resources. This is particularly useful for customers that create microservices. It is based on serverless computing, a mechanism that breaks workloads into small, event-driven resource components, and runs the code without the need to deliberately create and manage virtual machines. This enables organizations to execute code-based tasks on demand when trigged; the components exist only for as long as the assigned task runs. In this model, the provider handles the underlying server maintenance.

Organizations can also opt for a storage-as-a-service provider in the public cloud. The provider delivers a storage platform with offerings such bare-metal storage capacity, storage object and storage applications, such as backup and archiving.

Benefits and Challenges of Public Cloud Computing

Enterprises must weigh the advantages and drawbacks of public cloud adoption in order to determine whether it's the right fit.

Benefits of Public Cloud Computing

The cloud has many advantages over on-premises IT:

- Access to new technologies: Organizations that use large cloud providers get early and instant access to the IT industry's latest technologies, ranging from automatically updated applications to machine learning and AI. Many cloud customers lack the resources to obtain such access on their own.

- Virtually unlimited scalability: Cloud capacity and resources rapidly expand to meet user demands and traffic spikes. Public cloud users also achieve greater redundancy and high availability due to the providers' various, logically separated cloud locations. In addition to redundancy and availability, public cloud users receive faster connectivity between cloud services and end-users via their provider's network interfaces though bandwidth and latency issues are still common.

- Flexibility: The flexible and scalable nature of public cloud storage enables users to store high volumes of data and access them easily. Many organizations rely on the cloud for disaster recovery, to back up data and applications in case of emergency or outage. It's tempting to store all data indefinitely, but users should set up a data retention policy that regularly deletes old data from storage to avoid long-term storage costs and to maintain privacy.

- Analytics: Organizations should gather useful metrics on the data they store and resources they use. Doing so presents another benefit cloud data analytics. Public cloud services can perform analytics on high volumes and accommodate a variety of data types to present business insights.

Other public cloud benefits include access to the provider's reliable infrastructure and the abstraction of overhead management tasks. These enable IT staff to focus on tasks that are more important to the business, such as writing code for applications.

Challenges of Public Cloud Computing

While the public cloud presents many advantages, organizations also face a range of challenges and must separate cloud computing myths from realities:

- Runaway costs: Increasingly complex cloud costs and pricing models make it difficult for organizations to keep track of IT spending. The cloud is often cheaper than on-premises options, but organizations sometimes end up paying more for cloud. Pricey data egress fees make staying on a cloud budget even more challenging.

- Scarce cloud expertise: Another challenge is the skills gap among IT professionals in the cloud computing industry. Companies struggle to hire and retain staff with expertise in building and managing modern cloud applications. Without this expertise, organizations are ill-equipped to handle the complexities of modern IT demands. IT professionals that hope to fill these roles can better prepare for career opportunities by fine-tuning their cloud skills in areas such as architecture, operations and coding.

• Limited controls: Public cloud users also face the tradeoff of limited control over their IT stack since the provider can decide when and how to manage configurations. Other public cloud challenges include data separation problems due to multi-tenancy, latency issues for remote end-users and adherence to industry- and country-specific regulations.

Private Cloud

Private cloud is a cloud computing environment dedicated to a single customer. It combines many of the benefits of cloud computing with the security and control of on-premises IT infrastructure. Private cloud (also known as an internal cloud or corporate cloud) is a cloud computing environment in which all hardware and software resources are dedicated exclusively to, and accessible only by, a single customer. Private cloud combines many of the benefits of cloud computing including elasticity, scalability, and ease of service delivery with the access control, security, and resource customization of on-premises infrastructure.

Many companies choose private cloud over public cloud (cloud computing services delivered over infrastructure shared by multiple customers) because private cloud is an easier way (or the only way) to meet their regulatory compliance requirements. Others choose private cloud because their workloads deal with confidential documents, intellectual property, personally identifiable information (PII), medical records, financial data, or other sensitive data.

By building private cloud architecture according to cloud native principles, an organization gives itself the flexibility to easily move workloads to public cloud or run them within a hybrid cloud (mixed public and private cloud) environment whenever they're ready.

Working of Private Cloud

Private cloud is a single-tenant environment, meaning all resources are accessible to one customer only this is referred to as isolated access. Private clouds are typically hosted on-premises in the customer's data center. But, private clouds can also be hosted on an independent cloud provider's infrastructure or built on rented infrastructure housed in an offsite data center. Management models also vary the customer can manage everything itself or outsource partial or full management to a service provider.

Private Cloud Architecture

Single-tenant design aside, private cloud is based on the same technologies as other clouds technologies that enable the customer to provision and configure virtual servers and computing resources on demand in order to quickly and easily (or even automatically) scale in response to spikes in usage and traffic, to implement redundancy for high availability, and to optimize utilization of resources overall. These technologies include the following:

- Virtualization, which enables IT resources to be abstracted from their underlying physical hardware and pooled into unbounded resource pools of computing, storage, memory, and networking capacity that can then portioned among multiple virtual machines (VMs), containers, or other virtualized IT infrastructure elements. By removing the constraints of physical hardware, virtualization enables maximum utilization of hardware, allows hardware to be shared efficiently across multiple users and applications, and makes possible the scalability, agility, and elasticity of the cloud.

- Management software gives administrators centralized control over the infrastructure and applications running on it. This makes it possible to optimize security, availability, and resource utilization in the private cloud environment.

- Automation speeds tasks such as server provisioning and integrations that would otherwise need to be performed manually and repeatedly. Automation reduces the need for human intervention, making self-service resource delivery possible.

In addition, private cloud users can adopt cloud native application architectures and practices such as DevOps, containers, and microservices that can bring even greater efficiency and flexibility and enable a smooth transition to a public cloud or hybrid cloud environment in the future.

Virtual Private Cloud

A virtual private cloud (VPC) is a service from a public cloud provider that creates a private cloud-like environment on public cloud infrastructure. In a VPC, virtual network functions and security features give a customer the ability to define and control a logically isolated space in the public cloud, mimicking the private cloud's enhanced security within a multi-tenant environment.

VPC customers can benefit from the public cloud's resource availability, scalability, flexibility, and cost-effectiveness, all while retaining much of the security and control of private cloud. In most cases, a VPC will be less expensive to build and simpler to manage than an on-premises private cloud.

Managed Private Cloud

Several vendors are now offering fully managed private cloud solutions. This model differs from VPC in that a managed private cloud is a single-tenant environment. Responsibility for managing and maintaining the infrastructure is outsourced to a third-party service provider.

The physical hardware usually resides in the service provider's data center, although vendors also offer management services for infrastructure located in an enterprise's own data center. Managed private clouds allow for greater customization than is possible in a multi-tenant environment and incorporate the usual security benefits of a private cloud but are more expensive than self-managed infrastructures.

Hosted Private Cloud

This type of private cloud is hosted by a separate cloud service provider on-premises or in a data center, but the server is not shared with other organizations. The cloud service provider is responsible for configuring the network and maintaining the hardware for the private cloud, as well as keeping the software updated. This option provides the best of both worlds for organizations that require the security and availability of a private cloud but prefer not to invest in an in-house data center.

Private Cloud Storage

Also known as internal cloud storage, private cloud storage entails drawing upon cloud service delivery models to supply storage to an enterprise. Data is stored within the data center on a dedicated infrastructure, but access is delivered to business units and possibly partner organizations as a service. This allows the enterprise to take advantage of some of cloud computing's benefits such as elasticity and rapid provisioning while retaining a single-tenant architecture.

Public Cloud vs. Private Cloud

- Public cloud is used as a service via Internet by the users, whereas a private cloud, as the name conveys is deployed within certain boundaries like firewall settings and is completely managed and monitored by the users working on it in an organization.

- Users have to pay a monthly bill for public cloud services, but in private cloud money is charged on the basis of per GB usage along with bandwidth transfer fees.

- Public cloud functions on the prime principle of storage demand scalability, which means it requires no hardware device. On the contrary, no hardware is required even in private cloud, but the data stored in the private cloud can only be shared amongst users of an organization and third party sharing depends upon trust they build with them. It is also entirely monitored by the business entity where it is running.

The following diagram reviews the differences between public and private clouds:

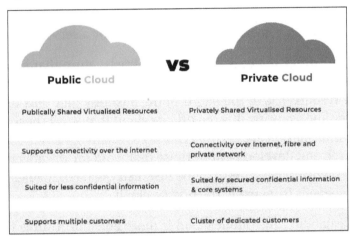

Any enterprises are beginning their cloud evaluation with a "private cloud." Researcher extended the definition of private cloud to be a "single tenant" cloud, as some enterprises may choose to use a single tenant cloud hosted at a service provider, versus hosting their cloud within their own data centers. In the figure below, we show two private clouds, connected via policy-based replication in two data centers. This provides the assurance of backup and disaster recovery that many enterprises require. A third location could easily be added for even higher levels of backup and disaster recovery.

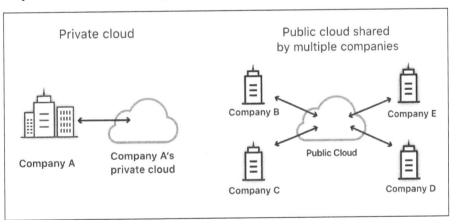

Private cloud inside an enterprise.

The growth of storage is driving increased costs, and the enterprise is on a continuous search to improve the way they can cost-effectively manage this growing data. The primary difference between hybrid cloud and private cloud is the extension of service provider oriented low cost cloud storage to the enterprise. The service provider based cloud may be a private cloud (single tenant) or a public cloud (multi-tenant). There are several implementations of hybrid cloud. The service provider cloud may enable enterprises to leverage the volume efficiencies of the service providers to realize additional savings. The private cloud, or enterprise cloud, is where the infrastructure is created or set up solely for one organization. Management of the infrastructure can be done in the comfort of the site of the organization itself. But if the company chooses, it can also be managed offsite, either as a hosted or managed cloud, by a service provider.

Public cloud, on the other hand, is the type of infrastructure that serves a number of tenants. Most of the tenants are small scale businesses and the general public. The ownership of the resources is in the hands of the business that sells the service. When it comes to privacy and security, it is the private cloud that works best. One can be sure that all data and information are secure. This is especially great for companies that do specialized research and development or those that work for the government. Furthermore, additional security measures may be installed. Also companies with huge databases can greatly benefit from using the private cloud.

On the issue of scalability, the public cloud is more efficient. Unlike the private cloud whose scalability potential is restricted or limited due to the company's limited emises, the public cloud shares more common resources which make it more scalable. The client business does not have to worry about additional servers as this is the job of the provider. Virtualization knowledge is another issue to consider. Though there have been attempts at creating a company's own private cloud, the problem comes in when there is the lack of expertise and experience of the employees. The staff that handles this area should be knowledgeable. This is not a problem for the public cloud.

Another important consideration is pricing. The private cloud is, obviously, more costly that the other one. If the company does not need the advanced security features and network latency, then the public cloud will do as it is more affordable. And for now, what is most necessary to do for companies is to start transferring their files to the cloud and be able to compete with the rest of the business world. The majority of public cloud deployments are generally used for web servers or development systems where security and compliance requirements of larger organizations and their customers is not an issue. Private cloud computing, on the other hand, by definition is a single-tenant environment where the hardware, storage and network are dedicated to a single client or company. The public cloud is defined as a multi-tenant environment, where you buy a "server slice" in a cloud computing environment that is shared with a number of other clients or tenants.

Private Cloud Computing Trades-Offs

- Security: Because private clouds are dedicated to a single organization, the hardware, data storage and network can be designed to assure high levels of security that cannot be accessed by other clients in the same data center.

- Compliance: Sarbanes Oxley, PCI and HIPAA compliance cannot be delivered through a public cloud deployment. Because the hardware, storage and network configuration is dedicated to a single client, compliance is much easier to achieve.

- Customizable: Hardware performance, network performance and storage performance can be specified and customized in the private cloud.

- Hybrid Deployments: If a dedicated server is required to run a high speed database application, that hardware can be integrated into a private cloud, in effect, hybridizing the solution between virtual servers and dedicated servers. This can't be achieved in a public cloud.

Challenges of a Private Cloud

There are a few constraints and challenges that would make the public cloud model more appealing to a lot of organizations. There are inherent challenges with private cloud that need to be addressed before an organization can venture down the path of building one.

- Upfront Capital Cost: One of the drawbacks of private clouds is that organizations still need to buy, build and manage the cloud infrastructure, which defeats the primary premise of cloud computing. One of the key value propositions of cloud computing is that it drastically reduces the upfront capital cost of in-house infrastructure, while providing the same or better service for a simple recurring operational cost. This benefit cannot be realized with private cloud infrastructures.

- Time and Resources: Not all organizations have the time or resources with in-house expertise to build the infrastructure and automation required to stand up and operate a private cloud. It involves much up-front investment in time and resources compared to simply going with a public cloud. However, there are many up and coming startups that are offering private cloud related services and products that organizations can use in their internal data center. While these products still need time to mature and become mainstream, this represents a significant shift towards the availability of the technology required to install and manage private cloud computing infrastructures. These product and service offerings could mitigate some of the risks and challenges and blur the line between a private and public cloud.

- Size of the organization: Not all organizations can afford to build a private cloud for the two reasons listed above. Crafting a business case for building a private cloud for a smaller organization is difficult, since building the in house infrastructure for the private cloud does not provide as much of a return on investment as larger cloud deployments do. The public cloud provides impressive benefits related to economies of scale, and smaller organizations will find it difficult to build a private cloud solution that can match that.

Hybrid Cloud

A hybrid cloud is a cloud computing environment that uses a mix of on-premises, private cloud and third-party, public cloud services with orchestration between these platforms. This typically involves a connection from an on-premises data center to a public cloud. The connection also can involve other private assets, including edge devices or other clouds.

Working of Hybrid Cloud

A hybrid cloud model allows enterprises to deploy workloads in private IT environments or public clouds and move between them as computing needs and costs change. This gives a business greater flexibility and more data deployment options. A hybrid cloud workload includes the network, hosting and web service features of an application.

While the terms are sometimes discussed interchangeably, there are key differences between hybrid and multi-cloud models. A hybrid cloud creates a single environment to operate both in on-premises, private resources and in public cloud resources such as those offered by AWS, Microsoft and Google. A multi-cloud environment consists of two or more public cloud providers but does not require a private or on-premises component.

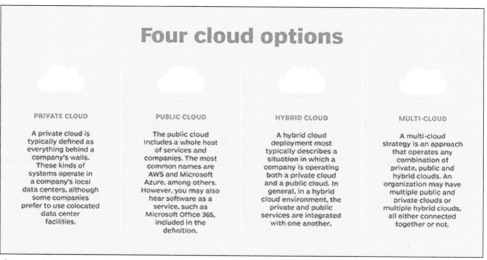

Understand the similarities and differences between the four cloud models. For many organizations, a hybrid cloud model provides the best of on-premises IT and cloud computing.

Benefits of Hybrid Cloud

Hybrid cloud computing enables an enterprise to deploy its most sensitive workloads in an on-premises cloud and to host less-critical resources on a third-party public cloud provider. This approach allows organizations to get the best of both private and public cloud models. The core benefits of hybrid cloud include the following:

- Flexibility: Users work with various types of data in disparate environments and adjust their infrastructure. A company can build a hybrid cloud that works for its needs, using traditional systems as well as the latest cloud technology, without a full commitment to a vendor. Organizations savvy with a hybrid cloud setup can migrate workloads to and from their traditional infrastructure and a vendor's public cloud whenever necessary.

- Cost management: With a private cloud, organizations own and operate the data center infrastructure, which requires significant capital expense and fixed costs. Alternatively, the public cloud offers resources and services that are accounted as variable and operational expenses. Hybrid cloud users can choose to run workloads in whichever environment is more cost effective.

- Agility and scalability: Hybrid cloud offers more resource options via a public cloud provider vs. an organization's physical data center. This makes it easier to provision, deploy and scale resources to meet demand spikes. When demand exceeds capacity of the local data center, an organization can burst the application to the public cloud to access extra scale and capacity.

- Resiliency and interoperability: To increase resiliency, a business can run workloads redundantly in both private and public environments. Components of one workload can also run in both environments and interoperate.

- Compliance: Compliance restrictions on where data can reside mean organizations in highly regulated industries cannot move all workloads to the public cloud. With hybrid cloud, organizations can keep data in a private environment while operating workloads in the cloud, or they can operate workloads in a private data center and move data to and from the public cloud as needed. This allows companies to meet regulatory requirements and still benefit from the elasticity of the cloud.

Other hybrid cloud advantages include consistency and support for greater standardization in IT management practices.

Hybrid Cloud Architecture

Establishing a hybrid cloud requires three main components:

- A public infrastructure as a service (IaaS) platform, such as Amazon Web Services, Microsoft Azure or Google Cloud Platform.

- Private computing resources, such as an on-premises data center.

- An adequate network connection to the hybrid cloud's private and public cloud environments.

Networking and Integration

A strong network connection is critical to a successful hybrid cloud strategy. Typically this involves a wide area network (WAN) or dedicated networking service for additional security. Consistently evaluate your connection and ensure it meets the uptime requirements specified in your service-level agreement (SLA) with a cloud provider.

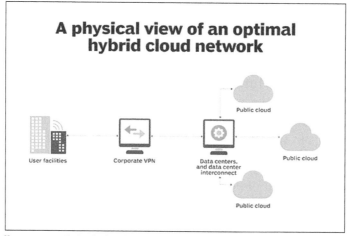

Ideally, a network for hybrid clouds connects applications to corporate data center and cloud resources outside the VPN.

An enterprise has no direct control over public cloud architecture. That means a business must adjust its resources and environments to make them compatible with its chosen public cloud platform's resources, services and application programming interfaces (APIs). This requires implementation of suitable hardware within the data center, including servers, storage, a local area network and load balancers. For an effective hybrid arrangement, these on-premises resources and environments must be able to integrate and interoperate with public cloud services and APIs.

There are two main approaches to hybrid cloud integration: Use the cloud as the front-end application hosting point, or create a unified elastic resource pool of data center and cloud functions. Consider the following questions to determine which integration strategy is right for you:

- What are my architecture's complete hybrid integration requirements?
- What combinations of technologies address my integration requirements?
- What is the most appropriate integration style or pattern for my use cases?
- Where does it make sense to deploy my integration platform?

Hybrid Cloud Platforms

Hybrid cloud architecture traditionally builds a virtualization layer or hypervisor on top of on-premises resources to create and support virtual machines and increasingly container-based workloads. On top of this, IT teams install a private cloud software layer, which delivers various cloud capabilities: self-service access to services such as compute or database instances, automation and orchestration, resilience and billing. This layer is integrated into services and APIs from public cloud providers.

A newer architectural approach involves public cloud providers offering hybrid cloud platforms that extend public cloud services into private data centers. This means everything is based on the same software stack. These hybrid cloud platforms deliver connections between public and private resources in different ways, but they often incorporate common industry technologies, such as Kubernetes to orchestrate container-based services.

Hybrid Cloud Use Cases

Before you implement a hybrid cloud model, review common hybrid cloud use cases to determine whether this approach fits company's IT needs.

- Digital transformation: Companies often want to modernize their IT infrastructure through public cloud adoption. Legacy applications or compliance factors, however, may preclude a business from entirely shutting down a private data center. Hybrid cloud enables companies with mixed data and application types to migrate parts of their IT infrastructure to the cloud and to retain on-premises applications that must remain in the data center.

- Disaster recovery: A hybrid cloud helps organizations fortify their disaster recovery strategy by replicating on-premises workloads and backing up data in the cloud. If there's a disruption in the data center, workloads fail over to the cloud environment and operate properly via on-demand cloud resources. However, implementation must be handled properly to avoid hybrid cloud backup challenges, such as bandwidth consumption and management complexity.

- Development and testing: It's cheaper and faster to develop and test applications in the public cloud because there's no need to purchase and set up on-premises physical hardware.

- Data processing: Hybrid cloud gives a company the option to use powerful public cloud services to run periodic analytical queries on locally stored data.

- Highly changeable workloads: Hybrid cloud is particularly valuable for dynamic or highly changeable workloads. For example, a transactional order-entry system that experiences significant seasonal demand spikes is a good hybrid cloud candidate.

- Exploring a cloud provider: Some organizations use a hybrid approach to evaluate a potential public cloud migration. An IT team can experiment with cloud tools on a small scale and learn how to work with the cloud provider before committing to a full public cloud adoption.

Hybrid Cloud Challenges

Despite these benefits, there are hybrid cloud challenges to consider:

- Compatibility: On-premises and public cloud environments work together in a hybrid cloud approach, but they are not fully compatible. It is difficult to synchronize them. For example, the back-end data center component of a hybrid cloud application cannot respond as quickly as the front-end public cloud component. This causes latency problems and other complexities.

- Data handling: Improper data placement and movement in a hybrid cloud can create security and cost challenges. To secure data in transit, encrypt all traffic. Meanwhile, if data is not located in the right environment, moving data across cloud environments triggers cloud network and egress fees that can quickly add up. Ensure that necessary workloads reside in public cloud storage to avoid unnecessary transfers and prevent spikes in charges.

- Complex access management: Authentication and authorization add to the hybrid cloud security challenges. Organizations need to adopt centralized protocols to access data in both private and public cloud environments. Use IAM and single sign-on tools, and assign permissions only when necessary to concentrate hybrid cloud access management.

- Skills gap: Hybrid cloud adoption requires users and IT staff to possess a specific set of technical skills. The expertise required to work with a public cloud differs from that for a private data center, and the learning curve to close that skills gap can lead to human error.

- Private cloud maintenance: A hybrid cloud's on-premises or private cloud component requires substantial investment, maintenance and expertise. Implementation of additional software, such as databases, helpdesk systems and other tools can further complicate a private cloud. Proper data planning, public cloud security tools and investment in employee training and cloud certifications can help mitigate some of the challenges associated with hybrid cloud adoption.

Hybrid Cloud Management

Because hybrid cloud architecture comprises multiple environments and types of components, cloud management is a complex task. Fortunately, there are strategies and tools to help resolve the complications of hybrid management and create a streamlined approach across environments. Implement hybrid cloud management practices to maximize control of your environments. For example, establish a cloud governance policy that defines standard processes for resource configurations, access control and other important operations. This will create a consistent, unified approach across the various components in your hybrid architecture.

Centralize control of on-premises and cloud-based resources with a hybrid cloud management tool set. These types of tools provide capabilities such as cost and performance monitoring, security, reporting and analytics. There are many third-party hybrid cloud management tools to choose from. Carefully evaluate hybrid cloud management tools before making your choice. Explore and test different features within your environment to select the tool that suits your organization's particular hybrid architecture.

Infrastructure-as-code tools can also help manage hybrid deployment. For example, Ansible, Puppet and HashiCorp's Terraform all provide hybrid cloud management capabilities. Adoption of containers and Kubernetes orchestration is another way to unify the resources in hybrid architecture.

Components of Hybrid Cloud Security

- Hybrid cloud security, like computer security in general, consists of three components: physical, technical, and administrative.

- Physical controls are for securing your actual hardware. Examples include locks, guards, and security cameras.

- Technical controls are protections designed into IT systems themselves, such as encryption, network authentication, and management software. Many of the strongest security tools for hybrid cloud are technical controls.

- Finally, administrative controls are programs to help people act in ways that enhance security, such as training and disaster planning.

Physical Controls for Hybrid Cloud Security

Hybrid clouds can span multiple locations, which makes physical security a special challenge. You can't build a perimeter around all your machines and lock the door. In the case of shared resources like a public cloud, you may have Service Level Agreements (SLAs) with your cloud provider that define which physical security standards will be met. For example, some public cloud providers have arrangements with government clients to restrict which personnel have access to the physical hardware. But even with good SLAs, you're giving up some level of control when you're relying on a public cloud provider. This means other security controls become even more important.

Technical Controls for Hybrid Cloud Security

Technical controls are the heart of hybrid cloud security. The centralized management of a hybrid cloud makes technical controls easier to implement. Some of the most powerful technical controls in your hybrid cloud toolbox are encryption, automation, orchestration, access control, and endpoint security.

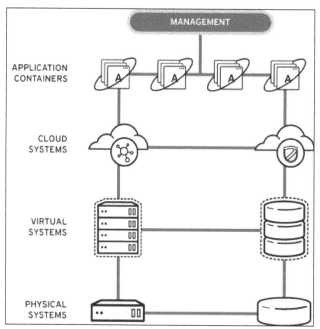

Hybrid Management Diagram.

Encryption

Encryption greatly reduces the risk that any readable data would be exposed even if a physical machine is compromised. You can encrypt data at rest and data in motion. Here's how:

- Protect your data at rest:

  - Full disk (partition encryption) protects your data while your computer is off. Try the Linux Unified Key Setup-on-disk (LUSK) format which can encrypt your hard drive partitions in bulk.

  - Hardware encryption that will protect the hard drive from unauthorized access. Try the Trusted Platform Module (TPM), which is a hardware chip that stores cryptographic keys. When the TPM is enabled, the hard drive is locked until the user is able to authenticate their login.

  - Encrypt root volumes without manually entering your passwords. If you have built a highly automated cloud environment, build upon that work with automated encryption. If you are using Linux, try the Network Bound Disk Encryption (NBDE), which works on both physical and virtual machines. Bonus: make TPM part of the NBDE and provide two layers of security (the NMDE will help protect networked environments, while the TPM will work on premises).

- Protect your data in motion:

  ○ Encrypt your network session. Data in motion is at a much higher risk of interception and alteration. Try the Internet Protocol Security (IPsec) which is an extension of the Internet Protocol that uses cryptography.

  ○ Select products that already implement security standards. Look for products that support the Federal Information Processing Standard (FIPS) Publication 140-2 which uses cryptographic modules to protect high-risk data.

Automation

To appreciate why automation is a natural fit for hybrid clouds, consider the drawbacks of manual monitoring and patching. Manual monitoring for security and compliance often has more risks than rewards. Manual patches and configuration management risk being implemented asynchronously. It also makes implementing self-service systems more difficult. If there is a security breach, records of manual patches and configurations risk being lost and can lead to team in-fighting and finger-pointing. Additionally, manual processes tend to be more error prone and take more time.

Automation, by contrast, allows you to stay ahead of risks, rather than react to them. Automation gives you the ability to set rules, share, and verify processes which ultimately make it easier to pass security audits. As you evaluate your hybrid cloud environments, think about automating the following processes:

- Monitoring your environments.

- Checking for compliance.

- Implementing patches.

- Implementing custom or regulatory security baselines.

Orchestration

Cloud orchestration goes a step further. You can think of automation as defining specific ingredients, and orchestration as a cookbook of recipes that bring the ingredients together. Orchestration makes it possible to manage cloud resources and their software components as a single unit, and then deploy them in an automated, repeatable way through a template. Orchestration's biggest boon to security is standardization. You can deliver the flexibility of the cloud while still making sure the systems deployed meet your standards for security and compliance.

Access Control

Hybrid clouds also depend on access control. Restrict user accounts to only the privileges they need and consider requiring two-factor authentication. Limiting access to users connected to a Virtual Private Network (VPN) can also help you maintain security standards.

Endpoint Security

Endpoint security often means using software to remotely revoke access or wipe sensitive data if a user's smartphone, tablet, or computer gets lost, stolen, or hacked. Users can connect to a hybrid cloud with personal devices from anywhere, making endpoint security an essential control. Adversaries may target your systems with phishing attacks on individual users and malware that compromises individual devices. We're listing it here as a technical control, but endpoint security combines physical, technical and administrative controls: Keep physical devices secure, use technical controls to limit the risks if a device falls into the wrong hands, and train users in good security practices.

Community Cloud

Community Cloud is a hybrid form of private cloud. They are multi-tenant platforms that enable different organizations to work on a shared platform.

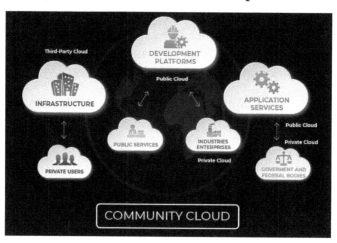

The purpose of this concept is to allow multiple customers to work on joint projects and applications that belong to the community, where it is necessary to have a centralized cloud infrastructure. In other words, Community Cloud is a distributed infrastructure that solves the specific issues of business sectors by integrating the services provided by different types of cloud solutions.

The communities involved in these projects, such as tenders, business organizations, and research companies, focus on similar issues in their cloud interactions. Their shared interests may include concepts and policies related to security and compliance considerations, and the goals of the project as well.

Community Cloud computing facilitates its users to identify and analyze their business demands better. Community Cloud may be hosted in a data center owned by one of the tenants, or by a third-party cloud services provider and can be either on-site or off-site.

Community Cloud Examples and Use Cases

Cloud providers have developed Community Cloud offerings, and some organizations are already seeing the benefits. The following list shows some of the main scenarios of the Community Cloud model that is beneficial to the participating organizations:

- Multiple governmental departments that perform transactions with one another can have their processing systems on shared infrastructure. This setup makes it cost-effective to the tenants, and can also reduce their data traffic.

- Federal agencies in the United States. Government entities in the U.S. that share similar requirements related to security levels, audit, and privacy can use Community Cloud. As it is community-based, users are confident enough to invest in the platform for their projects.

- Multiple companies may need a particular system or application hosted on cloud services. The cloud provider can allow various users to connect to the same environment and segment their sessions logically. Such a setup removes the need to have separate servers for each client who has the same intentions.

- Agencies can use this model to test applications with high-end security needs rather than using a Public Cloud. Given the regulatory measures associated with Community Clouds, this could be an opportunity to test features of a Public Cloud offering.

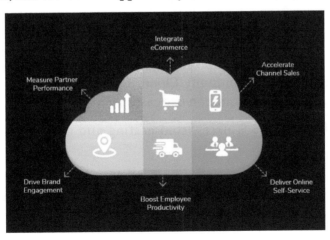

Benefits of Community Clouds

Community Cloud provides benefits to organizations in the community, individually as well as collectively. Organizations do not have to worry about the security concerns linked with Public Cloud because of the closed user group. This recent cloud computing model has great potential for businesses seeking cost-effective cloud services to collaborate on joint projects, as it comes with multiple advantages:

- Openness and Impartiality: Community Clouds are open systems, and they remove the dependency organizations have on cloud service providers. Organizations can achieve many benefits while avoiding the disadvantages of both public and private clouds.

- Flexibility and Scalability:

  ○ Ensures compatibility among each of its users, allowing them to modify properties according to their individual use cases. They also enable companies to interact with their remote employees and support the use of different devices, be it a smartphone or a tablet. This makes this type of cloud solution more flexible to users' demands.

  ○ Consists of a community of users and, as such, is scalable in different aspects such as hardware resources, services, and manpower. It takes into account demand growth, and you only have to increase the user-base.

- High Availability and Reliability: Your cloud service must be able to ensure the availability of data and applications at all times. Community Clouds secure your data in the same way as any other cloud service, by replicating data and applications in multiple secure locations to protect them from unforeseen circumstances. Cloud possesses redundant infrastructure to make sure data is available whenever and wherever you need it. High availability and reliability are critical concerns for any type of cloud solution.

- Security and Compliance: Two significant concerns discussed when organizations rely on cloud computing are data security and compliance with relevant regulatory authorities. Compromising each other's data security is not profitable to anyone in a Community Cloud. Users can configure various levels of security for their data. Common use cases:

  ○ The ability to block users from editing and downloading specific datasets.

  ○ Making sensitive data subject to strict regulations on who has access to Sharing sensitive data unique to a particular organization would bring harm to all the members involved.

  ○ What devices can store sensitive data.

- Convenience and Control: Conflicts related to convenience and control do not arise in a Community Cloud. Democracy is a crucial factor the Community Cloud offers as all tenants share and own the infrastructure and make decisions collaboratively. This setup allows organizations to have their data closer to them while avoiding the complexities of a Private Cloud.

- Less Work for the IT Department: Having data, applications, and systems in the cloud means that you do not have to manage them entirely. This convenience eliminates the need for tenants to employ extra human resources to manage the system. Even in a self-managed solution, the work is divided among the participating organizations.

- Environment Sustainability: In the Community Cloud, organizations use a single platform for all their needs, which dissuades them from investing in separate cloud facilities. This shift introduces a symbiotic relationship between broadening and shrinking the use of cloud among clients. With the reduction of organizations using different clouds, resources are used more efficiently, thus leading to a smaller carbon footprint.

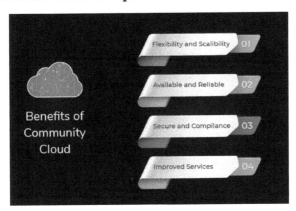

In addition to the direct benefits, it helps users avoid most of the disadvantages of Private and Public Cloud solutions. They allow users to avoid the higher cost of private clouds and the uncertainty of Public Clouds.

Community Cloud Challenges

The biggest concerns regarding Community Cloud are cloud security considerations and trust. No standard cloud model exists for defining best practices and identifying security liabilities of the data and applications which would reside on these servers. Since this type of cloud is relatively new and still evolving, users may hesitate to go into the whole dilemma of abandoning the current approach.

Security Considerations

Multiple organizations will access and control the infrastructure in a Community Cloud, requiring specialized security configurations:

- Every participant in the community has authorized access to the data. Therefore, organizations must make sure they do not share restricted data.

- Rules and regulations related to compliance within a Community Cloud can be confusing. The systems of one organization may have to adhere to the rules and regulations of other organizations involved in the community as well.

- Agreements among the member organizations in a Community Cloud are vital. For example, just because all the organizations have shared access to audit logs does not mean that every organization has to go through them. Having an agreement on who performs such tasks will not only save time and workforce needs but also help to avoid ambiguity.

The security concerns regarding Community Clouds are not unique to them but apply to any other type of Public Cloud as well. As such, it is safe to say that Community Cloud solutions offer a unique opportunity to organizations that wish to work on joint projects.

What to Consider Before Adopting a Community Cloud Approach

Community Clouds address industry-specific requirements while delivering the cost-effectiveness of a Public cloud. So the answer to the question "What is a Community Cloud" will depend on the individual needs of the collaborating organizations. If you are looking for a cost-effective approach which deals with fewer complexities in a cloud environment, and at the same time ensures the security of your applications, Community Cloud computing is the way to go. However, there are certain things that you should clarify before moving on to this model:

- The economic model of the cloud offering concerning the payments of the maintenance and capitals costs.

- Availability and Service Level Agreements (SLA).

- How tenants handle security issues and regulations when sharing data among participating organizations.

- Service Outage information.

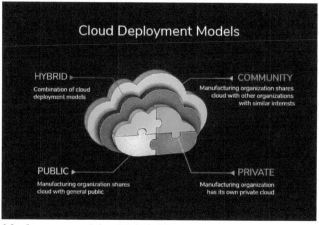

Diagram of deployment models with hybrid, community, public, and private cloud.

There is no guarantee as to whether this model of Cloud Computing will be as popular as Public Cloud. The beauty of the Community Cloud model is that it can cater to the needs of a specific group of users.

Cloud Service Models

The three main cloud service models are software as a service (SaaS), platform as a service (PaaS), and infrastructure as a service (IaaS). Each service model has its own benefits and drawbacks. One thing you must be careful with when you choose a service model is what you as the customer will be responsible for. Whether you are using a cloud provider or not, you must always ensure that you have accounted for the maintenance and monitoring of your systems and applications. The only difference with a cloud model is that there are certain aspects that the provider will be responsible for.

Software as a Service (SaaS)

Software as a service (SaaS) allows users to connect to and use cloud-based apps over the Internet. Common examples are email, calendaring and office tools. SaaS provides a complete software solution which you purchase on a pay-as-you-go basis from a cloud service provider. You rent the use of an app for your organisation and your users connect to it over the Internet, usually with a web browser. All of the underlying infrastructure, middleware, app software and app data are located in the service provider's data center. The service provider manages the hardware and software and with the appropriate service agreement, will ensure the availability and the security of the app and your data as well. SaaS allows your organisation to get quickly up and running with an app at minimal upfront cost.

Characteristics of SaaS

A good way to understand the SaaS model is by thinking of a bank, which protects the privacy of each customer while providing service that is reliable and secure on a massive scale. A bank's customers all use the same financial systems and technology without worrying about anyone accessing their personal information without authorization. A "bank" meets the key characteristics of the SaaS model:

- Multitenant Architecture: A multitenant architecture, in which all users and applications share a single, common infrastructure and code base that is centrally maintained. Because SaaS vendor clients are all on the same infrastructure and code base, vendors can innovate more quickly and save the valuable development time previously spent on maintaining numerous versions of outdated code.

- Easy Customisation: The ability for each user to easily customise applications to fit their business processes without affecting the common infrastructure. Because of the way SaaS is architected, these customisations are unique to each company or user and are always preserved through upgrades. That means SaaS providers can make upgrades more often, with less customer risk and much lower adoption cost.

- Better Access: Improved access to data from any networked device while making it easier to manage privileges, monitor data use, and ensure everyone sees the same information at the same time.

- SaaS Harnesses the Consumer Web: Anyone familiar with Amazon.com or My Yahoo! will be familiar with the Web interface of typical SaaS applications. With the SaaS model, you can customise with point-and-click ease, making the weeks or months it takes to update traditional business software seem hopelessly old fashioned.

- SaaS Trends: Organisations are now developing SaaS integration platforms (or SIPs) for building additional SaaS applications. The consulting firm Saugatuck Technology calls this the "third wave" in software adoption: when SaaS moves beyond standalone software functionality to become a platform for mission-critical applications.

Advantages of SaaS

SaaS offers many potential advantages over the traditional models of business software installation, including:

- Lower up-front cost: SaaS is generally subscription-based and has no up-front license fees resulting in lower initial costs. The SaaS provider manages the IT infrastructure that is running the software, which brings down fees for hardware and software maintenance.

- Quick set up and deployment: SaaS application is already installed and configured in the cloud. This minimizes common delays resulting from often lengthy traditional software deployment.

- Easy upgrades: The SaaS providers deal with hardware and software updates, deploying upgrades centrally to the hosted applications and removing this workload and responsibility from you.

- Accessibility: All you need to access a SaaS application is a browser and an internet connection. This is generally available on a wide range of devices and from anywhere in the world, making SaaS more accessible than the traditional business software installation.

- Scalability: SaaS providers generally offer many subscription options and flexibility to change subscriptions as and when needed, e.g. when your business grows, or more users need to access the service.

SaaS, and more widely cloud computing, can help you make the most of a limited IT budget while giving you access to the latest technology and professional support. However, you should consider some potential disadvantages before making a final decision.

Disadvantages of SaaS

SaaS model sometimes has certain shortcomings, including:

- Lack of control: In-house software application gives businesses a higher degree of control than hosted solutions where control resides with a third party. Typically everyone has to use the latest version of the software application and cannot defer upgrades or changes in the features.

- Security and data concerns: Access management and the privacy of sensitive information is a major consideration around cloud and hosted services.

- Limited range of applications: While SaaS is becoming more popular, there are still many applications that don't offer a hosted platform.

- Connectivity requirement: Since the SaaS model is based on web delivery, if your internet service fails, you will lose access to your software or data.

- Performance: SaaS may run at somewhat slower speeds than on-premise client or server applications, so it's worth keeping performance in mind your software isn't hosted on a local machine.

Infrastructure as a Service (IaaS)

Infrastructure as a service (IaaS) is a form of cloud computing that provides virtualized computing resources over the internet. IaaS is one of the three main categories of cloud computing services, alongside software as a service (SaaS) and platform as a service (PaaS). In the IaaS model, the cloud provider manages IT infrastructures such as storage, server and networking resources, and delivers them to subscriber organizations via virtual machines accessible through the internet. IaaS can have many benefits for organizations, such as potentially making workloads faster, easier, more flexible and more cost efficient.

IaaS Architecture

In an IaaS service model, a cloud provider hosts the infrastructure components that are traditionally present in an on-premises data center. This includes servers, storage and networking hardware, as well as the virtualization or hypervisor layer. IaaS providers also supply a range of services to accompany those infrastructure components. These can include the following:

- Detailed billing.
- Monitoring.

- Log access.

- Security.

- Load balancing.

- Clustering.

- Storage resiliency, such as backup, replication and recovery.

These services are increasingly policy-driven, enabling IaaS users to implement greater levels of automation and orchestration for important infrastructure tasks. For example, a user can implement policies to drive load balancing to maintain application availability and performance.

Working of IaaS

IaaS customers access resources and services through a wide area network (WAN), such as the internet, and can use the cloud provider's services to install the remaining elements of an application stack. For example, the user can log in to the IaaS platform to create virtual machines (VMs); install operating systems in each VM; deploy middleware, such as databases; create storage buckets for workloads and backups; and install the enterprise workload into that VM. Customers can then use the provider's services to track costs, monitor performance, balance network traffic, troubleshoot application issues and manage disaster recovery.

Any cloud computing model requires the participation of a provider. The provider is often a third-party organization that specializes in selling IaaS. Amazon Web Services (AWS) and Google Cloud Platform (GCP) are examples of independent IaaS providers. A business might also opt to deploy a private cloud, becoming its own provider of infrastructure services.

Advantages of IaaS

Organizations choose IaaS because it is often easier, faster and more cost-efficient to operate a workload without having to buy, manage and support the underlying infrastructure. With IaaS, a business can simply rent or lease that infrastructure from another business. IaaS is an effective cloud service model for workloads that are temporary, experimental or that change unexpectedly. For example, if a business is developing a new software product, it might be more cost-effective to host and test the application using an IaaS provider.

Once the new software is tested and refined, the business can remove it from the IaaS environment for a more traditional, in-house deployment. Conversely, the business could commit that piece of software to a long-term IaaS deployment if the costs of a long-term commitment are less. In general, IaaS customers pay on a per-user basis, typically by the hour, week or month. Some IaaS providers also charge customers based on the amount of virtual machine space they use. This pay-as-you-go model eliminates the capital expense of deploying in-house hardware and software. When a business cannot use third-party providers, a private cloud built on premises can still offer the control and scalability of IaaS though the cost benefits no longer apply.

Disadvantages of IaaS

Despite its flexible, pay-as-you-go model, IaaS billing can be a problem for some businesses. Cloud billing is extremely granular, and it is broken out to reflect the precise usage of services. It is common for users to experience sticker shock or finding costs to be higher than expected when reviewing the bills for every resource and service involved in application deployment. Users should monitor their IaaS environments and bills closely to understand how IaaS is being used and to avoid being charged for unauthorized services.

Insight is another common problem for IaaS users. Because IaaS providers own the infrastructure, the details of their infrastructure configuration and performance are rarely transparent to IaaS users. This lack of transparency can make systems management and monitoring more difficult for users. IaaS users are also concerned about service resilience. The workload's availability and performance are highly dependent on the provider. If an IaaS provider experiences network bottlenecks or any form of internal or external downtime, the users' workloads will be affected. In addition, because IaaS is a multi-tenant architecture, the noisy neighbor issue can negatively impact users' workloads.

Platform as a Service (PaaS)

In cloud computing, Platform as a Service (PaaS) represents a link between "software as a service" (SaaS) and "infrastructure as a service" (IaaS). While IaaS only provides the infrastructure that companies need for their work, PaaS goes one step further and offers a package of useful tools so you can start developing apps. This means, you can design, test, revise, and deploy the product to your users: all this is possible with platform as a service. Well-known platform as a service solutions include Salesforce's Google App Engine (GAE), Microsoft Azure, and force.com.

Structure of PaaS

PaaS's offerings consist of basic infrastructure such as servers, operating systems, storage space, and middleware, i.e. programs that interconnect multiple applications. In addition, there are resources such as development tools, programming languages, database management systems, and container techniques. The various solutions contained on the platform are either the provider's proprietary developments or come from third parties. Their purpose is to enable customers to develop new web applications quickly and conveniently.

If you use PaaS, you no longer have to worry about buying and managing the infrastructure or purchasing the solutions required for development, but can focus completely on programming your application and on your customers. The resulting programs can then be made available as software as a service via the cloud. These can be, for example, commercial apps or internal software that are only intended for use within the company itself.

Working Principles of PaaS

With platform as a service, you basically develop your product as you would in a self-built development environment. Once the code is created, you transfer it to the platform, where it is deployed and executed in a container that meets the resource requirements. Here, you can see changes instantly. Many PaaS services are able to run multiple versions of a program at the same time e.g. you can create live test environments or execute roll backs from previous versions.

Web hosting services are a simple example of how platform as a service works. As a customer, you create the code and enter it into the web hosting service. This executes the code and displays the web page you created. You don't have to worry about storage space, maintenance, or database setup. However, PaaS offerings can also be much more complex and include many other features.

Special Features of PaaS

If you use platform as a service, only certain programming languages are available. So you need to choose a provider that supports the languages you use. Pay close attention to the requirements of your own project and which programming languages are used by the individual PaaS solutions.

Also consider what services you will probably need in the future if the applications you develop are successful and generate more traffic. Your service must remain stable even in the event of a sudden influx of users poor performance has a negative impact on your company because it leads to long loading times. And this in turn leads to customer dissatisfaction. The services you book can usually be upscaled, but the price increases as well. You should consider these costs before choosing a provider.

When is Platform as a Service Used?

In addition to app development, there are other application areas in which PaaS is frequently used:

- To develop or extend new programming interfaces (APIs).

- It can also be used to analyze extensive data to better predict demand for specific products.

- PaaS can also be used to access or set up a business process management platform that stores business rules or service level agreements.

- The platform can also be used to manage critical business data and provide an overview of data, even if it is stored redundantly on different systems.

- In addition, platform as a service can act as a communication platform to deliver voice, video, or messaging content.

- As Database PaaS, the service is also used for automated databases.

- The Internet of Things, in particular, is considered to be a future growth area. This plays an important role for cloud services, as PaaS environments are also suitable for developing new applications that can be used for the Internet of Things.

Types of PaaS

In view of the wide range of platform as service solutions on offer, it is hardly possible to assign clear categories to these. This is because the individual models sometimes differ greatly and are tailored to different needs. Nevertheless, there are certain characteristics that can be used to identify different types.

For example, a distinction is made between application PaaS (aPaaS) and integration and governance PaaS (iPaaS). The first model describes the deployment of apps that have a graphical interface for operation. For example, this could be a program for internal use in the company that employees can access and use via the cloud.

iPaaS, on the other hand, aims to integrate cloud services, with the platform ensuring that middleware is no longer required to provide applications. An example of this is the Anypoint Platform developed by MuleSoft. The pure application provisioning, on the other hand, allows neither the development nor the testing of apps, but only their operation.

In addition, there are the open PaaS offers. This refers to applications such as Google App Engine, which make it possible to work in an open source environment and for which the programming languages, databases, servers, or operating systems are not predefined.

Advantages and Disadvantages of PaaS

PaaS has a lot to offer to companies in need of significant application development throughout the course of business. Some businesses may only really need one of the IaaS providers, some SaaS applications, just another service provider. However, there are many factors to consider when considering implementing a PaaS model to business.

Advantages of PaaS

As with other cloud computing solutions, like the SaaS and IaaS model, there's a lot to love about PaaS opportunities for companies in need.

- Faster Development: In many cases, speed is an important part of coding and development. When products need to be rolled out quickly, managing in-house resources can be a drain on productivity, leading to corner cutting or delays. Due to the ease of use of PaaS solutions, projects can be completed on an accelerated timeline without compromising quality.

- Easier Training: With one platform that can cater to many jobs, it's easy to get staff members up and running without significant training requirements. This can ensure all developers and coders are on the same page throughout all projects.

- Multi-platform capabilities: As PaaS solutions aren't specific to one device or network, like many on-site development platforms are, companies can design applications and programs across operating systems and devices, like desktop computers and mobile phones. This can also ensure compatibility.

- Sophisticated Abilities: In many cases, on-site development platforms are limited based on the in-house technology available. This can mean out of date tools that require significant workarounds to achieve the right results. Due to the web-based nature of PaaS options, updates and upgrades are rolled out automatically to provide access to the best tools at all times.

- Remote Work: Due to the web-based nature of cloud solutions and cloud hosting, designers are no longer limited to on-site technology. PaaS products can be accessed anywhere at any time on any device, making it easy for team members to collaborate from anywhere in the world.

- Comprehensive Experience: PaaS products are designed to offer comprehensive and complete solutions, from brainstorming to implementation. Due to the ease of use and available opportunities, companies taking advantage of PaaS are guaranteed support that can make managing the application lifecycle fast and easy.

Disadvantages of PaaS

Despite the advantages, PaaS products aren't right for everyone. Before moving forward, be sure to take these potential downsides into consideration. Be aware that some of these challenges are related to particular PaaS providers versus all PaaS providers and thus may not apply universally.

- Security: Security is up to the cloud provider, leaving businesses essentially vulnerable to the whims of others. While this can be fine for those who choose a private cloud experience with customized security protocols, those who use public cloud PaaS products, like those hosted through Microsoft Azure, in conjunction with a public cloud infrastructure must settle with whatever security policies are in place with no opportunity to upgrade or enhance offerings.

- Infrastructure Challenges: As PaaS is not an infrastructure function, performance often depends on a company's own infrastructure. If the available options cannot meet the demands of a PaaS solution or are otherwise unsuitable for cloud computing, other issues may arise. This can mean an investment in updating on-site infrastructure or switching to an IaaS product.

- Compatibility Issues: While cloud computing opportunities are intended to be as user-friendly and compatible as possible, if a company's existing operations aren't compatible with current hardware, traditional software, or cloud-based software, users may run into challenges. In general, PaaS products are customized by the provider, not the user, so users must accept whatever defaults a provider chooses, regardless of potential incompatibilities, whether technological or operational.

- Lack of Scalability: All cloud solutions are scalable to some degree, but PaaS options are less flexible than, say, IaaS solutions. The overall technology is a little more rigid, making use challenging for those who see big growth on the horizon. This can also be problematic for companies that see significant seasonality and experience periods of unusually high demand throughout the year.

References

- Public-cloud: techtarget.com, Retrieved 18, February 2020

- Introduction-to-private-cloud: ibm.com, Retrieved 23, June 2020

- Private-Vs-Public-Cloud-258253155: researchgate.net, Retrieved 05, March 2020

- Hybrid-cloud: techtarget.com, Retrieved 25, July 2020

- What-is-hybrid-cloud-security: redhat.com, Retrieved 02, April 2020

- Advantages-and-disadvantages-software-service-saas: nibusinessinfo.co.uk, Retrieved 22, February 2020

- Infrastructure-as-a-Service-IaaS: techtarget.com, Retrieved 21, August 2020

- Paas-platform-as-a-service: ionos.com, Retrieved 13, May 2020

3

Cloud Storage

The digital data in cloud computing is physically stored in multiple servers which are managed and owned by hosting companies. It involves keeping the data safe and accessible. The topics elaborated in this chapter will help in gaining a better perspective about the different aspects of data storage in cloud computing such as object storage and cooperative storage cloud.

Cloud storage is a model of data storage in which the digital data is stored in logical pools, the physical storage spans multiple servers (and often locations), and the physical environment is typically owned and managed by a hosting company. These cloud storage providers are responsible for keeping the data available and accessible, and the physical environment protected and running. People and organizations buy or lease storage capacity from the providers to store user, organization, or application data.

Cloud storage services may be accessed through a co-located cloud computer service, a web service application programming interface (API) or by applications that utilize the API, such as cloud desktop storage, a cloud storage gateway or Web-based content management systems.

History

Cloud computing is believed to have been invented by Joseph Carl Robnett Licklider in the 1960s with his work on ARPANET to connect people and data from anywhere at any time.

In 1983, CompuServe offered its consumer users a small amount of disk space that could be used to store any files they chose to upload.

In 1994, AT&T launched PersonaLink Services, an online platform for personal and business communication and entrepreneurship. The storage was one of the first to be all web-based, and referenced in their commercials as, "you can think of our electronic meeting place as the cloud." Amazon Web Services introduced their cloud storage service AWS S3 in 2006, and has gained widespread recognition and adoption as the storage supplier to popular services such as Smugmug, Dropbox, Synaptop and Pinterest. In 2005, Box announced an online file sharing and personal cloud content management service for businesses.

Architecture

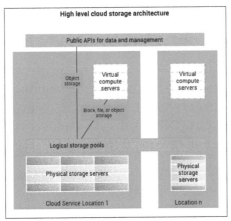

A high level architecture of cloud storage.

Cloud storage is based on highly virtualized infrastructure and is like broader cloud computing in terms of accessible interfaces, near-instant elasticity and scalability, multi-tenancy, and metered resources. Cloud storage services can be utilized from an off-premises service (Amazon S3) or deployed on-premises (ViON Capacity Services).

Cloud storage typically refers to a hosted object storage service, but the term has broadened to include other types of data storage that are now available as a service, like block storage.

Object storage services like Amazon S3 and Microsoft Azure Storage, object storage software like Openstack Swift, object storage systems like EMC Atmos, EMC ECS and Hitachi Content Platform, and distributed storage research projects like OceanStore and VISION Cloud are all examples of storage that can be hosted and deployed with cloud storage characteristics.

Cloud storage is:

- Made up of many distributed resources, but still acts as one, either in a federated or a cooperative storage cloud architecture.

- Highly fault tolerant through redundancy and distribution of data.

- Highly durable through the creation of versioned copies.

- Typically eventually consistent with regard to data replicas.

Advantages

- Companies need only pay for the storage they actually use, typically an average of consumption during a month. This does not mean that cloud storage is less expensive, only that it incurs operating expenses rather than capital expenses.

- Businesses using cloud storage can cut their energy consumption by up to 70% making them a more green business. Also at the vendor level they are dealing with higher levels of energy so they will be more equipped with managing it in order to keep their own costs down as well.

- Organizations can choose between off-premises and on-premises cloud storage options, or a mixture of the two options, depending on relevant decision criteria that is complementary to initial direct cost savings potential; for instance, continuity of operations (COOP), disaster recovery (DR), security (PII, HIPAA, SARBOX, IA/CND), and records retention laws, regulations, and policies.

- Storage availability and data protection is intrinsic to object storage architecture, so depending on the application, the additional technology, effort and cost to add availability and protection can be eliminated.

- Storage maintenance tasks, such as purchasing additional storage capacity, are offloaded to the responsibility of a service provider.

- Cloud storage provides users with immediate access to a broad range of resources and applications hosted in the infrastructure of another organization via a web service interface.

- Cloud storage can be used for copying virtual machine images from the cloud to on-premises locations or to import a virtual machine image from an on-premises location to the cloud image library. In addition, cloud storage can be used to move virtual machine images between user accounts or between data centers.

- Cloud storage can be used as natural disaster proof backup, as normally there are 2 or 3 different backup servers located in different places around the globe.

Potential Concerns

Attack Surface Area

Outsourcing data storage increases the attack surface area.

1. When data has been distributed it is stored at more locations increasing the risk of unauthorized physical access to the data. For example, in cloud based architecture, data is replicated and moved frequently so the risk of unauthorized data recovery increases dramatically. Such as in the case of disposal of old equipment, reuse of drives, reallocation of storage space. The manner that data is replicated depends on the service level a customer chooses and on the service provided. When encryption is in place it can ensure confidentiality. Crypto-shredding can be used when disposing of data (on a disk).

2. The number of people with access to the data who could be compromised (i.e. bribed, or coerced) increases dramatically. A single company might have a small

team of administrators, network engineers and technicians, but a cloud storage company will have many customers and thousands of servers and therefore a much larger team of technical staff with physical and electronic access to almost all of the data at the entire facility or perhaps the entire company. Encryption keys that are kept by the service user, as opposed to the service provider limit the access to data by service provider employees. As for sharing the multiple data with multiple users in cloud, a large number of keys has to be distributed to users via secure channels for decryption, also it has to be securely stored and managed by the users in their devices. And storing these keys requires rather expensive secure storage. To overcome that Key-aggregate cryptosystem can be used.

3. It increases the number of networks over which the data travels. Instead of just a local area network (LAN) or storage area network (SAN), data stored on a cloud requires a WAN (wide area network) to connect them both.

4. By sharing storage and networks with many other users/customers it is possible for other customers to access your data. Sometimes because of erroneous actions, faulty equipment, a bug and sometimes because of criminal intent. This risk applies to all types of storage and not only cloud storage. The risk of having data read during transmission can be mitigated through encryption technology. Encryption in transit protects data as it is being transmitted to and from the cloud service. Encryption at rest protects data that is stored at the service provider. Encrypting data in an on-premises cloud service on-ramp system can provide both kinds of encryption protection.

Supplier Stability

Companies are not permanent and the services and products they provide can change. Outsourcing data storage to another company needs careful investigation and nothing is ever certain. Contracts set in stone can be worthless when a company ceases to exist or its circumstances change. Companies can:

1. Go bankrupt.

2. Expand and change their focus.

3. Be purchased by other larger companies.

4. Be purchased by a company headquartered in or move to a country that negates compliance with export restrictions and thus necessitates a move.

5. Suffer an irrecoverable disaster.

Accessibility

- Performance for outsourced storage is likely to be lower than local storage, depending on how much a customer is willing to spend for WAN bandwidth.

- Reliability and availability depends on wide area network availability and on the level of precautions taken by the service provider. Reliability should be based on hardware as well as various algorithms used.

- Its a given a multiplicity of data storage.

Other Concerns

- Security of stored data and data in transit may be a concern when storing sensitive data at a cloud storage provider.

- Users with specific records-keeping requirements, such as public agencies that must retain electronic records according to statute, may encounter complications with using cloud computing and storage. For instance, the U.S. Department of Defense designated the Defense Information Systems Agency (DISA) to maintain a list of records management products that meet all of the records retention, personally identifiable information (PII), and security (Information Assurance; IA) requirements.

- Cloud storage is a rich resource for both hackers and national security agencies. Because the cloud holds data from many different users and organizations, hackers see it as a very valuable target.

- Piracy and copyright infringement may be enabled by sites that permit filesharing. For example, the CodexCloud ebook storage site has faced litigation from the owners of the intellectual property uploaded and shared there, as have the GrooveShark and YouTube sites it has been compared to.

- The legal aspect, from a regulatory compliance standpoint, is of concern when storing files domestically and especially internationally.

Object Storage

Object storage (also known as object-based storage) is a computer data storage architecture that manages data as objects, as opposed to other storage architectures like file systems which manage data as a file hierarchy and block storage which manages data as blocks within sectors and tracks. Each object typically includes the data itself, a variable amount of metadata, and a globally unique identifier. Object storage can be implemented at multiple levels, including the device level (object storage device), the system level, and the interface level. In each case, object storage seeks to enable capabilities not addressed by other storage architectures, like interfaces that can be directly programmable by the application, a namespace that can span multiple instances of physical hardware, and data management functions like data replication and data distribution at object-level granularity.

Object storage systems allow retention of massive amounts of unstructured data. Object storage is used for purposes such as storing photos on Facebook, songs on Spotify, or files in online collaboration services, such as Dropbox.

History

In 1995, research led by Garth Gibson on Network Attached Secure Disks first promoted the concept of splitting less common operations, like namespace manipulations, from common operations, like reads and writes, to optimize the performance and scale of both. In the same year, 1995, a Belgium company - FilePool - was established to build the basis for archiving functions. Object storage was proposed at Gibson's Carnegie Mellon University lab as a research project in 1996 . Another key concept was abstracting the writes and reads of data to more flexible data containers (objects). Fine grained access control through object storage architecture was further described by one of the NASD team, Howard Gobioff, who later was one of the inventors of the Google File System. Other related work includes the Coda filesystem project at Carnegie Mellon, which started in 1987, and spawned the Lustre file system. There is also the OceanStore project at UC Berkeley, which started in 1999.

Centera, debuted in 2002. The technology. called content-addressable storage, was developed at Filepool, acquired by EMC Corporation in 2001.

Development

From 1999 to 2013, at least $300 million of venture financing was related to object storage, including vendors like Amplidata, Bycast, Cleversafe, Cloudian, Nirvanix, and Scality. This does not include engineering from systems vendors like DataDirect Networks (WOS), Dell EMC Elastic Cloud Storage, Centera, Atmos, HDS (HCP), IBM, NetApp (StorageGRID), Redhat GlusterFS, cloud services vendors like Amazon (AWS S3), Microsoft (Microsoft Azure) and Google (Google Cloud Storage), or open source development at Lustre, OpenStack (Swift), MogileFS, Ceph and OpenIO. An article written illustrating products' timeline was published in July 2016.

Architecture

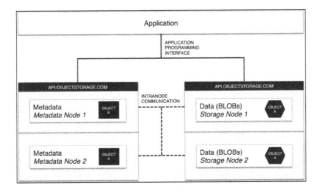

Abstraction of Storage

One of the design principles of object storage is to abstract some of the lower layers of storage away from the administrators and applications. Thus, data is exposed and managed as objects instead of files or blocks. Objects contain additional descriptive properties which can be used for better indexing or management. Administrators do not have to perform lower level storage functions like constructing and managing logical volumes to utilize disk capacity or setting RAID levels to deal with disk failure.

Object storage also allows the addressing and identification of individual objects by more than just file name and file path. Object storage adds a unique identifier within a bucket, or across the entire system, to support much larger namespaces and eliminate name collisions.

Inclusion of Rich Custom Metadata within the Object

Object storage explicitly separates file metadata from data to support additional capabilities: As opposed to fixed metadata in file systems (filename, creation date, type, etc.), object storage provides for full function, custom, object-level metadata in order to:

- Capture application-specific or user-specific information for better indexing purposes.

- Support data management policies (e.g. a policy to drive object movement from one storage tier to another).

- Centralize management of storage across many individual nodes and clusters.

- Optimize metadata storage (e.g. encapsulated, database or key value storage) and caching/indexing (when authoritative metadata is encapsulated with the metadata inside the object) independently from the data storage (e.g. unstructured binary storage).

Additionally, in some object-based file system implementations:

- The file system clients only contact metadata servers once when the file is opened and then get content directly via object storage servers (vs. block-based file systems which would require constant metadata access).

- Data objects can be configured on a per-file basis to allow adaptive stripe width, even across multiple object storage servers, supporting optimizations in bandwidth and I/O.

Object-based storage devices (OSD) as well as some software implementations (e.g., Caringo Swarm) manage metadata and data at the storage device level;

- Instead of providing a block-oriented interface that reads and writes fixed sized blocks of data, data is organized into flexible-sized data containers, called objects.

- Each object has both data (an uninterpreted sequence of bytes) and metadata (an extensible set of attributes describing the object); physically encapsulating both together benefits recoverability.

- The command interface includes commands to create and delete objects, write bytes and read bytes to and from individual objects, and to set and get attributes on objects.

- Security mechanisms provide per-object and per-command access control.

Programmatic Data Management

Object storage provides programmatic interfaces to allow applications to manipulate data. At the base level, this includes CRUD functions for basic read, write and delete operations. Some object storage implementations go further, supporting additional functionality like object versioning, object replication, and movement of objects between different tiers and types of storage. Most API implementations are ReST-based, allowing the use of many standard HTTP calls.

Implementation

Object-based Storage Devices

Object storage at the protocol and device layer was proposed 20 years ago and approved for the SCSI command set nearly 10 years ago as "Object-based Storage Device Commands" (OSD), but has not been productized until the development of the Seagate Kinetic Open Storage platform. The SCSI command set for Object Storage Devices was developed by a working group of the Storage Networking Industry Association (SNIA) for the T10 committee of the International Committee for Information Technology Standards (INCITS). T10 is responsible for all SCSI standards.

Object-based File Systems

Some distributed file systems use an object-based architecture, where file metadata is stored in metadata servers and file data is stored in object storage servers. File system client software interacts with the distinct servers, and abstracts them to present a full file system to users and applications. IBM Spectrum Scale (also known as GPFS), Dell EMC Elastic Cloud Storage, Ceph, XtreemFS, and Lustre are examples of this type of object storage.

Archive Storage

Some early incarnations of object storage were used for archiving, as implementations were optimized for data services like immutability, not performance. EMC Centera and Hitachi HCP (formerly known as HCAP) are two commonly cited object storage products for archiving. Another example is Quantum Lattus Object Storage Platform.

Cloud Storage

The vast majority of cloud storage available in the market leverages an object storage architecture. Two notable examples are Amazon Web Services S3, which debuted in 2005, and Rackspace Files (whose code was released as OpenStack Swift).

"Captive" Object Storage

Some large internet companies developed their own software when object storage products were not commercially available or use cases were very specific. Facebook famously invented their own object storage software, code-named Haystack, to address their particular massive scale photo management needs efficiently.

Hybrid Storage

A few object storage systems, such as Ceph, GlusterFS, Cloudian, IBM Spectrum Scale, and Scality support Unified File and Object (UFO) storage, allowing some clients to store objects on a storage system while simultaneously other clients store files on the same storage system. While "hybrid storage" is not a widely accepted term for this concept, interoperable interfaces to the same set of data is becoming available in some object storage products.

Virtual Object Storage

In addition to object storage systems that own the managed files, some systems provide an object abstraction on top of one or more traditional filesystem based solutions. These solutions do not own the underlaying raw storage, but instead actively mirror the filesystem changes and replicate them in their own object catalog, alongside any metadata that can be automatically extracted from the files. Users can then contribute additional metadata through the virtual object storage APIs. A global namespace and replication capabilities both inside and across filesystems are typically supported.

Notable examples in this category are Nirvana, and its open-source cousin iRODS.

Most products in this category have recently extended their capabilities to support other Object Store solutions as well.

Object Storage Systems

More general purpose object storage systems came to market around 2008. Lured by the incredible growth of "captive" storage systems within web applications like Yahoo

Mail and the early success of cloud storage, object storage systems promised the scale and capabilities of cloud storage, with the ability to deploy the system within an enterprise, or at an aspiring cloud storage service provider. Notable examples of object storage systems include NetApp StorageGRID, EMC Atmos, OpenStack Swift, Scality RING, Caringo Swarm (formerly CAStor), Cloudian, OpenIO, and Minio.

Market Adoption

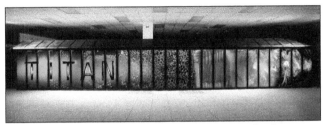

The Titan supercomputer at Oak Ridge National Laboratory.

One of the first object storage products, Lustre, is used in 70% of the Top 100 supercomputers and ~50% of the Top 500. As of June 16, 2013, this includes 7 of the top 10, including the current fastest system on the list - China's Tianhe-2 and the second fastest, the Titan supercomputer at Oak Ridge National Laboratory (pictured on the right).

Object storage systems had good adoption in the early 2000s as an archive platform, particularly in the wake of compliance laws like Sarbanes-Oxley. After five years in the market, EMC's Centera product claimed over 3,500 customers and 150 petabytes shipped by 2007. Hitachi's HCP product also claims many petabyte-scale customers. Newer object storage systems have also gotten some traction, particularly around very large custom applications like eBay's auction site, where EMC Atmos is used to manage over 500 million objects a day. As of March 3, 2014, EMC claims to have sold over 1.5 exabytes of Atmos storage. On July 1, 2014, Los Alamos National Lab chose the Scality RING as the basis for a 500 petabyte storage environment, which would be among the largest ever.

"Captive" object storage systems like Facebook's Haystack have scaled impressively. In April 2009, Haystack was managing 60 billion photos and 1.5 petabytes of storage, adding 220 million photos and 25 terabytes a week. Facebook more recently stated that they were adding 350 million photos a day and were storing 240 billion photos. This could equal as much as 357 petabytes.

Cloud storage has become pervasive as many new web and mobile applications choose it as a common way to store binary data. As the storage backend to many popular applications like Smugmug and Dropbox, AWS S3 has grown to massive scale, citing over 2 trillion objects stored in April 2013. Two months later, Microsoft claimed that they stored even more objects in Azure at 8.5 trillion. By April 2014, Azure claimed over 20 trillion objects stored. Windows Azure Storage manages Blobs (user files), Tables (structured storage), and Queues (message delivery) and counts them all as objects.

Market Analysis

IDC has begun to assess the object-based storage market annually using its MarketScape methodology. IDC describes the MarketScape as: "...a quantitative and qualitative assessment of the characteristics that assess a vendor's current and future success in the said market or market segment and provide a measure of their ascendancy to become a Leader or maintain a leadership. IDC MarketScape assessments are particularly helpful in emerging markets that are often fragmented, have several players, and lack clear leaders."

In 2013, IDC rated Cleversafe, Scality, DataDirect Networks, Amplidata, and EMC as leaders. In 2014, it rated Scality, Cleversafe, DataDirect Networks, Hitachi Data Systems, Amplidata, EMC, and Cloudian as leaders.

Object-based Storage Device Standards

OSD Version 1

In the first version of the OSD standard, objects are specified with a 64-bit partition ID and a 64-bit object ID. Partitions are created and deleted within an OSD, and objects are created and deleted within partitions. There are no fixed sizes associated with partitions or objects; they are allowed to grow subject to physical size limitations of the device or logical quota constraints on a partition.

An extensible set of attributes describe objects. Some attributes are implemented directly by the OSD, such as the number of bytes in an object and the modify time of an object. There is a special policy tag attribute that is part of the security mechanism. Other attributes are uninterpreted by the OSD. These are set on objects by the higher-level storage systems that use the OSD for persistent storage. For example, attributes might be used to classify objects, or to capture relationships among different objects stored on different OSDs.

A list command returns a list of identifiers for objects within a partition, optionally filtered by matches against their attribute values. A list command can also return selected attributes of the listed objects.

Read and write commands can be combined, or piggy-backed, with commands to get and set attributes. This ability reduces the number of times a high-level storage system has to cross the interface to the OSD, which can improve overall efficiency.

OSD Version 2

A second generation of the SCSI command set, "Object-Based Storage Devices - 2" (OSD-2) added support for snapshots, collections of objects, and improved error handling.

A snapshot is a point in time copy of all the objects in a partition into a new partition.

The OSD can implement a space-efficient copy using copy-on-write techniques so that the two partitions share objects that are unchanged between the snapshots, or the OSD might physically copy the data to the new partition. The standard defines clones, which are writeable, and snapshots, which are read-only.

A collection is a special kind of object that contains the identifiers of other objects. There are operations to add and delete from collections, and there are operations to get or set attributes for all the objects in a collection. Collections are also used for error reporting. If an object becomes damaged by the occurrence of a media defect (i.e., a bad spot on the disk) or by a software error within the OSD implementation, its identifier is put into a special error collection. The higher-level storage system that uses the OSD can query this collection and take corrective action as necessary.

Differences between Key-Value and Object Stores

A traditional block storage interface uses a series of fixed size blocks which are numbered starting at 0. Data must be that exact fixed size and can be stored in a particular block which is identified by its logical block number (LBN). Later, one can retrieve that block of data by specifying its unique LBN.

With a key/value store, data is identified by a key rather than a LBN. A key might be "cat" or "olive" or "42". It can be an arbitrary sequence of bytes of arbitrary length. Data (called a value in this parlance) does not need to be a fixed size and also can be an arbitrary sequence of bytes of arbitrary length. One stores data by presenting the key and data (value) to the data store and can later retrieve the data by presenting the key. This concept is seen in programming languages. Python calls them dictionaries, Perl calls them hashes, Java and C++ call them maps, etc. Several data stores also implement key/value stores such as Memcached, Redis and CouchDB.

Object stores are similar to key/value stores in two respects. First, the object identifier or URL (the equivalent of the key) can be an arbitrary string. Second, data is may be of an arbitrary size.

There are, however, a few key differences between key/value stores and object stores. First, object stores also allow one to associate a limited set of attributes (metadata) with each piece of data. The key, value and set of attributes is referred to as an object. Second, object stores are optimized for large amount of data (hundreds of megabytes or even gigabytes), whereas for key/value stores the value is expected to be relatively small (kilobytes). Finally, object stores usually offer weaker consistency guarantees such as eventual consistency, whereas key/value stores offer strong consistency.

Unfortunately, the border between an object store and a key/value store is blurred, with key/value stores being sometimes loosely referred to as object stores.

File Hosting Service

A file hosting service, cloud storage service, online file storage provider, or cyberlocker is an Internet hosting service specifically designed to host user files. It allows users to upload files that could then be accessed over the internet from a different computer, tablet, smart phone or other networked device, by the same user or possibly by other users, after a password or other authentication is provided. Typically, the services allow HTTP access, and sometimes FTP access. Related services are content-displaying hosting services (i.e. video and image), virtual storage, and remote backup.

Uses

Personal File Storage

Personal file storage services are aimed at private individuals, offering a sort of "network storage" for personal backup, file access, or file distribution. Users can upload their files and share them publicly or keep them password-protected.

Document-sharing services allow users to share and collaborate on document files. These services originally targeted files such as PDFs, word processor documents, and spreadsheets. However many remote file storage services are now aimed at allowing users to share and sychronize all types of files across all the devices they use.

File Sync and Sharing Services

File syncing and sharing services are file hosting services which allow users to create special folders on each of their computers or mobile devices, which the service then synchronizes so that it appears to be the same folder regardless of which computer is used to view it. Files placed in this folder also are typically accessible through a website and mobile apps, and can be easily shared with other users for viewing or collaboration.

Such services have become popular via consumer products such as Dropbox and Google Drive.

Content Caching

Content providers who potentially encounter bandwidth congestion issues may use services specialized in distributing cached or static content. It is the case for companies with a major Internet presence.

Storage Charges

Some online file storage services offer space on a per-gigabyte basis, and sometimes include a bandwidth cost component as well. Usually these will be charged monthly or yearly; for example, Carbonite. Some companies offer the service for free, relying on advertising revenue. Some hosting services do not place any limit on how much space the user's account can consume. Some services require a software download which makes files only available on computers which have that software installed, others allow users to retrieve files through any web browser. With the increased inbox space offered by webmail services, many users have started using their webmail service as an online drive. Some sites offer free unlimited file storage but have a limit on the file size. Some sites offer additional online storage capacity in exchange for new customer referrals.

One-click Hosting

One-click hosting, sometimes referred to as cyberlocker, generally describes web services that allow internet users to easily upload one or more files from their hard drives (or from a remote location) onto the one-click host's server free of charge.

Most such services simply return a URL which can be given to other people, who can then fetch the file later. In many cases these URLs are predictable allowing potential misuse of the service. As of 2005 these sites have drastically increased in popularity, and subsequently, many of the smaller, less efficient sites have failed. Although one-click hosting can be used for many purposes, this type of file sharing has, to a degree, come to compete with P2P filesharing services.

The sites make money through advertising or charging for premium services such as increased downloading capacity, removing any wait restrictions the site may have or prolonging how long uploaded files remain on the site. Premium services include facilities like unlimited downloading, no waiting, maximum download speed etc. Many such sites implement a CAPTCHA to prevent automated downloading. Several programs aid in downloading files from these one-click hosts; examples are JDownloader, FreeRapid, Mipony, Tucan Manager and CryptLoad.

Use for Copyright Infringement

File hosting services may be used as a means to distribute or share files without consent of the copyright owner. In such cases one individual uploads a file to a file hosting service, which others can then download. Legal assessments can be very diverse.

For example, in the case of Swiss-German file hosting service RapidShare, in 2010 the US government's congressional international anti-piracy caucus declared the site a "notorious illegal site", claiming that the site was "overwhelmingly used for the global exchange of illegal movies, music and other copyrighted works". But in the legal case *Atari Europe S.A.S.U. v. Rapidshare AG* in Germany, the Düsseldorf higher regional court examined claims related to alleged infringing activity and reached the conclusion on appeal that "most people utilize RapidShare for legal use cases" and that to assume otherwise was equivalent to inviting "a general suspicion against shared hosting services and their users which is not justified". The court also observed that the site removes copyrighted material when asked, does not provide search facilities for illegal material, noted previous cases siding with RapidShare, and after analysis the court concluded that the plaintiff's proposals for more strictly preventing sharing of copyrighted material – submitted as examples of anti-piracy measures RapidShare might have adopted – were found to be "unreasonable or pointless".

By contrast in January 2012 the United States Department of Justice seized and shut down the file hosting site Megaupload.com and commenced criminal cases against its owners and others. Their indictment concluded that Megaupload differed from other online file storage businesses, suggesting a number of design features of its operating model as being evidence showing a criminal intent and venture. Examples cited included reliance upon advertising revenue and other activities showing the business was funded by (and heavily promoted) downloads and not storage, defendants' communications helping users who sought infringing material, and defendants' communications discussing their own evasion and infringement issues. As of 2014 the case has not yet been heard.

The file hosting site Putlocker has been noted by the Motion Picture Association of America for being a major piracy threat, and Alfred Perry of Paramount Pictures listed Putlocker as one of the "top 5 rogue cyberlocker services", alongside Wupload, File-Serve, Depositfiles, and MediaFire.

Security

The emergence of cloud storage services have prompted much discussion on security. Security, as it relates to cloud storage can be broken down into.

Access and Integrity Security

Deals with the questions: Will the user be able to continue accessing their data? Who else can access it? Who can change it?

Whether the user is able to continue accessing their data depends on a large number of factors, ranging from the location and quality of their internet connection and the physical integrity of the provider's data center to the financial stability of the storage provider.

The question of who can access and, potentially, change their data ranges from what physical access controls are in place in the provider's data center to what technical steps have been taken, such as access control, encryption, etc.

Many cloud storage services state that they either encrypt data before it is uploaded or while it is stored. While encryption is generally regarded as best practice in cloud storage how the encryption is implemented is very important.

Consumer-grade, public file hosting and synchronization services are popular, but for business use, they create the concern that corporate information is exported to devices and cloud services that are not controlled by the organization.

Data Encryption

Secret key encryption is sometimes referred to as zero knowledge, meaning that only the user has the encryption key needed to decrypt the data. Since data is encrypted using the secret key, identical files encrypted with different keys will be different. To be truly zero knowledge, the file hosting service must not be able to store the user's passwords or see their data even with physical access to the servers. For this reason, secret key encryption is considered the highest level of access security in cloud storage. This form of encryption is rapidly gaining popularity, with companies such as SpiderOak being entirely zero knowledge file storage and sharing.

Since secret key encryption results in unique files, it makes data deduplication impossible and therefore may use more storage space.

Convergent encryption derives the key from the file content itself and means an identical file encrypted on different computers result in identical encrypted files. This enables the cloud storage provider to de-duplicate data blocks, meaning only one instance of a unique file (such as a document, photo, music or movie file) is actually stored on the cloud servers but made accessible to all uploaders. A third party who gained access to the encrypted files could thus easily determine if a user has uploaded a particular file simply by encrypting it themselves and comparing the outputs.

Some point out that there is a theoretical possibility that organizations such as the RIAA, MPAA, or a government could obtain a warrant for US law enforcement to access the cloud storage provider's servers and gain access to the encrypted files belonging to a user. By demonstrating to a court how applying the convergent encryption methodology to an unencrypted copyrighted file produces the same encrypted file as that possessed by the user would appear to make a strong case that the user is guilty of possessing the file in question and thus providing evidence of copyright infringement by the user.

There is, however, no easily accessible public record of this having been tried in court as of May 2013 and an argument could be made that, similar to the opinion expressed by Attorney Rick G. Sanders of Aaron | Sanders PLLC in regards to the iTunes Match "Honeypot" discussion, that a warrant to search the cloud storage provider's servers would be hard to obtain without other, independent, evidence establishing probable cause for copyright infringement. Such legal restraint would obviously not apply to the Secret Police of an oppressive government who could potentially gain access to the encrypted files through various forms of hacking or other cybercrime.

Ownership Security

Deals with the questions: Who owns the data the user uploads? Will the act of uploading change the ownership?

Cloud Storage Gateway

A cloud storage gateway is a network appliance or server which resides at the customer premises and translates cloud storage APIs such as SOAP or REST to block-based storage protocols such as iSCSI or Fibre Channel or file-based interfaces such as NFS or SMB.

According to a 2011 report by Gartner Group, cloud gateways were expected to increase the use of cloud storage by lowering monthly charges and eliminating the concern of data security.

Market

The cloud storage gateway market was estimated at $74 million in 2012, up from $11 million at the end of 2010.

One analyst predicted in 2013 that the cloud storage gateway market might reach US$860 million by 2016. In January 2013, some vendors were CTERA Networks, Emulex, Panzura, Riverbed Technology, Seven10, Sonian Inc., StorSimple, Avere Systems and TwinStrata.

Characteristics

Unlike the cloud storage services which they complement, cloud storage gateways use standard network protocols which integrate with existing applications. Cloud storage gateways can also serve as intermediaries to multiple cloud storage providers. Some cloud storage gateways also include additional storage features such as backup and recovery, caching, compression, encryption, storage de-duplication and provisioning.

SOAP

SOAP (originally Simple Object Access Protocol) is a protocol specification for exchanging structured information in the implementation of web services in computer networks. Its purpose is to induce extensibility, neutrality and independence. It uses XML Information Set for its message format, and relies on application layer protocols, most often Hypertext Transfer Protocol (HTTP) or Simple Mail Transfer Protocol (SMTP), for message negotiation and transmission.

SOAP allows processes running on disparate operating systems (such as Windows and Linux) to communicate using Extensible Markup Language (XML). Since Web protocols like HTTP are installed and running on all operating systems, SOAP allows clients to invoke web services and receive responses independent of language and platforms.

Characteristics

SOAP provides the Messaging Protocol layer of a web services protocol stack for web services. It is an XML-based protocol consisting of three parts:

- an envelope, which defines the message structure and how to process it.

- a set of encoding rules for expressing instances of application-defined datatypes.

- a convention for representing procedure calls and responses.

SOAP has three major characteristics:

1. *extensibility* (security and WS-Addressing are among the extensions under development).

2. *neutrality* (SOAP can operate over any protocol such as HTTP, SMTP, TCP, UDP, or JMS).

3. *independence* (SOAP allows for any programming model).

As an example of what SOAP procedures can do, an application can send a SOAP request to a server that has web services enabled—such as a real-estate price database—with the parameters for a search. The server then returns a SOAP response (an XML-formatted document with the resulting data), e.g., prices, location, features. Since the generated data comes in a standardized machine-parsable format, the requesting application can then integrate it directly.

The SOAP architecture consists of several layers of specifications for:

- message format.

- Message Exchange Patterns (MEP).

- underlying transport protocol bindings.

- message processing models.

- protocol extensibility.

SOAP evolved as a successor of XML-RPC, though it borrows its transport and interaction neutrality from Web Service Addressing and the envelope/header/body from elsewhere (probably from WDDX).

History

SOAP was designed as an object-access protocol in 1998 by Dave Winer, Don Box, Bob Atkinson, and Mohsen Al-Ghosein for Microsoft, where Atkinson and Al-Ghosein were working. Due to politics within Microsoft, the specification was not made available until it was submitted to IETF 13 September 1999. Because of Microsoft's hesitation, Dave Winer shipped XML-RPC in 1998.

The submitted Internet Draft did not reach RFC status and is therefore not considered a "standard" as such. Version 1.1 of the specification was published as a W3C Note on 8 May 2000. Since version 1.1 did not reach W3C Recommendation status, it can not be considered a "standard" either. Version 1.2 of the specification, however, became a W3C recommendation on June 24, 2003.

The SOAP specification was maintained by the XML Protocol Working Group of the World Wide Web Consortium until the group was closed 10 July 2009. *SOAP* originally stood for "Simple Object Access Protocol" but version 1.2 of the standard dropped this acronym.

After SOAP was first introduced, it became the underlying layer of a more complex set of Web services, based on Web Services Description Language (WSDL), XML schema and Universal Description Discovery and Integration (UDDI). These different services, especially UDDI, have proved to be of far less interest, but an appreciation of them gives a complete understanding of the expected role of SOAP compared to how web services have actually evolved.

SOAP Terminology

SOAP specification can be broadly defined to be consisting of the following 3 conceptual components: Protocol concepts, encapsulation concepts and Network concepts.

Protocol Concepts

- SOAP: The set of rules formalizing and governing the format and processing rules for information exchanged between a SOAP sender and a SOAP receiver.

- SOAP Nodes: These are physical/logical machines with processing units which are used to transmit/forward, receive and process SOAP messages. These are analogous to Node (networking).

- SOAP Roles: Over the path of a SOAP message, all nodes assume a specific role. The role of the node defines the action that the node performs on the message it receives. For example, a role *"none"* means that no node will process the SOAP header in any way and simply transmit the message along its path.

- SOAP protocol binding : A SOAP message needs to work in conjunction with other protocols to be transferred over a network. For example, a SOAP message could use TCP as a lower layer protocol to transfer messages. These bindings are defined in the SOAP protocol binding framework.

- SOAP features: SOAP provides a messaging framework only. However, it can be extended to add features such as reliability, security etc. There are rules to be followed when adding features to the SOAP framework.

- SOAP module : A collection of specifications regarding the semantics of SOAP header to describe any new features being extended upon SOAP. A module needs to realize 0 or more features. SOAP requires modules to adhere to prescribed rules.

Data Encapsulation Concepts

- SOAP message: Represents the information being exchanged between 2 soap nodes.

- SOAP envelope : As per its name, it is the enclosing element of an XML message identifying it as a SOAP message.

- SOAP header block: A SOAP header can contain more than one of these blocks, each being a discrete computational block within the header. In general, the SOAP *role* information is used to target nodes on the path. A header block is said to be targeted at a SOAP node if the SOAP role for the header block is the name of a role in which the SOAP node operates. (ex: A SOAP header block with role attribute as *ultimateReceiver* is targeted only at the destination node which has this role. A header with a role attribute as *next* is targeted at each intermediary as well as the destination node.)

- SOAP header : A collection of one or more header blocks targeted at each SOAP receiver.

- SOAP body : Contains the body of the message intended for the SOAP receiver. The interpretation and processing of SOAP body is defined by header blocks.

- SOAP fault: In case a SOAP node fails to process a SOAP message, it adds the fault information to the SOAP fault element. This element is contained within the SOAP body as a child element.

Message Sender and Receiver Concepts

- SOAP sender: The node that transmits a SOAP message.

- SOAP receiver : The node receiving a SOAP message. (Could be an intermediary or the destination node.)

- SOAP message path : The path consisting of all the nodes that the SOAP message traversed to reach the destination node.

- Initial SOAP sender: This is the node which originated the SOAP message to be transmitted. This is the root of the SOAP message path.

- SOAP intermediary: All the nodes in between the SOAP originator and the intended SOAP destination. It processes the SOAP header blocks targeted at it and acts to forward a SOAP message towards an ultimate SOAP receiver.

- Ultimate SOAP receiver: The destination receiver of the SOAP message. This node is responsible for processing the message body and any header blocks targeted at it.

Specification

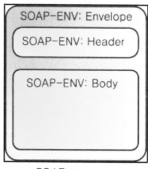

SOAP structure

The SOAP specification defines the messaging framework, which consists of:

- The *SOAP processing model* defining the rules for processing a SOAP message.

- The *SOAP extensibility model* defining the concepts of SOAP features and SOAP modules.

- The *SOAP underlying protocol binding* framework describing the rules for defining a binding to an underlying protocol that can be used for exchanging SOAP messages between SOAP nodes.

- The *SOAP message construct* defining the structure of a SOAP message.

SOAP Building Blocks

A SOAP message is an ordinary XML document containing the following elements:

Element	Description	Required
Envelope	Identifies the XML document as a SOAP message.	Yes
Header	Contains header information.	No
Body	Contains call, and response information.	Yes
Fault	Provides information about errors that occurred while processing the message.	No

Transport Methods

Both SMTP and HTTP are valid application layer protocols used as transport for SOAP, but HTTP has gained wider acceptance as it works well with today's internet infrastructure; specifically, HTTP works well with network firewalls. SOAP may also be used over HTTPS (which is the same protocol as HTTP at the application level, but uses an encrypted transport protocol underneath) with either simple or mutual authentication; this is the advocated WS-I method to provide web service security as stated in the WS-I Basic Profile 1.1.

This is a major advantage over other distributed protocols like GIOP/IIOP or DCOM, which are normally filtered by firewalls. SOAP over AMQP is yet another possibility that some implementations support. SOAP also has an advantage over DCOM that it is unaffected by security rights configured on the machines that require knowledge of both transmitting and receiving nodes. This lets SOAP be loosely coupled in a way that is not possible with DCOM. There is also the SOAP-over-UDP OASIS standard.

Message Format

XML Information Set was chosen as the standard message format because of its widespread use by major corporations and open source development efforts. Typically, XML Information Set is serialized as XML. A wide variety of freely available tools significantly eases the transition to a SOAP-based implementation. The somewhat lengthy syntax of XML can be both a benefit and a drawback. While it promotes readability for humans, facilitates error detection, and avoids interoperability problems such as byte-order (endianness), it can slow processing speed and can be cumbersome. For example, CORBA, GIOP, ICE, and DCOM use much shorter, binary message formats. On the other hand, hardware appliances are available to accelerate processing of XML messages. Binary XML is also being explored as a means for streamlining the throughput requirements of XML. XML messages by their self-documenting nature usually have more 'overhead' (headers, footers, nested tags, delimiters) than actual data in contrast to earlier protocols where the overhead was usually a relatively small percentage of the overall message.

In financial messaging SOAP was found to result in a 2–4 times larger message than previous protocols FIX (Financial Information Exchange) and CDR (Common Data Representation).

XML Information Set does not have to be serialized in XML. For instance, CSV and JSON XML-infoset representations exist. There is also no need to specify a generic transformation framework. The concept of SOAP bindings allows for specific bindings for a specific application. The drawback is that both the senders and receivers have to support this newly defined binding.

Example Message (Encapsulated in HTTP)

```
POST /InStock HTTP/1.1

Host: www.example.org

Content-Type: application/soap+xml; charset=utf-8

Content-Length: 299

SOAPAction: "http://www.w3.org/2003/05/soap-envelope"

<?xml version="1.0"?>

<soap:Envelope    xmlns:soap="http://www.w3.org/2003/05/soap-envelope"
xmlns:m="http://www.example.org/stock/Surya">

  <soap:Header>

  </soap:Header>

  <soap:Body>

    <m:GetStockPrice>

      <m:StockName>GOOGLE</m:StockName>

    </m:GetStockPrice>

   </soap:Body>

</soap:Envelope>
```

Technical Critique

Advantages

- SOAP's neutrality characteristic explicitly makes it suitable for use with any transport protocol. Implementations often use HTTP as a transport protocol, but other popular transport protocols can be used. For example, SOAP can also be used over SMTP, JMS and message queues.

- SOAP, when combined with HTTP post/response exchanges, tunnels easily through existing firewalls and proxies, and consequently doesn't require modifying the widespread computing and communication infrastructures that exist for processing HTTP post/response exchanges.

- SOAP has available to it all the facilities of XML, including easy internationalization and extensibility with XML Namespaces.

Disadvantages

- When using standard implementations and the default SOAP/HTTP binding, the XML infoset is serialized as XML. To improve performance for the special case of XML with embedded binary objects, the Message Transmission Optimization Mechanism was introduced.

- When relying on HTTP as a transport protocol and not using WS-Addressing or an ESB, the roles of the interacting parties are fixed. Only one party (the client) can use the services of the other.

- The verbosity of the protocol, slow parsing speed of XML, and lack of a standardized interaction model led to the domination in the field by services using the HTTP protocol more directly. For example, REST.

Representational State Transfer

Representational state transfer (REST) or RESTful web services is one way of providing interoperability between computer systems on the Internet. REST-compliant Web services allow requesting systems to access and manipulate textual representations of Web resources using a uniform and predefined set of stateless operations. Other forms of Web service exist, which expose their own arbitrary sets of operations such as WSDL and SOAP.

"Web resources" were first defined on the World Wide Web as documents or files identified by their URLs, but today they have a much more generic and abstract definition encompassing every thing or entity that can be identified, named, addressed or handled, in any way whatsoever, on the Web. In a RESTful Web service, requests made to a resource's URI will elicit a response that may be in XML, HTML, JSON or some other defined format. The response may confirm that some alteration has been made to the stored resource, and it may provide hypertext links to other related resources or collections of resources. Using HTTP, as is most common, the kind of operations available include those predefined by the HTTP verbs GET, POST, PUT, DELETE and so on.

By making use of a stateless protocol and standard operations, REST systems aim for fast performance, reliability, and the ability to grow, by re-using components that can be managed and updated without affecting the system as a whole, even while it is running.

The term *representational state transfer* was introduced and defined in 2000 by Roy Fielding in his doctoral dissertation. Fielding used REST to design HTTP 1.1 and Uniform Resource Identifiers (URI). The term is intended to evoke an image of how a well-designed Web application behaves: it is a network of Web resources (a virtual state-machine) where the user progresses through the application by selecting links, such as /user/tom, and operations such as GET or DELETE (state transitions), resulting in the next resource (representing the next state of the application) being transferred to the user for their use.

History

Roy Fielding speaking at OSCON 2008.

REST was defined by Roy Fielding in his 2000 PhD dissertation "Architectural Styles and the Design of Network-based Software Architectures" at UC Irvine. Fielding developed the REST architectural style in parallel with HTTP 1.1 of 1996–1999, based on the existing design of HTTP 1.0 of 1996.

In a retrospective look at the development of REST, Roy Fielding said:

Throughout the HTTP standardization process, I was called on to defend the design choices of the Web. That is an extremely difficult thing to do within a process that accepts proposals from anyone on a topic that was rapidly becoming the center of an entire industry. I had comments from well over 500 developers, many of whom were distinguished engineers with decades of experience, and I had to explain everything from the most abstract notions of Web interaction to the finest details of HTTP syntax. That process honed my model down to a core set of principles, properties, and constraints that are now called REST.

Architectural Properties

The architectural properties affected by the constraints of the REST architectural style are:

- Performance - component interactions can be the dominant factor in user-perceived performance and network efficiency.

- Scalability to support large numbers of components and interactions among components. Roy Fielding, one of the principal authors of the HTTP specification, describes REST's effect on scalability as follows:

  REST's client–server separation of concerns simplifies component implementation, reduces the complexity of connector semantics, improves the effectiveness of performance tuning, and increases the scalability of pure server components. Layered system constraints allow intermediaries—proxies, gateways, and firewalls—to be introduced at various points in the communication without changing the interfaces between components, thus allowing them to assist in communication translation or improve performance via large-scale, shared caching. REST enables intermediate processing by constraining messages to be self-descriptive: interaction is stateless between requests, standard methods and media types are used to indicate semantics and exchange information, and responses explicitly indicate cacheability.

- Simplicity of a uniform Interface.

- Modifiability of components to meet changing needs (even while the application is running).

- Visibility of communication between components by service agents.

- Portability of components by moving program code with the data.

- Reliability is the resistance to failure at the system level in the presence of failures within components, connectors, or data.

Architectural Constraints

There are six guiding constraints that define a RESTful system. These constraints restrict the ways that the server may process and respond to client requests so that, by operating within these constraints, the service gains desirable non-functional properties, such as performance, scalability, simplicity, modifiability, visibility, portability, and reliability. If a service violates any of the required constraints, it cannot be considered RESTful.

The formal REST constraints are as follows:

Client-server

The first constraints added to our hybrid style are those of the client-server architectural style. Separation of concerns is the principle behind the client-server constraints. By separating the user interface concerns from the data storage concerns, we improve the portability of the user interface across multiple platforms and improve scalability by simplifying the server components. Perhaps most significant to the Web, however, is that the separation allows the components to evolve independently, thus supporting the Internet-scale requirement of multiple organizational domains.

Stateless

The client–server communication is constrained by no client context being stored on the server between requests. Each request from any client contains all the information necessary to service the request, and session state is held in the client. The session state can be transferred by the server to another service such as a database to maintain a persistent state for a period and allow authentication. The client begins sending requests when it is ready to make the transition to a new state. While one or more requests are outstanding, the client is considered to be *in transition*. The representation of each application state contains links that may be used the next time the client chooses to initiate a new state-transition.

Cacheable

As on the World Wide Web, clients and intermediaries can cache responses. Responses must therefore, implicitly or explicitly, define themselves as cacheable or not to prevent clients from reusing stale or inappropriate data in response to further requests. Well-managed caching partially or completely eliminates some client–server interactions, further improving scalability and performance.

Layered System

A client cannot ordinarily tell whether it is connected directly to the end server, or to an intermediary along the way. Intermediary servers may improve system scalability by enabling load balancing and by providing shared caches. They may also enforce security policies.

Code on Demand (Optional)

Servers can temporarily extend or customize the functionality of a client by transferring executable code. Examples of this may include compiled components such as Java applets and client-side scripts such as JavaScript.

Uniform Interface

The uniform interface constraint is fundamental to the design of any REST service. It simplifies and decouples the architecture, which enables each part to evolve independently. The four constraints for this uniform interface are:

Identification of Resources

Individual resources are identified in requests, for example using URIs in Web-based REST systems. The resources themselves are conceptually separate from the representations that are returned to the client. For example, the server may send data from its database as HTML, XML or JSON, none of which are the server's internal representation.

Manipulation of Resources through Representations

When a client holds a representation of a resource, including any metadata attached, it has enough information to modify or delete the resource.

Self-descriptive Messages

Each message includes enough information to describe how to process the message. For example, which parser to invoke may be specified by an Internet media type (previously known as a MIME type).

Hypermedia as the Engine of Application State (HATEOAS)

Having accessed an initial URI for the REST application—analogous to a human Web user accessing the home page of a website—a REST client should then be able to use server-provided links dynamically to discover all the available actions and resources it needs. As access proceeds, the server responds with text that includes hyperlinks to other actions that are currently available. There is no need for the client to be hard-coded with information regarding the structure or dynamics of the REST service.

Applied to Web Services

Web service APIs that adhere to the REST architectural constraints are called RESTful APIs. HTTP-based RESTful APIs are defined with the following aspects:

- base URL, such as `http://api.example.com/resources/`

- an internet media type that defines state transition data elements (e.g., Atom, microformats, application/vnd.collection+json, etc.) The current representation tells the client how to compose requests for transitions to all the next available application states. This could be as simple as a URL or as complex as a Java applet.

- standard HTTP methods (e.g., OPTIONS, GET, PUT, POST, and DELETE).

Relationship between URL and HTTP Methods

The following table shows how HTTP methods are typically used in a RESTful API:

HTTP methods				
Uniform Resource Locator (URL)	GET	PUT	POST	DELETE
Collection, such as http://api.example.com/resources/	List the URIs and perhaps other details of the collection's members.	Replace the entire collection with another collection.	Create a new entry in the collection. The new entry's URI is assigned automatically and is usually returned by the operation.	Delete the entire collection.

| Element, such as http://api. example.com/resources/ item17 | Retrieve a representation of the addressed member of the collection, expressed in an appropriate Internet media type. | Replace the addressed member of the collection, or if it does not exist, create it. | Not generally used. Treat the addressed member as a collection in its own right and create a new entry within it. | Delete the addressed member of the collection. |

The GET method is a safe method (or *nullipotent*), meaning that calling it produces no side-effects: retrieving or accessing a record does not change it. The PUT and DELETE methods are idempotent, meaning that the state of the system exposed by the API is unchanged no matter how many times more than once the same request is repeated.

Unlike SOAP-based Web services, there is no "official" standard for RESTful Web APIs. This is because REST is an architectural style, while SOAP is a protocol. REST is not a standard in itself, but RESTful implementations make use of standards, such as HTTP, URI, JSON, and XML. Many developers also describe their APIs as being RESTful, even though these APIs actually don't fulfill all of the architectural constraints described above (especially the uniform interface constraint).

iSCSI

In computing, iSCSI is an acronym for Internet Small Computer Systems Interface, an Internet Protocol (IP)-based storage networking standard for linking data storage facilities. It provides block-level access to storage devices by carrying SCSI commands over a TCP/IP network. iSCSI is used to facilitate data transfers over intranets and to manage storage over long distances. It can be used to transmit data over local area networks (LANs), wide area networks (WANs), or the Internet and can enable location-independent data storage and retrieval.

The protocol allows clients (called *initiators*) to send SCSI commands (*CDBs*) to storage devices (*targets*) on remote servers. It is a storage area network (SAN) protocol, allowing organizations to consolidate storage into storage arrays while providing clients (such as database and web servers) with the illusion of locally attached SCSI disks. It mainly competes with Fibre Channel, but unlike traditional Fibre Channel which usually requires dedicated cabling, iSCSI can be run over long distances using existing network infrastructure. iSCSI was pioneered by IBM and Cisco in 1998 and submitted as a draft standard in March 2000.

Concepts

In essence, iSCSI allows two hosts to negotiate and then exchange SCSI commands using Internet Protocol (IP) networks. By doing this, iSCSI takes a popular high-performance local storage bus and emulates it over a wide range of networks, creating a storage area network (SAN). Unlike some SAN protocols, iSCSI requires no dedicated cabling; it can be run over existing IP infrastructure. As a result, iSCSI is often seen as a low-cost alternative to Fibre Channel, which requires dedicated infrastructure except in its FCoE (Fibre Channel over Ethernet) form. However, the performance of an iSCSI SAN deployment can be severely degraded if not operated on a dedicated network or subnet (LAN or VLAN), due to competition for a fixed amount of bandwidth.

Although iSCSI can communicate with arbitrary types of SCSI devices, system administrators almost always use it to allow server computers (such as database servers) to access disk volumes on storage arrays. iSCSI SANs often have one of two objectives:

Storage Consolidation

Organizations move disparate storage resources from servers around their network to central locations, often in data centers; this allows for more efficiency in the allocation of storage, as the storage itself is no longer tied to a particular server. In a SAN environment, a server can be allocated a new disk volume without any changes to hardware or cabling.

Disaster Recovery

Organizations mirror storage resources from one data center to a remote data center, which can serve as a hot standby in the event of a prolonged outage. In particular, iSCSI SANs allow entire disk arrays to be migrated across a WAN with minimal configuration changes, in effect making storage "routable" in the same manner as network traffic.

Initiator

An *initiator* functions as an iSCSI client. An initiator typically serves the same purpose to a computer as a SCSI bus adapter would, except that, instead of physically cabling SCSI devices (like hard drives and tape changers), an iSCSI initiator sends SCSI commands over an IP network. An initiator falls into two broad types:

A software initiator uses code to implement iSCSI. Typically, this happens in a kernel-resident device driver that uses the existing network card (NIC) and network stack to emulate SCSI devices for a computer by speaking the iSCSI protocol. Software initiators are available for most popular operating systems and are the most common method of deploying iSCSI.

A hardware initiator uses dedicated hardware, typically in combination with firmware running on that hardware, to implement iSCSI. A hardware initiator mitigates the overhead of iSCSI and TCP processing and Ethernet interrupts, and therefore may improve the performance of servers that use iSCSI. An iSCSI host bus adapter (more commonly,

HBA) implements a hardware initiator. A typical HBA is packaged as a combination of a Gigabit (or 10 Gigabit) Ethernet network interface controller, some kind of TCP/IP offload engine (TOE) technology and a SCSI bus adapter, which is how it appears to the operating system. An iSCSI HBA can include PCI option ROM to allow booting from an iSCSI SAN.

An *iSCSI offload engine*, or *iSOE card*, offers an alternative to a full iSCSI HBA. An iSOE "offloads" the iSCSI initiator operations for this particular network interface from the host processor, freeing up CPU cycles for the main host applications. iSCSI HBAs or iSOEs are used when the additional performance enhancement justifies the additional expense of using an HBA for iSCSI, rather than using a software-based iSCSI client (initiator). iSOE may be implemented with additional services such as TCP offload engine (TOE) to further reduce host server CPU usage.

Target

The iSCSI specification refers to a storage resource located on an iSCSI server (more generally, one of potentially many *instances* of iSCSI storage nodes running on that server) as a *target*.

An iSCSI target is often a dedicated network-connected hard disk storage device, but may also be a general-purpose computer, since as with initiators, software to provide an iSCSI target is available for most mainstream operating systems.

Common deployment scenarios for an iSCSI target include:

Storage Array

In a data center or enterprise environment, an iSCSI target often resides in a large storage array. These arrays can be in the form of commodity hardware with free-software-based iSCSI implementations, or as commercial products such as in CloudByte, StorTrends, Pure Storage, HP StorageWorks, EqualLogic, Tegile Systems, Nimble storage, Reduxio, IBM Storwize family, Isilon, NetApp filer, EMC Corporation NS-series, CX4, VNX, VNXe, VMAX, Hitachi Data Systems HNAS, or Pivot3 vSTAC.

A storage array usually provides distinct iSCSI targets for numerous clients.

Software Target

Nearly all modern mainstream server operating systems (such as BSD, Linux, Solaris or Windows Server) can provide iSCSI target functionality, either as a built-in feature or with supplemental software. Some specific-purpose operating systems implement iSCSI target support.

Logical Unit Number

In SCSI terminology, LUN stands for *logical unit*, which are specified by unique *logical unit numbers*. A LUN represents an individually addressable (logical) SCSI device that is part of a physical SCSI device (target). In an iSCSI environment, LUNs are essentially numbered disk drives. An initiator negotiates with a target to establish connectivity to a LUN; the result is an iSCSI connection that emulates a connection to a SCSI hard disk. Initiators treat iSCSI LUNs the same way as they would a raw SCSI or IDE hard drive; for instance, rather than mounting remote directories as would be done in NFS or CIFS environments, iSCSI systems format and directly manage filesystems on iSCSI LUNs.

In enterprise deployments, LUNs usually represent subsets of large RAID disk arrays, often allocated one per client. iSCSI imposes no rules or restrictions on multiple computers sharing individual LUNs; it leaves shared access to a single underlying filesystem as a task for the operating system.

Network Booting

For general data storage on an already-booted computer, any type of generic network interface may be used to access iSCSI devices. However, a generic consumer-grade network interface is not able to boot a diskless computer from a remote iSCSI data source. Instead, it is commonplace for a server to load its initial operating system from a TFTP server or local boot device, and then use iSCSI for data storage once booting from the local device has finished.

A separate DHCP server may be configured to assist interfaces equipped with network boot capability to be able to boot over iSCSI. In this case, the network interface looks for a DHCP server offering a PXE or bootp boot image. This is used to kick off the iSCSI remote boot process, using the booting network interface's MAC address to direct the computer to the correct iSCSI boot target. One can then use a software-only approach to load a small boot program which can in turn mount a remote iSCSI target as if it was a local SCSI drive and then fire the boot process from said iSCSI target. This can be achieved using an existing Preboot Execution Environment (PXE) boot ROM, which is available on many wired Ethernet adapters. The boot code can also be loaded from CD/DVD, floppy disk (or floppy disk image) and USB storage, or it can replace existing PXE boot code on adapters that can be re-flashed. The most popular free software to offer iSCSI boot support is iPXE.

Most Intel Ethernet controllers for servers support iSCSI boot.

Addressing

iSCSI uses TCP (typically TCP ports 860 and 3260) for the protocols itself, with higher-level names used to address the objects within the protocol. Special names refer to both iSCSI initiators and targets. iSCSI provides three name-formats.

iSCSI Qualified Name (IQN)

Format: The iSCSI Qualified Name is documented in RFC 3720, with further examples of names in RFC 3721. Briefly, the fields are:

- literal iqn (iSCSI Qualified Name).

- date (yyyy-mm) that the naming authority took ownership of the domain.

- reversed domain name of the authority (e.g. org.alpinelinux, com.example, to.yp.cr).

- Optional ":" prefixing a storage target name specified by the naming authority.

From the RFC:

Type	Date	Naming Auth	String defined by *example.com* Naming Authority
iqn	1992-01	com.example	storage:diskarrays-sn-a8675309
iqn	1992-01	com.example	
iqn	1992-01	com.example	storage.tape1.sys1.xyz
iqn	1992-01	com.example	storage.disk2.sys1.xyz

Extended Unique Identifier (EUI)

Format: eui.{EUI-64 bit address} (e.g. eui.02004567A425678D)

T11 Network Address Authority (NAA)

Format: naa.{NAA 64 or 128 bit identifier} (e.g. naa.52004567BA64678D)

IQN format addresses occur most commonly. They are qualified by a date (yyyy-mm) because domain names can expire or be acquired by another entity.

The IEEE Registration authority provides EUI in accordance with the EUI-64 standard. NAA is part OUI which is provided by the IEEE Registration Authority. NAA name formats were added to iSCSI in RFC 3980, to provide compatibility with naming conventions used in Fibre Channel and Serial Attached SCSI (SAS) storage technologies.

Usually, an iSCSI participant can be defined by three or four fields:

- Hostname or IP Address (e.g., "iscsi.example.com").

- Port Number (e.g., 3260).

- iSCSI Name (e.g., the IQN "iqn.2003-01.com.ibm:00.fcd0ab21.shark128").

- An optional CHAP Secret (e.g., "secretsarefun").

iSNS

iSCSI initiators can locate appropriate storage resources using the Internet Storage Name Service (iSNS) protocol. In theory, iSNS provides iSCSI SANs with the same management model as dedicated Fibre Channel SANs. In practice, administrators can satisfy many deployment goals for iSCSI without using iSNS.

Security

Authentication

iSCSI initiators and targets prove their identity to each other using CHAP, which includes a mechanism to prevent cleartext passwords from appearing on the wire. By itself, CHAP is vulnerable to dictionary attacks, spoofing, and reflection attacks. If followed carefully, the best practices for using CHAP within iSCSI reduce the surface for these attacks and mitigate the risks.

Additionally, as with all IP-based protocols, IPsec can operate at the network layer. The iSCSI negotiation protocol is designed to accommodate other authentication schemes, though interoperability issues limit their deployment.

Logical Network Isolation

To ensure that only valid initiators connect to storage arrays, administrators most commonly run iSCSI only over logically isolated backchannel networks. In this deployment architecture, only the management ports of storage arrays are exposed to the general-purpose internal network, and the iSCSI protocol itself is run over dedicated network segments or virtual LANs (VLAN). This mitigates authentication concerns; unauthorized users are not physically provisioned for iSCSI, and thus cannot talk to storage arrays. However, it also creates a transitive trust problem, in that a single compromised host with an iSCSI disk can be used to attack storage resources for other hosts.

Physical Network Isolation

While iSCSI can be logically isolated from the general network using VLANs only, it is still no different from any other network equipment and may use any cable or port as long as there is a completed signal path between source and target. Just a single cabling mistake by a network technician can compromise the barrier of logical separation, and an accidental bridging may not be immediately detected because it does not cause network errors.

In order to further differentiate iSCSI from the regular network and prevent cabling mistakes when changing connections, administrators may implement self-defined color-or-coding and labeling standards, such as only using yellow-colored cables for the iSCSI connections and only blue cables for the regular network, and clearly labeling ports and switches used only for iSCSI.

While iSCSI could be implemented as just a VLAN cluster of ports on a large multi-port switch that is also used for general network usage, the administrator may instead choose to use physically separate switches dedicated to iSCSI VLANs only, to further prevent the possibility of an incorrectly connected cable plugged into the wrong port bridging the logical barrier.

Authorization

Because iSCSI aims to consolidate storage for many servers into a single storage array, iSCSI deployments require strategies to prevent unrelated initiators from accessing storage resources. As a pathological example, a single enterprise storage array could hold data for servers variously regulated by the Sarbanes–Oxley Act for corporate accounting, HIPAA for health benefits information, and PCI DSS for credit card processing. During an audit, storage systems must demonstrate controls to ensure that a server under one regime cannot access the storage assets of a server under another.

Typically, iSCSI storage arrays explicitly map initiators to specific target LUNs; an initiator authenticates not to the storage array, but to the specific storage asset it intends to use. However, because the target LUNs for SCSI commands are expressed both in the iSCSI negotiation protocol and in the underlying SCSI protocol, care must be taken to ensure that access control is provided consistently.

Confidentiality and Integrity

For the most part, iSCSI operates as a cleartext protocol that provides no cryptographic protection for data in motion during SCSI transactions. As a result, an attacker who can listen in on iSCSI Ethernet traffic can:

- Reconstruct and copy the files and filesystems being transferred on the wire.

- Alter the contents of files by injecting fake iSCSI frames.

- Corrupt filesystems being accessed by initiators, exposing servers to software flaws in poorly tested filesystem code.

These problems do not occur only with iSCSI, but rather apply to any SAN protocol without cryptographic security. IP-based security protocols, such as IPsec, can provide standards-based cryptographic protection to this traffic, generally at a severe performance penalty.

Implementations

Operating Systems

The dates in the following table denote the first appearance of a native driver in each operating system. Third-party drivers for Windows and Linux were available as early as 2001, specifically for attaching IBM's IP Storage 200i appliance.

OS	First release date	Version	Features
i5/OS	2006-10	i5/OS V5R4M0	Target, Multipath
VMware ESX	2006-06	ESX 3.0, ESX 4.0, ESXi 5.x, ESXi 6.x	Initiator, Multipath
AIX	2002-10	AIX 5.3 TL10, AIX 6.1 TL3	Initiator, Target
Windows	2003-06	2000, XP Pro, 2003, Vista, 2008, 2008 R2, Windows 7, Windows 8, Windows Server 2012, Windows 8.1, Windows Server 2012 R2, Windows 10, Windows Server 2016	Initiator, Target, Multipath
NetWare	2003-08	NetWare 5.1, 6.5, & OES	Initiator, Target
HP-UX	2003-10	HP 11i v1, HP 11i v2, HP 11i v3	Initiator
Solaris	2002-05	Solaris 10, OpenSolaris	Initiator, Target, Multipath, iSER
Linux	2005-06	2.6.12, 3.1	Initiator (2.6.12), Target (3.1), Multipath, iSER, VAAI
OpenBSD	2009-10	4.9	Initiator
NetBSD	2002-06	4.0, 5.0	Initiator (5.0), Target (4.0)
FreeBSD	2008-02	7.0	Initiator (7.0), Target (10.0), Multipath, iSER, VAAI
OpenVMS	2002-08	8.3-1H1	Initiator, Multipath
macOS	2008-07	10.4—	N/A

Targets

Most iSCSI targets involve disk, though iSCSI tape and medium-changer targets are popular as well. So far, physical devices have not featured native iSCSI interfaces on a component level. Instead, devices with Parallel SCSI or Fibre Channel interfaces are bridged by using iSCSI target software, external bridges, or controllers internal to the device enclosure.

Alternatively, it is possible to virtualize disk and tape targets. Rather than representing an actual physical device, an emulated virtual device is presented. The underlying implementation can deviate drastically from the presented target as is done with virtual tape library (VTL) products. VTLs use disk storage for storing data written to virtual tapes. As with actual physical devices, virtual targets are presented by using iSCSI target software, external bridges, or controllers internal to the device enclosure.

In the security products industry, some manufacturers use an iSCSI RAID as a target, with the initiator being either an IP-enabled encoder or camera.

Converters and Bridges

Multiple systems exist that allow Fibre Channel, SCSI and SAS devices to be attached to an IP network for use via iSCSI. They can be used to allow migration from older storage technologies, access to SANs from remote servers and the linking of SANs over IP networks. An iSCSI gateway bridges IP servers to Fibre Channel SANs. The TCP connection is terminated at the gateway, which is implemented on a Fibre Channel switch or as a standalone appliance.

Fibre Channel

Fibre Channel, or FC, is a high-speed network technology (commonly running at 1, 2, 4, 8, 16, 32, and 128 gigabit per second rates) primarily used to connect computer data storage to servers. Fibre Channel is mainly used in storage area networks (SAN) in commercial data centers. Fibre Channel networks form a switched fabric because they operate in unison as one big switch. Fibre Channel typically runs on optical fiber cables within and between data centers.

Most block storage runs over Fibre Channel Fabrics and supports many upper level protocols. Fibre Channel Protocol (FCP) is a transport protocol that predominantly transports SCSI commands over Fibre Channel networks. Mainframe computers run the FICON command set over Fibre Channel because of its high reliability and throughput. Fibre Channel can be used for flash memory being transported over the NVMe interface protocol.

Etymology

To promote the fiber optic aspects of the technology and to make a unique name, the industry decided to use the British English spelling *fibre* for the standard.

History

Fibre Channel is standardized in the T11 Technical Committee of the International Committee for Information Technology Standards (INCITS), an American National Standards Institute (ANSI)-accredited standards committee. Fibre Channel started in 1988, with ANSI standard approval in 1994, to merge the benefits of multiple physical layer implementations including SCSI, HIPPI and ESCON.

Fibre Channel was designed as a serial interface to overcome limitations of the SCSI and HIPPI interfaces. FC was developed with leading edge multi-mode fiber technologies that overcame the speed limitations of the ESCON protocol. By appealing to the large base of SCSI disk drives and leveraging mainframe technologies, Fibre Channel developed economies of scale for advanced technologies and deployments became economical and widespread.

Initially, the standard also ratified lower speed Fibre Channel versions with 132.8125 Mbit/s ("12,5 MB/s»), 265.625 Mbit/s («25 MB/s»), and 531.25 Mbit/s («50 MB/s») that were already growing out of use at the time. Fibre Channel saw adoption at 1 Gigabit/s Fibre Channel (1GFC) and its success grew with each successive speed. Fibre Channel has doubled in speed every few years since 1996.

Fibre channel has seen active development since its inception, with numerous speed improvements on a variety of underlying transport media. For example, the following table shows native Fibre Channel speeds:

Fibre Channel Variants					
NAME	Line-rate (gigabaud)	Line coding	Nominal throughput per direction; MB/s	Net throughput per direction; MB/s	Availability
1GFC	1.0625	8b10b	100	103.2	1997
2GFC	2.125	8b10b	200	206.5	2001
4GFC	4.25	8b10b	400	412.9	2004
8GFC	8.5	8b10b	800	825.8	2005
10GFC	10.51875	64b66b	1,200	1,239	2008
16GFC	14.025	64b66b	1,600	1,652	2011
32GFC "Gen 6"	28.05	64b66b	3,200	3,303	2016
128GFC "Gen 6"	28.05 ×4	64b66b	12,800	13,210	2016

In addition to a cutting edge physical layer, Fibre Channel also added support for any number of "upper layer" protocols, including ATM, IP and FICON, with SCSI being the predominant usage.

Topologies

There are three major Fibre Channel topologies, describing how a number of ports are connected together. A *port* in Fibre Channel terminology is any entity that actively communicates over the network, not necessarily a hardware port. This port is usually implemented in a device such as disk storage, an HBA on a server or a Fibre Channel switch.

- Point-to-point (FC-FS-3). Two devices are connected directly to each other. This is the simplest topology, with limited connectivity.

- Arbitrated Loop (*FC-AL-2*). In this design, all devices are in a loop or ring, similar to token ring networking. Adding or removing a device from the loop causes all activity on the loop to be interrupted. The failure of one device causes a break in the ring. Fibre Channel hubs exist to connect multiple devices together and may bypass failed ports. A loop may also be made by cabling each port to the next in a ring.

- o A minimal loop containing only two ports, while appearing to be similar to point-to-point, differs considerably in terms of the protocol.

- o Only one pair of ports can communicate concurrently on a loop.

- o Maximum speed of 8GFC.

- o Arbitrated Loop has been rarely used after 2010.

- Switched Fabric (*FC-SW-6*). In this design, all devices are connected to Fibre Channel switches, similar conceptually to modern Ethernet implementations. Advantages of this topology over point-to-point or Arbitrated Loop include:

- o The Fabric can scale to tens of thousands of ports.

- o The switches manage the state of the Fabric, providing optimized paths via Fabric Shortest Path First (FSPF).

- o The traffic between two ports flows through the switches and not through any other ports like in Arbitrated Loop.

- o Failure of a port is isolated to a link and should not affect operation of other ports.

- o Multiple pairs of ports may communicate simultaneously in a Fabric.

Attribute	Point-to-Point	Arbitrated Loop	Switched Fabric
Max ports	2	127	~16777216 (2^{24})
Address size	N/A	8-bit ALPA	24-bit port ID
Side effect of port failure	Link fails	Loop fails (until port bypassed)	N/A
Access to medium	Dedicated	Arbitrated	Dedicated

Layers

Fibre Channel does not follow the OSI model layering, and is split into five layers:

- FC-4 – Protocol-mapping layer, in which upper level protocols such as SCSI, IP or FICON, are encapsulated into Information Units (IUs) for delivery to FC-2. Current FC-4s include FCP-4, FC-SB-5, and FC-NVMe;

- FC-3 – Common services layer, a thin layer that could eventually implement functions like encryption or RAID redundancy algorithms; multiport connections;

- FC-2 – Signaling Protocol, defined by the Fibre Channel Framing and Signaling 4 (FC-FS-4) standard, consists of the low level Fibre Channel protocols; port to port connections;

- FC-1 – Transmission Protocol, which implements line coding of signals;

- FC-0 – PHY, includes cabling, connectors etc.

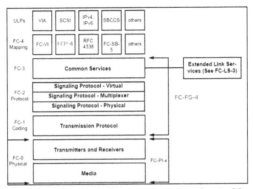

Fibre Channel is a layered technology that starts at the physical layer and progresses through the protocols to the upper level protocols like SCSI and SBCCS.

This diagram from FC-FS-4 defines the layers.

Layers FC-0 are defined in Fibre Channel Physical Interfaces (FC-PI-6), the physical layers of Fibre Channel.

Fibre Channel products are available at 1, 2, 4, 8, 10, 16 and 32 and 128 Gbit/s; these protocol flavors are called accordingly 1GFC, 2GFC, 4GFC, 8GFC, 10GFC, 16GFC, 32GFC or 128GFC. The 32GFC standard was approved by the INCITS T11 committee in 2013, and those products became available in 2016. The 1GFC, 2GFC, 4GFC, 8GFC designs all use 8b/10b encoding, while the 10GFC and 16GFC standard uses 64b/66b encoding. Unlike the 10GFC standards, 16GFC provides backward compatibility with 4GFC and 8GFC since it provides exactly twice the throughput of 8GFC or four times that of 4GFC.

Ports

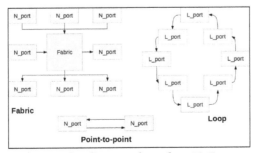

FC topologies and port types: This diagram shows how N_Ports can be connected to a fabric or to another N_Port. A Loop Port (L_Port) communicates through a shared loop and is rarely used anymore.

Fibre Channel ports come in a variety of logical configurations. The most common types of ports are:

- N_Port (Node port) An N_Port is typically an HBA port that connects to a switch's F_Port or another N_Port. Nx_Port communicating through a PN_Port that is not operating a Loop Port State Machine.

- F_Port (Fabric port) An F_Port is a switch port that is connected to an N_Port.

- E_Port (Expansion port) Switch port that attaches to another E_Port to create an Inter-Switch Link.

Fibre Channel Loop protocols create multiple types of Loop Ports:

- L_Port (Loop port) FC_Port that contains Arbitrated Loop functions associated with the Arbitrated Loop topology.

- FL_Port (Fabric Loop port) L_Port that is able to perform the function of an F_Port, attached via a link to one or more NL_Ports in an Arbitrated Loop topology.

- NL_Port (Node Loop port) PN_Port that is operating a Loop port state machine.

If a port can support loop and non-loop functionality, the port is known as:

- Fx_Port switch port capable of operating as an F_Port or FL_Port.

- Nx_Port end point for Fibre Channel frame communication, having a distinct address identifier and Name_Identifier,providing an independent set of FC-2V functions to higher levels, and having the ability to act as an Originator, a Responder, or both.

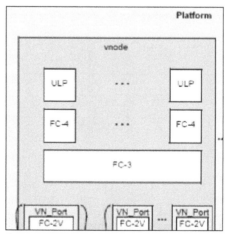

A Port has a physical structure as well as logical or virtual structure. This diagram shows how a virtual port may have multiple physical ports and vice versa.

Ports have virtual components and physical components and are described as:

- PN_Port entity that includes a Link_Control_Facility and one or more Nx_Ports.

- VF_Port (Virtual F_Port) instance of the FC-2V sublevel that connects to one or more VN_Ports.

- VN_Port (Virtual N_Port) instance of the FC-2V sublevel. VN_Port is used when it is desired to emphasize support for multiple Nx_Ports on a single Multiplexer (e.g., via a single PN_Port).

- VE_Port (Virtual E_Port) instance of the FC-2V sublevel that connects to another VE_Port or to a B_Port to create an Inter-Switch Link.

The following types of ports are also used in Fibre Channel:

- A_Port (Adjacent port) combination of one PA_Port and one VA_Port operating together.

- B_Port (Bridge Port) Fabric inter-element port used to connect bridge devices with E_Ports on a Switch.

- D_Port (Diagnostic Port) A configured port used to perform diagnostic tests on a link with another D_Port.

- EX_Port A type of E_Port used to connect to an FC router fabric.

- G_Port (Generic Fabric port) Switch port that may function either as an E_Port, A_Port, or as an F_Port.

- GL_Port (Generic Fabric Loop port) Switch port that may function either as an E_Port, A_Port, or as an Fx_Port.

- PE_Port LCF within the Fabric that attaches to another PE_Port or to a B_Port through a link.

- PF_Port LCF within a Fabric that attaches to a PN_Port through a link.

- TE_Port (Trunking E_Port) A trunking expansion port that expands the functionality of E ports to support VSAN trunking, Transport quality of service (QoS) parameters, and Fibre Channel trace (fctrace) feature.

- U_Port (Universal port) A port waiting to become another port type

- VA_Port (Virtual A_Port) instance of the FC-2V sublevel of Fibre Channel that connects to another VA_Port.

- VEX_Port VEX_Ports are no different from EX_Ports, except underlying transport is IP rather than FC.

Media and Modules

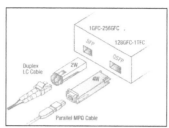

Fibre Channel predominantly uses the SFP module with the LC connector and duplex cabling, but 128GFC uses the QSFP28 module and the MPO connectors and ribbon cabling.

The Fibre Channel physical layer is based on serial connections that use corresponding modules. The small form-factor pluggable transceiver (SFP) module and its enhanced version SFP+ are common form factors for ports, supporting a variety of distances via multi-mode and single-mode fiber as shown in the table below. The SFP module uses duplex fiber cabling that has LC connectors.

The quad small form-factor pluggable (QSFP) module began being used for 4-lane implementations of 128GFC. The QSFP uses either the LC connector for 128GFC-CWDM4 or an MPO connector for 128GFC-SW4 or 128GFC-PSM4. The MPO cabling uses 8- or 12-fiber cabling infrastructure that connects to another 128GFC port or may be broken out into four duplex LC connections to 32GFC SFP+ ports. Fibre Channel switches use either SFP or QSFP modules.

Fiber Type	Speed (MB/s)	Transmitter	Medium variant	Distance
Single-mode Fiber (SMF)	12,800	1,310 nm longwave light	128GFC-PSM4	0.5m - 0.5 km
		1,270, 1,290, 1,310 and 1,330 nm long-wave light	128GFC-CWDM4	0.5 m – 2 km
	3,200	1,310 nm longwave light	3200-SM-LC-L	0.5 m - 10 km
	1,600	1,310 nm longwave light	1600-SM-LC-L	0.5 m – 10 km
		1,490 nm longwave light	1600-SM-LZ-I	0.5 m – 2 km
	800	1,310 nm longwave light	800-SM-LC-L	2 m – 10 km
			800-SM-LC-I	2 m – 1.4 km
	400	1,310 nm longwave light	400-SM-LC-L	2 m – 10 km
			400-SM-LC-M	2 m – 4 km
			400-SM-LL-I	2 m – 2 km
	200	1,550 nm longwave light	200-SM-LL-V	2 m – 50 km
		1,310 nm longwave light	200-SM-LC-L	2 m – 10 km
			200-SM-LL-I	2 m – 2 km
	100	1,550 nm longwave light	100-SM-LL-V	2 m – 50 km
		1,310 nm longwave light	100-SM-LL-L 100-SM-LC-L	2 m – 10 km
			100-SM-LL-I	2 m – 2 km

Fiber Type	Speed (MB/s)	Transmitter	Medium variant	Distance
Multimode Fiber (MMF)	12,800	850 nm shortwave light	128GFC-SW4	0 – 100 m
	3,200		3200-SN	0 – 100 m
	1,600		1600-M5F-SN-I	0.5 m – 125 m
			1600-M5E-SN-I	0.5–100 m
			1600-M5-SN-S	0.5–35 m
			1600-M6-SN-S	0.5–15 m
	800		800-M5F-SN-I	0.5–190 m
			800-M5E-SN-I	0.5–150 m
			800-M5-SN-S	0.5–50 m
			800-M6-SN-S	0.5–21 m
	400		400-M5F-SN-I	0.5–400 m
			400-M5E-SN-I	0.5–380 m
			400-M5-SN-I	0.5–150 m
			400-M6-SN-I	0.5–70 m
	200		200-M5E-SN-I	0.5–500 m
			200-M5-SN-I	0.5–300 m
			200-M6-SN-I	0.5–150 m
	100		100-M5E-SN-I	0.5–860 m
			100-M5-SN-I	0.5–500 m
			100-M6-SN-I	0.5–300 m
			100-M5-SL-I	2–500 m
			100-M6-SL-I	2–175 m

Multimode fiber	Fiber diameter	FC media designation
OM1	62.5 µm	M6
OM2	50 µm	M5
OM3	50 µm	M5E
OM4	50 µm	M5F

Modern Fibre Channel devices support SFP transceiver, mainly with LC (Lucent Connector) fiber connector. Older 1GFC devices used GBIC transceiver, mainly with SC (Subscriber Connector) fiber connector.

Fibre Channel Storage Area Networks

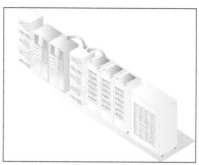

The Fibre Channel SAN connects servers to storage via Fibre Channel switches.

The goal of Fibre Channel is to create a storage area network (SAN) to connect servers to storage.

The SAN is a dedicated network that enables multiple servers to access the same storage. Enterprise storage uses the SAN to backup to tape libraries while the storage is still accessible to the server. Servers may access storage from multiple storage devices over the network as well.

SANs are often designed with dual fabrics to increase fault tolerance. Two completely separate fabrics are operational and if the primary fabric fails, then the second fabric becomes the primary.

Fibre Channel Switches

Fibre Channel switch with SFP+ modules and LC optical fiber connectors with Optical Multimode 3 (OM3) fiber (aqua).

Fibre Channel switches can be divided into two classes. These classes are not part of the standard, and the classification of every switch is a marketing decision of the manufacturer:

- Directors offer a high port-count in a modular (slot-based) chassis with no single point of failure (high availability).

- Switches are typically smaller, fixed-configuration (sometimes semi-modular), less redundant devices.

A fabric consisting entirely of one vendors products is considered to be *homogeneous*. This is often referred to as operating in its "native mode" and allows the vendor to add proprietary features which may not be compliant with the Fibre Channel standard.

If multiple switch vendors are used within the same fabric it is *heterogeneous*, the switches may only achieve adjacency if all switches are placed into their interoperability modes. This is called the "open fabric" mode as each vendor's switch may have to disable its proprietary features to comply with the Fibre Channel standard.

Some switch manufacturers offer a variety of interoperability modes above and beyond the "native" and "open fabric" states. These "native interoperability" modes allow switches to operate in the native mode of another vendor and still maintain some of the proprietary behaviors of both. However, running in native interoperability mode may still disable some proprietary features and can produce fabrics of questionable stability.

Fibre Channel Host Bus Adapters

Dual port 8Gb FC host bus adapter card.

Fibre Channel HBAs, as well as CNAs, are available for all major open systems, computer architectures, and buses, including PCI and SBus. Some are OS dependent. Each HBA has a unique World Wide Name (WWN), which is similar to an Ethernet MAC address in that it uses an Organizationally Unique Identifier (OUI) assigned by the IEEE. However, WWNs are longer (8 bytes). There are two types of WWNs on a HBA; a node WWN (WWNN), which can be shared by some or all ports of a device, and a port WWN (WWPN), which is necessarily unique to each port.

Network File System

Network File System (NFS) is a distributed file system protocol originally developed by Sun Microsystems in 1984, allowing a user on a client computer to access files over a computer network much like local storage is accessed. NFS, like many other protocols, builds on the Open Network Computing Remote Procedure Call (ONC RPC) system. The NFS is an open standard defined in Request for Comments (RFC), allowing anyone to implement the protocol.

Versions and Variations

Sun used version 1 only for in-house experimental purposes. When the development team added substantial changes to NFS version 1 and released it outside of Sun, they decided to release the new version as v2, so that version interoperation and RPC version fallback could be tested.

NFSv2

Version 2 of the protocol (defined in RFC 1094, March 1989) originally operated only over User Datagram Protocol (UDP). Its designers meant to keep the server side stateless, with locking (for example) implemented outside of the core protocol. People involved in the creation of NFS version 2 include Russel Sandberg, Bob Lyon, Bill Joy, Steve Kleiman, and others.

The Virtual File System interface allows a modular implementation, reflected in a simple protocol. By February 1986, implementations were demonstrated for operating systems such as System V release 2, DOS, and VAX/VMS using Eunice. NFSv2 only allows the first 2 GB of a file to be read due to 32-bit limitations.

NFSv3

Version 3 (RFC 1813, June 1995) added:

- support for 64-bit file sizes and offsets, to handle files larger than 2 gigabytes (GB);

- support for asynchronous writes on the server, to improve write performance;

- additional file attributes in many replies, to avoid the need to re-fetch them;

- a READDIRPLUS operation, to get file handles and attributes along with file names when scanning a directory;

- assorted other improvements.

The first NFS Version 3 proposal within Sun Microsystems was created not long after the release of NFS Version 2. The principal motivation was an attempt to mitigate the performance issue of the synchronous write operation in NFS Version 2. By July 1992, implementation practice had solved many shortcomings of NFS Version 2, leaving only lack of large file support (64-bit file sizes and offsets) a pressing issue. This became an acute pain point for Digital Equipment Corporation wih the intodution of a 64-bit version of Ultrix to support their newly released 64-bit RISC processor, the Alpha 21064. At the time of introduction of Version 3, vendor support for TCP as a transport-layer protocol began increasing. While several vendors had already added support for NFS Version 2 with TCP as a transport, Sun Microsystems added support for TCP as a transport for NFS at the same time it added support for Version 3. Using TCP as a transport made using NFS over a WAN more feasible, and allowed the use of larger read and write transfer sizes beyond the 8 KB limit imposed by User Datagram Protocol (UDP).

NFSv4

Version 4 (RFC 3010, December 2000; revised in RFC 3530, April 2003 and again in RFC 7530, March 2015), influenced by Andrew File System (AFS) and Server Message Block (SMB, also termed CIFS), includes performance improvements, mandates strong security, and introduces a stateful protocol. Version 4 became the first version developed with the Internet Engineering Task Force (IETF) after Sun Microsystems handed over the development of the NFS protocols.

NFS version 4.1 (RFC 5661, January 2010) aims to provide protocol support to take advantage of clustered server deployments including the ability to provide scalable parallel access to files distributed among multiple servers (pNFS extension). NFS version 4.2 (RFC 7862) was published in November 2016.

Other Extensions

WebNFS, an extension to Version 2 and Version 3, allows NFS to integrate more easily into Web-browsers and to enable operation through firewalls. In 2007 Sun Microsystems open-sourced their client-side WebNFS implementation.

Various side-band protocols have become associated with NFS. Note:

- the byte-range advisory Network Lock Manager (NLM) protocol (added to support UNIX System V file locking APIs).

- the remote quota-reporting (RQUOTAD) protocol, which allows NFS users to view their data-storage quotas on NFS servers.

- NFS over RDMA, an adaptation of NFS that uses remote direct memory access (RDMA) as a transport.

- NFS-Ganesha, an NFS server, running in user-space and supporting the CephFS FSAL (File System Abstraction Layer) using libcephfs.

Platforms

NFS is often used with Unix operating systems (such as Solaris, AIX, HP-UX), Apple's macOS, and Unix-like operating systems (such as Linux and FreeBSD). It is also available to operating systems such as Acorn RISC OS, the classic Mac OS, OpenVMS, MS-DOS, Microsoft Windows, Novell NetWare, and IBM AS/400. Alternative remote file access protocols include the Server Message Block (SMB, also termed CIFS), Apple Filing Protocol (AFP), NetWare Core Protocol (NCP), and OS/400 File Server file system (QFileSvr.400).

SMB and NetWare Core Protocol (NCP) occur more often than NFS on systems running Microsoft Windows; AFP occurs more often than NFS in Apple Macintosh systems; and QFileSvr.400 occurs more often in AS/400 systems. Haiku recently added NFSv4 support as part of a Google Summer of Code project.

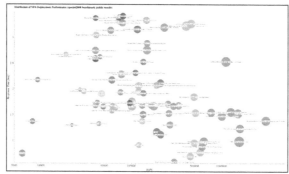

NFS specint2008 performance comparison, as of 22 November 2013.

Typical Implementation

Assuming a Unix-style scenario in which one machine (the client) needs access to data stored on another machine (the NFS server):

1. The server implements NFS daemon processes, running by default as nfsd, to make its data generically available to clients.

2. The server administrator determines what to make available, exporting the names and parameters of directories, typically using the /etc/exports configuration file and the exportfs command.

3. The server security-administration ensures that it can recognize and approve validated clients.

4. The server network configuration ensures that appropriate clients can negotiate with it through any firewall system.

5. The client machine requests access to exported data, typically by issuing a mount command. (The client asks the server (rpcbind) which port the NFS server is using, the client connects to the NFS server (nfsd), nfsd passes the request to mountd)

6. If all goes well, users on the client machine can then view and interact with mounted filesystems on the server within the parameters permitted.

Note that automation of the NFS mounting process may take place — perhaps using /etc/fstab and/or automounting facilities.

Protocol Development

During the development of the ONC protocol (called SunRPC at the time), only Apollo's Network Computing System (NCS) offered comparable functionality. Two competing groups developed over fundamental differences in the two remote procedure call systems. Arguments focused on the method for data-encoding — ONC's External Data Representation (XDR) always rendered integers in big-endian order, even if both peers of the connection had little-endian machine-architectures, whereas NCS's method attempted to avoid byte-swap whenever two peers shared a common endianness in their machine-architectures. An industry-group called the Network Computing Forum formed (March 1987) in an (ultimately unsuccessful) attempt to reconcile the two network-computing environments.

Later, Sun and AT&T announced they would jointly develop AT&T's UNIX System V Release 4. This caused many of AT&T's other licensees of UNIX System to become concerned that this would put Sun in an advantaged position, and ultimately led to Digital Equipment, HP, IBM, and others forming the Open Software Foundation (OSF) in 1988. Ironically, Sun and AT&T had formerly competed over Sun's NFS versus AT&T's Remote File System (RFS), and the quick adoption of NFS over RFS by Digital Equipment, HP, IBM, and many other computer vendors tipped the majority of users in favor of NFS. NFS interoperability was aided by events called "Connectathons" starting in 1986 that allowed vendor-neutral testing of implementations with each other. OSF adopted the Distributed Computing Environment (DCE) and the DCE Distributed File System (DFS) over Sun/ONC RPC and NFS. DFS used DCE as the RPC, and DFS derived from the Andrew File System (AFS); DCE itself derived from a suite of technologies, including Apollo's NCS and Kerberos.

1990s

Sun Microsystems and the Internet Society (ISOC) reached an agreement to cede "change control" of ONC RPC so that the ISOC's engineering-standards body, the Internet Engineering Task Force (IETF), could publish standards documents (RFCs) related to ONC RPC protocols and could extend ONC RPC. OSF attempted to make DCE RPC an IETF standard, but ultimately proved unwilling to give up change control. Later, the IETF chose to extend ONC RPC by adding a new authentication flavor based on Generic Security Services Application Program Interface (GSSAPI), RPCSEC GSS, to meet IETF requirements that protocol standards have adequate security.

Later, Sun and ISOC reached a similar agreement to give ISOC change control over NFS, although writing the contract carefully to exclude NFS version 2 and version 3. Instead, ISOC gained the right to add new versions to the NFS protocol, which resulted in IETF specifying NFS version 4 in 2003.

2000s

By the 21st century, neither DFS nor AFS had achieved any major commercial success as compared to SMB-CIFS or NFS. IBM, which had formerly acquired the primary commercial vendor of DFS and AFS, Transarc, donated most of the AFS source code to the free software community in 2000. The OpenAFS project lives on. In early 2005, IBM announced end of sales for AFS and DFS.

In January, 2010, Panasas proposed an NFSv4.1 based on their *Parallel NFS* (pNFS) technology claiming to improve data-access parallelism capability. The NFSv4.1 protocol defines a method of separating the filesystem meta-data from file data location; it goes beyond the simple name/data separation by striping the data amongst a set of data servers. This differs from the traditional NFS server which holds the names of files and their data under the single umbrella of the server. Some products are multi-node NFS servers, but the participation of the client in separation of meta-data and data is limited.

The NFSv4.1 pNFS server is a set of server resources or components; these are assumed to be controlled by the meta-data server.

The pNFS client still accesses one meta-data server for traversal or interaction with the namespace; when the client moves data to and from the server it may directly interact with the set of data servers belonging to the pNFS server collection. The NFSv4.1 client can be enabled to be a direct participant in the exact location of file data and to avoid solitary interaction with one NFS server when moving data.

In addition to pNFS, NFSv4.1 provides:

- Sessions.
- Directory Delegation and Notifications.
- Multi-server Namespace.
- access control lists and discretionary access control.
- Retention Attributions.
- SECINFO_NO_NAME.

Cloud E-commerce

Cloud e-commerce refers to the process of outsourcing of a remote network of servers hosted on the Internet to use application services, store, and process data. Essentially, it is a cloud-based e-commerce solution versus software installed on a local server.

Cloud e-commerce provides a wide range of benefits over traditional on-premise storage used for commerce. Within the last years, the cloud has gained popularity due to reduced complexity and lower cost of maintenance. Nowadays, cloud e-commerce has become one of the most optimal solutions on the market.

Scalability on Demand

The extreme traffic variability in e-commerce with its seasonal spikes creates a unique workload for e-commerce hosting. Required hardware capacity must conform to the traffic peaks (ex. Black Friday, Cyber Monday, etc.). But for most of the year, the servers are not in use.

The cloud offers an elastic solution, that allows for substantial variations in workload and meets the needs for seasonal or even hourly promotional spikes in traffic, including unpredictable outbreaks. This way cloud e-commerce store resources can be scaled up and down to support your actual needs.

The other side of scalability is business growth. An increase in store's popularity, integration of new services and further store evolution force the infrastructure to grow accordingly. A flexible platform at the heart of your e-commerce solution, as well as scalable environment responds quickly to business challenges and opportunities.

Cloud allows to avoid physical superstructure. The e-commerce business doesn't have to purchase additional equipment and hire new maintenance staff.

Reliable Pro Protection

When hosting your business in the cloud, the e-commerce website doesn't need to worry about maintaining and monitoring servers. Security and protection of network, physical facilities, applications, including data encryption and customers' personal data safety can be excluded from the list of concerns. E-commerce cloud vendors take all the risks. The cloud hosting providers complete a third-party certification, and proper security is a priority for them. Besides, constant accessibility of ecommerce storefront and regular data backup ensure that the e-commerce store will be available without any data loss in case of an emergency.

Cost-effective Performance

Cloud fits e-commerce solutions perfectly because the business pays for resources only when it needs them. A cloud-based solution may save a company over 70% of the costs associated with building static environments scaled for traffic peaks - the hardware that may only be in use a few days a year.

Easy Accessibility from any Place

If the e-commerce project operates in multiple countries, a cloud-based e-commerce solution offers clear advantages considering the speed required to roll out and manage an e-commerce application. With cloud-based e-commerce, there's a remote network of servers that responds dynamically to business demands to deliver content fast no matter where your customer is.

How to Pick a Service for your Commerce?

The cloud computing service categories fall under several distinct categories. Each of these models or their combinations allows users to create the perfect foundation for the e-commerce suite.

IaaS (Infrastructure as a Service)

This type of cloud service focuses on providing on-demand data storage on disks and virtual servers. Customers purchase a remote data center infrastructure service instead of having to purchase their own hardware.

Examples include cloud services offered by established well-known brands, such as Amazon, Microsoft, and others.

PaaS (Platform as a Service)

A cloud development platform that allows its users to develop, manage, and launch applications within a self-service portal with a ready-to-use cloud computing infrastructure. Most platforms provide the basics so that you don't have to start from scratch. The operating system is supported and frequently upgraded, and the services for your e-commerce solution can be built, using certain modules.

Examples of Platform-as-a-Service are Google App Engine, Cloudfy, and Cloudsuite.

SaaS (Software as a Service)

Software-as-a-Service means that a third-party hosting service provider gives clients access to various software solutions on a pay-as-you-go basis.

This service type is very popular among e-commerce vendors. Modern applications allow your business to improve its customer experience and expand the online store with advanced features, such as smart shopping cart or mobile-friendly applications.

Among the most popular SaaS solutions are Salesforce, NetSuite, Slack and others.

An optimal choice for an e-commerce business willing to use cloud, however, would be a solution that combines a platform with a ready-to-use set of software tools. In other words, PaaS and SaaS built specifically for e-commerce. Examples of cloud e-commerce solutions include:

- Magento

- Demandware

- Commerce Cloud from Oracle

- Commerce Cloud from SalesForce

Enterprise e-commerce cloud solutions can be based on different public clouds, including Azure from Microsoft, Google Cloud or AWS from Amazon.

Cooperative Storage Cloud

A cooperative storage cloud is a decentralized model of networked online storage where data is stored on multiple computers (nodes), hosted by the participants cooperating in the cloud. For the cooperative scheme to be viable, the total storage contributed in aggregate must be at least equal to the amount of storage needed by end users. However, some nodes may contribute less storage and some may contribute more. There may be reward models to compensate the nodes contributing more.

Unlike a traditional storage cloud, a cooperative does not directly employ dedicated servers for the actual storage of the data, thereby eliminating the need for a significant dedicated hardware investment. Each node in the cooperative runs specialized software which communicates with a centralized control and orchestration server, thereby allowing the node to both consume and contribute storage space to the cloud. The centralized control and orchestration server requires several orders of magnitude less resources (storage, computing power, and bandwidth) to operate, relative to the overall capacity of the cooperative.

Data Security

Files hosted in the cloud are fragmented and encrypted before leaving the local machine. They are then distributed randomly using a load balancing and geo-distribution algorithm to other nodes in the cooperative. Users can add an additional layer of security and reduce storage space by compressing and encrypting files before they are copied to the cloud.

Data Redundancy

In order to maintain data integrity and high availability across a relatively unreliable set of computers over a wide area network like the Internet, the source node will add some level of redundancy to each data block. This allows the system to recreate the entire block even if some nodes are temporarily unavailable (due to loss of network connectivity, the machine being powered off or a hardware failure). The most storage and bandwidth efficient forms of redundancy use erasure coding techniques like

Reed-Solomon. A simple, less CPU intensive but more expensive form of redundancy is duplicate copies.

Flexible Contribution

Due to bandwidth or hardware constraints some nodes may not be able to contribute as much space as they consume in the cloud. On the other hand, nodes with large storage space and limited or no bandwidth constraints may contribute more than they consume, thereby the cooperative can always stay in balance.

Examples

The University of California's OceanStore project, MIT's Chord, is a non-commercial example.

Sia is a fully distributed system using a blockchain where a cryptocurrency is exchanged for storage, and a daemon that can act both as a file host and as a "renter" of storage, using Merkle trees to provide strong guarantees that hosts will only get paid if they successfully hold data for the duration of a "storage contract". Data is encrypted and spread among hosts in a redundant manner, using erasure coding, to maximize availability. According to one of its creators, Sia was the first platform of its kind to launch an end-user product.

On June 1, 2016 Minebox GMBH announced that their forthcoming Minebox Networked Attached Storage device (NAS) will utilize the Sia network to persist its backups. Users of the Minebox will also be able to rent their free disk space via Sia.

Storj is another example: based on the Bitcoin blockchain technology and a peer-to-peer architecture, it intends to provide cloud storage to people. It is currently developing two applications to achieve this goal: *MetaDisk*, which lets the user upload files to the network, and *DriveShare*, allowing users to rent out their storage space to MetaDisk users.

A partly centralized system was operated by Symform, Inc., a startup company based in Seattle. Symform generated and kept the keys used to encrypt and decrypt, and since it also decided which server will host which parts of a file, users have to trust Symform not to share those with any other party or misuse the information. Symform discontinued its service on Jul 31, 2016.

References

- Sanjay Ghemawat; Howard Gobioff; Shun-Tak Leung (October 2003). "The Google File System" (PDF). Google. Retrieved 20, June 2020

- Richardson, Leonard; Amundsen, Mike (2013), RESTful Web APIs, O'Reilly Media, ISBN 978-1-449-35806-8, Retrieved 13, May 2020

- Subashini, S.; Kavitha, V. (2011-01-01). "A survey on security issues in service delivery models of cloud computing". Journal of Network and Computer Applications. 34 (1): 1–11. doi:10.1016/j.jnca.2010.07.006

- Preston, W. Curtis (2002). "Fibre Channel Architecture". Using SANs and NAS. Sebastopol, CA: O'Reilly Media. pp. 19–39. ISBN 978-0-596-00153-7. OCLC 472853124

- Butler, Brandon (2 June 2014). "Cloud's worst-case scenario: What to do if your provider goes belly up". Network World. Retrieved 25, July 2020

- Mesnier, Mike; Gregory R. Ganger; Erik Riedel (August 2003). "Object-Based Storage" (PDF). IEEE Communications Magazine: 84–90. doi:10.1109/mcom.2003.1222722. Retrieved 21, August 2020

- Thomas Erl, Benjamin Carlyle, Cesare Pautasso, Raj Balasubramanian (2013). "5.1". In Thomas Erl. SOA with REST. Prentice Hall. ISBN 978-0-13-701251-0

- Sandoval, Greg (31 March 2012). "MPAA wants more criminal cases brought against 'rogue' sites". CNET. Retrieved 01, April 2020

- "Box.net lets you store, share, work in the computing cloud". Silicon Valley Business Journal. December 6, 2009. Retrieved 26, January 2020

- Mellor, Chris (6 January 2015). "IDC: Who's HOT and who's NOT (in object storage) in 2014". The Register. Retrieved 13, May 2020

- Hirsch, Frederick; Kemp, John; Ilkka, Jani (2007). Mobile Web Services: Architecture and Implementation. John Wiley & Sons. p. 27. ISBN 9780470032596. Retrieved 01, February 2020

Distributed Systems and Computing

Distributed systems refer to the systems which have multiple components situated on different machines which are in communication with each other and coordinate their actions in such a manner that it appears as a single coherent system to the end user. This chapter discusses in detail the different aspects of distributed systems and computing.

Distributed Systems

A distributed system is a collection of independent components located on different machines that share messages with each other in order to achieve common goals. As such, the distributed system will appear as if it is one interface or computer to the end-user. The hope is that together, the system can maximize resources and information while preventing failures, as if one system fails, it won't affect the availability of the service.

Working of Distributed Systems

The most important functions of distributed computing are:

- Resource sharing: Whether it's the hardware, software or data that can be shared.

- Openness: How open is the software designed to be developed and shared with each other.

- Concurrency: Multiple machines can process the same function at the same time.

- Scalability: How do the computing and processing capabilities multiply when extended to many machines.

- Fault tolerance: How easy and quickly can failures in parts of the system be detected and recovered.

- Transparency: How much access does one node have to locate and communicate with other nodes in the system.

Modern distributed systems have evolved to include autonomous processes that might run on the same physical machine, but interact by exchanging messages with each other.

Examples of Distributed Systems

- Networks: The earliest example of a distributed system happened in the 1970s when ethernet was invented and LAN (local area networks) were created. For the first time computers would be able to send messages to other systems with a local IP address. Peer-to-peer networks evolved and e-mail and then the Internet as we know it continue to be the biggest, ever growing example of distributed systems. As the internet changed from IPv4 to IPv6, distributed systems have evolved from "LAN" based to "Internet" based.

- Telecommunication Networks: Telephone and cellular networks are also examples of distributed networks. Telephone networks have been around for over a century and it started as an early example of a peer to peer network. Cellular networks are distributed networks with base stations physically distributed in areas called cells. As telephone networks have evolved to VOIP (voice over IP), it continues to grow in complexity as a distributed network.

- Distributed Real-time Systems: Many industries use real-time systems that are distributed locally and globally. Airlines use flight control systems, Uber and Lyft use dispatch systems, manufacturing plants use automation control systems, logistics and e-commerce companies use real-time tracking systems.

- Parallel Processing: There used to be a distinction between parallel computing and distributed systems. Parallel computing was focused on how to run software on multiple threads or processors that accessed the same data and memory. Distributed systems meant separate machines with their own processors and memory. With the rise of modern operating systems, processors and cloud services these days, distributed computing also encompasses parallel processing.

- Distributed artificial intelligence: Distributed Artificial Intelligence is a way to use large scale computing power and parallel processing to learn and process very large data sets using multi-agents.

- Distributed Database Systems: A distributed database is a database that is located over multiple servers and/or physical locations. The data can either be replicated or duplicated across systems. Most popular applications use a distributed database and need to be aware of the homogenous or heterogenous nature of the distributed database system. A homogenous distributed database means that each system has the same database management system and data model. They are easier to manage and scale performance by adding new nodes and locations. Heterogenous distributed databases allow for multiple data models, different database management systems. Gateways are used to translate the data between nodes and usually happen as a result of merging applications and systems.

Advantages of Distributed Systems

The ultimate goal of a distributed system is to enable the scalability, performance and high availability of applications. Major benefits include:

- Unlimited Horizontal Scaling: Machines can be added whenever required.

- Low Latency: Having machines that are geographically located closer to users, it will reduce the time it takes to serve users.

- Fault Tolerance: If one server or data centre goes down, others could still serve the users of the service.

Disadvantages of Distributed Systems

Every engineering decision has tradeoffs. Complexity is the biggest disadvantage of distributed systems. There are more machines, more messages, more data being passed between more parties which leads to issues with:

- Data Integration and Consistency: Being able to synchronize the order of changes to data and states of the application in a distributed system is challenging, especially when there nodes are starting, stopping or failing.

- Network and Communication Failure: Messages may not be delivered to the right nodes or in the incorrect order which lead to a breakdown in communication and functionality.

- Management Overhead: More intelligence, monitoring, logging, load balancing functions need to be added for visibility into the operation and failures of the distributed systems.

Distributed Computing

The term "distributed computing" describes a digital infrastructure in which a network of computers solves pending computational tasks. Despite being physically separated, these autonomous computers work together closely in a process where the work is divvied up. The hardware being used is secondary to the method here. In addition to high-performance computers and workstations used by professionals, you can also integrate minicomputers and desktop computers used by private individuals.

Distributed hardware cannot use a shared memory due to being physically separated, so the participating computers exchange messages and data (e.g. computation results) over a network. This inter-machine communication occurs locally over an intranet (e.g. in a data center) or across the country and world via the internet. Messages are transferred using internet protocols such as TCP/IP and UDP.

In line with the principle of transparency, distributed computing strives to present it-self externally as a functional unit and to simplify the use of technology as much as possible. For example, users searching for a product in the database of an online shop perceive the shopping experience as a single process and do not have to deal with the modular system architecture being used. In short, distributed computing is a combination of task distribution and coordinated interactions. The goal is to make task management as efficient as possible and to find practical flexible solutions.

Functioning of Distributed System

In distributed computing, a computation starts with a special problem-solving strategy. A single problem is divided up and each part is processed by one of the computing units. Distributed applications running on all the machines in the computer network handle the operational execution.

Distributed applications often use client-server architecture. Clients and servers share the work and cover certain application functions with the software installed on them. A product search is carried out using the following steps: (1) The client acts as an input instance and a user interface that receives the user request and processes it so that it can be sent on to a server. (2) The remote server then carries out the main part of the search function and searches a database. The search results are prepared on the server-side to be sent back to the client and are communicated to the client over the network. In the end, the results are displayed on the user's screen.

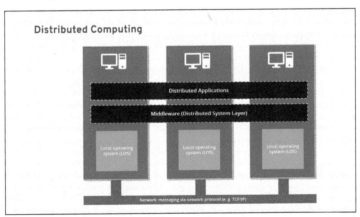

Distributed applications can solve problems across devices in a computer network. When used in conjunction with middleware, they can optimize operational interactions with locally accessible hardware and software.

Middleware services are often integrated into distributed processes. Acting as a special software layer, middleware defines the (logical) interaction patterns between partners and ensures communication, and optimal integration in distributed systems. It provides interfaces and services that bridge gaps between different applications and enables and monitors their communication (e.g. through communication controllers). For operational implementation, middleware provides a proven method for cross-device inter-process communication called remote procedure call (RPC) which is frequently used in client-server architecture for product searches involving database queries.

This integration function, which is in line with the transparency principle, can also be viewed as a translation task. Technically heterogeneous application systems and platforms normally cannot communicate with one another. Middleware helps them to "speak one language" and work together productively. In addition to cross-device and cross-platform interaction, middleware also handles other tasks like data management. It controls distributed applications' access to functions and processes of operating systems that are available locally on the connected computer.

Types of Distributed Computing

Distributed computing is a multifaceted field with infrastructures that can vary widely. It is thus nearly impossible to define all types of distributed computing. However, this field of computer science is commonly divided into three subfields:

- Cloud computing.

- Grid computing.

- Cluster computing.

Cloud computing uses distributed computing to provide customers with highly scalable cost-effective infrastructures and platforms. Cloud providers usually offer their resources through hosted services that can be used over the internet. A number of different service models have established themselves on the market:

- Software as a service (SaaS): In the case of SaaS, the customer uses the cloud provider's applications and associated infrastructure (e.g. servers, online storage, computing power). The applications can be accessed with a variety of devices via a thin client interface (e.g. a browser-based web app). Maintenance and administration of the outsourced infrastructure is handled by the cloud provider.

- Platform as a service (PaaS): In the case of PaaS, a cloud-based environment is provided (e.g. for developing web applications). The customer retains control over the applications provided and can configure customized user settings while the technical infrastructure for distributed computing is handled by the cloud provider.

- Infrastructure as a service (IaaS): In the case of IaaS, the cloud provider supplies a technical infrastructure which users can access via public or private networks. The provided infrastructure may include the following components: servers, computing and networking resources, communication devices (e.g. routers, switches, and firewalls), storage space, and systems for archiving and securing data. As for the customer, they retain control over operating systems and provided applications.

Grid computing is based on the idea of a supercomputer with enormous computing power. However, computing tasks are performed by many instances rather than just one. Servers and computers can thus perform different tasks independently of one another. Grid computing can access resources in a very flexible manner when performing tasks. Normally, participants will allocate specific resources to an entire project at night when the technical infrastructure tends to be less heavily used.

One advantage of this is that highly powerful systems can be quickly used and the computing power can be scaled as needed. There is no need to replace or upgrade an expensive supercomputer with another pricey one to improve performance. Since grid computing can create a virtual supercomputer from a cluster of loosely interconnected computers, it is specialized in solving problems that are particularly computationally intensive. This method is often used for ambitious scientific projects and decrypting cryptographic codes.

Cluster computing cannot be clearly differentiated from cloud and grid computing. It is a more general approach and refers to all the ways in which individual computers and their computing power can be combined together in clusters. Examples of this include server clusters, clusters in big data and in cloud environments, database clusters, and application clusters. Computer networks are also increasingly being used in high-performance computing which can solve particularly demanding computing problems.

Different types of distributed computing can also be defined by looking at the system architectures and interaction models of a distributed infrastructure. Due to the complex system architectures in distributed computing, the term distributed systems is more often used. The following are some of the more commonly used architecture models in distributed computing:

- Client-server model.

- Peer-to-peer model.

- Multilayered model (multi-tier architectures).

- Service-oriented architecture (SOA).

The client-server model is a simple interaction and communication model in distributed computing. In this model, a server receives a request from a client, performs the necessary processing procedures, and sends back a response (e.g. a message, data, computational results).

A peer-to-peer architecture organizes interaction and communication in distributed computing in a decentralized manner. All computers (also referred to as nodes) have the same rights and perform the same tasks and functions in the network. Each computer is thus able to act as both a client and a server. One example of peer-to-peer architecture is cryptocurrency blockchains.

When designing a multilayered architecture, individual components of a software system are distributed across multiple layers (or tiers), thus increasing the efficiency and flexibility offered by distributed computing. This system architecture can be designed as two-tier, three-tier or n-tier architecture depending on its intended use and is often found in web applications.

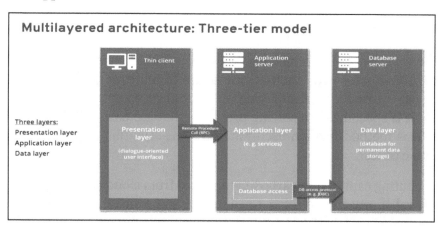

In a multilayered architecture, a database request is processed by dividing up the work. The layers are located on different computers that perform specific tasks and act as the client or server.

A service-oriented architecture (SOA) focuses on services and is geared towards addressing the individual needs and processes of company. This allows individual services to be combined into a bespoke business process. For example, an SOA can cover the entire process of "ordering online" which involves the following services: "taking the order", "credit checks" and "sending the invoice". Technical components (e.g. servers, databases, etc.) are used as tools but are not the main focus here. In this type of distributed computing, priority is given to ensuring that services are effectively combined, work together well, and are smartly organized with the aim of making business processes as efficient and smooth as possible.

In a service-oriented architecture, extra emphasis is placed on well-defined interfaces that functionally connect the components and increase efficiency. These can also benefit from the system's flexibility since services can be used in a number of ways in different contexts and reused in business processes. Service-oriented architectures using distributed computing are often based on web services.

Advantages of Distributed Computing

Distributed computing has many advantages. It allows companies to build an affordable high-performance infrastructure using inexpensive off-the-shelf computers with microprocessors instead of extremely expensive mainframes. Large clusters can even outperform individual supercomputers and handle high-performance computing tasks that are complex and computationally intensive. Since distributed computing system architectures are comprised of multiple (sometimes redundant) components, it is easier to compensate for the failure of individual components (i.e. increased partition tolerance). Thanks to the high level of task distribution, processes can be outsourced and the computing load can be shared (i.e. load balancing).

Many distributed computing solutions aim to increase flexibility which also usually increases efficiency and cost-effectiveness. To solve specific problems, specialized platforms such as database servers can be integrated. For example, SOA architectures can be used in business fields to create bespoke solutions for optimizing specific business processes. Providers can offer computing resources and infrastructures worldwide, which makes cloud-based work possible. This allows companies to respond to customer demands with scaled and needs-based offers and prices.

Distributed computing's flexibility also means that temporary idle capacity can be used for particularly ambitious projects. Users and companies can also be flexible in their hardware purchases since they are not restricted to a single manufacturer. Another major advantage is its scalability. Companies are able to scale quickly and at a moment's notice or gradually adjust the required computing power to the demand as they grow organically. If you choose to use your own hardware for scaling, you can steadily expand your device fleet in affordable increments.

Despite its many advantages, distributed computing also has some disadvantages, such as the higher cost of implementing and maintaining a complex system architecture. In addition, there are timing and synchronization problems between distributed instances that must be addressed. In terms of partition tolerance, the decentralized approach does have certain advantages over a single processing instance. However, the distributed computing method also gives rise to security problems, such as how data becomes vulnerable to sabotage and hacking when transferred over public networks. Distributed infrastructures are also generally more error-prone since there are more interfaces and potential sources for error at the hardware and software level. Problem and error troubleshooting is also made more difficult by the infrastructure's complexity.

Uses of Distributed Computing

Distributed computing has become an essential basic technology involved in the digitalization of both our private life and work life. The internet and the services it offers would not be possible if it were not for the client-server architectures of distributed systems. Every Google search involves distributed computing with supplier instances around the world working together to generate matching search results. Google Maps and Google Earth also leverage distributed computing for their services.

Distributed computing methods and architectures are also used in email and conferencing systems, airline and hotel reservation systems as well as libraries and navigation systems. In the working world, the primary applications of this technology include automation processes as well as planning, production, and design systems. Social networks, mobile systems, online banking, and online gaming (e.g. multiplayer systems) also use efficient distributed systems.

Additional areas of application for distributed computing include e-learning platforms, artificial intelligence, and e-commerce. Purchases and orders made in online shops are usually carried out by distributed systems. In meteorology, sensor and monitoring systems rely on the computing power of distributed systems to forecast natural disasters. Many digital applications today are based on distributed databases.

Particularly computationally intensive research projects that used to require the use of expensive supercomputers (e.g. the Cray computer) can now be conducted with more cost-effective distributed systems. The volunteer computing project SETI@home has been setting standards in the field of distributed computing since 1999 and still are today in 2020. Countless networked home computers belonging to private individuals have been used to evaluate data from the Arecibo Observatory radio telescope in Puerto Rico and support the University of California, Berkeley in its search for extraterrestrial life. A unique feature of this project was its resource-saving approach. The analysis software only worked during periods when the user's computer had nothing to do. After the signal was analyzed, the results were sent back to the headquarters in Berkeley.

Communication in Distributed Computing

First let us look at a more problem-oriented view of what are the entities that need to contact each other in a distributed environment.

- Objects: In object-oriented approaches, objects are the base entities that can interact with each other. The mechanism of interaction is typically the interface exposed by objects. Interface definition language or IDL is defined to access the methods of an object.

- Components: Usage of objects has exposed certain problems and usage of components has been proposed to resolve these. Components are object-like entities that provide abstract functions. In addition these also specify any and all dependencies they may have. This provides a more complete contract for system construction.

- Web Services: Web services are very important for distributed system, especially cloud-based systems. These are closely related to objects and components in the sense that the functionalities are encapsulated and are exposed only through specific interfaces. Web services are in the core of service oriented architecture and World Wide Web. One important characteristic of web services is their capabilities to be discovered that make them particularly useful.

Distributed Communication Paradigms

Now we take a look at the different paradigms that are typically used in a distributed system for the communication of the entities in a distributed environment. There are three main types of communication paradigms:

- Interprocess communication.

- Remote Invocation.

- Indirect communication.

The first of the three is interprocess communication refers to three mechanisms, viz., the message-passing, socket programming and multicast communication. Socket programming is the basic method of network communication. Message-passing is a low-level communication method, using which processes can communicate with each other. Message-passing primitives require certain protocols and support.

Message Passing

Message passing involves the passing of messages between processes using simple primitives to send and receive messages. It requires the programmer to know the message and the names of the source and destination processes. First let us look at a simple form of message passing syntax is using send() and receive() primitives. The simple message passing using send() and receive() can be explained using high level language primitives. The syntax of send() is send(receiver, message) where 'receiver' is the process id of the receiving process along with the IP-address of the node where this process is located and 'message' is the data that is to be communicated. Syntax of receive() is receive(sender, message), where 'sender' is the process id of the sending process along with the IP-address of the node from which the message is to be received and 'message' indicates the buffer to store the received message. The other parameter 'message' is the data that need to be sent by the sender.

Usage of this form requires that the application programmer should be aware of the process id as well as the IP address of the destination process along with the exact message that need to be sent. In the receiving process, the application programmer must be aware of the possible sender processes, the process id and the IP address of these processes and possible size of the message to be sent. The sender process will build the message send() and communicate it to the OS of the node where the process is running, called the local OS. The local OS communicates the message over the network to the OS of the node where the receiving process is running, called the remote OS. The remote OS will deliver the message to the 'receiving' process that should have already executed the receive() message.

Message

Let us first understand the term message thoroughly. A distributed system is "one in which components located at networked computers communicate and coordinate their actions only by passing messages." We take the meaning of the term message as is used here. Message is information that the sending process wishes to pass to the receiving process. It does not specify the form of data representation and does not impose any restriction on its usage. Therefore, the only restriction is imposed on its size by the underlying network using which the two OSs interact.

Networking

A collection of computing devices that are connected in various ways in order to communicate and share resources is termed as computer networking. Typically, in a networked environment, communicating components, i.e., the computers are connected using different transmission media such as wired and wireless channels, cable and fibre channels etc., with the help of routers, hubs, bridges, switches along with suitable network interfaces. There are various software components that have to be built in the system for the networking to work. These include protocol stacks, communication handlers and drivers. All these constitute what is known as the communication subsystem that aid passing the necessary messages from sender to the receiver. We call the computing nodes connected to this communication subsystem as hosts or nodes.

- Client Server Protocol: The most popular and useful architecture in a networked environment is the client server architecture. This model consists of two entities: one of these is called the client and the other the server. Communication between these two entities constitute the interaction based on which the distribute system can be implemented. In a typical scenario, client would initiate the interaction by sending a request and the server is to fulfill the request and send a reply back to the client. A server has the capability of accepting multiple requests from different clients and process these and send back appropriate responses to appropriate clients, thereby needing a many to one communication environment. Networking protocols are used for this purpose.

Internet

"The Internet is the global system of interconnected computer networks that use the Internet protocol suite (TCP/IP) to link billions of devices worldwide. It is a network of networks." The Internet is called the network of networks. It is constructed from various networks to represent a single communication subsystem that allows devices or nodes connected to different networks to communicate with each other. A network is built to connect the nodes attached to that network. This is also called a subnet. The Internet is built by connecting many such subnets to facilitate the communication between the nodes attached to different subnets. The infrastructure required to build the Internet consists of suitable architecture along with the required software and hardware components.

In this respect, a valid question that can be raised is who owns the Internet or rather to whom does it belong? No single person or company owns the Internet or even controls it entirely. As a network of networks, this wide-area network consists of multiple smaller networks, which belongs to specific organization or even to specific persons. The job at the Internet level is to specify how these smaller networks are to be connected together, and hence it does not belong to anyone.

TCP/IP Protocol

Communication using the networking should follow specific protocols. These are called the network protocols, which are nothing but a set of rules that are observed by all parties ensuring that communication occurs efficiently for all. Perhaps of all the protocols available, the most popular one is the Transmission Control Protocol/Internet Protocol or TCP/IP. This is for communication over the Internet. We should take a look at the most well-known of the network protocols developed by the International Organization for Standardization (ISO) called the Open Systems Interconnection reference model (OSI model). It consists of seven layers.

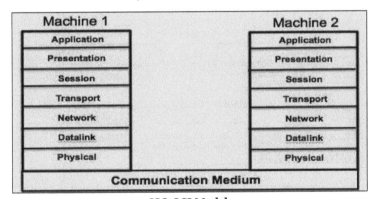

ISO OSI Model.

TCP/IP follows OSI protocols but contains fewer layers. This makes TCP/IP more efficient, although it also lends greater complexity to the implementation of this protocol. Figure below shows the layers in TCP/IP.

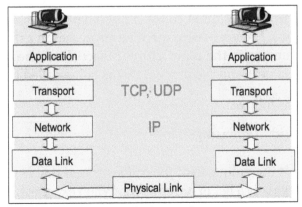

TCP/IP Protocol.

Two layers in the above figure are particularly interesting; the Network layer and the Transport layer. Internet Protocol (IP) is the choice of protocol that is run in this layer in this suit. The job of the Network layer is to transmit data and it is possible to run IP over any protocol run in the Data Link layer making it a flexible layer. The IP has no assurance of correctness in it. Hence use of IP guarantees nothing to its users.

On the other hand, the next higher layer, the Transport layer can run one of the two protocols available, viz., Transmission Control Protocol (TCP) or User Datagram Protocol (UDP). While TCP is a connection-oriented and reliable protocol, UDP is a connectionless unreliable protocol. However, reliability of TCP comes at the cost of a higher overhead and hence there are applications like multimedia applications and video conferencing where typically UDP is used.

Remote Procedure Call

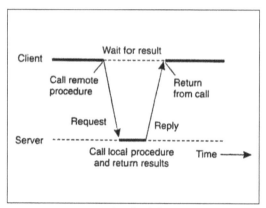

RPC Principle.

The simplicity of procedure call between two processes in a single-machine environment attracted the attention of researchers and a similar mechanism was developed for processes or entities running in different machines in a distributed environment as well. This mechanism is called remote procedure call or RPC. RPC helps in making distributed programming look similar to conventional programming, thereby bridging the gap between the two. Processes can call other processes in a different machine as if they are procedures running in the same address space. Here the process that is giving the call is the 'caller' process and the process that is being called is the 'callee' process.

The syntax of RPC is as follows:

      call < process_id > (< message >);

where < process_id > is the unique id of the callee process that is running in a different machine and < message > is a list of parameters. When executed, this call ensures that the < message > is sent to the called process identified by < process_id >. As a result of this call, the callee process executes the procedure (i.e., the parameters) and sends the result back to the caller process. In RPC semantic, the caller process that executes the "call", should remain in a waiting state and should not execute any other code till the reply from callee has arrived. This is why RPC is called a blocking protocol. Also going by our earlier description of client and server, it is easy to see that the callee process is the client and the called process is the server.

RPC Implementation

The idea behind RPC is to give the caller an illusion and make call to the remote procedure look as much as possible like a local one. RPC provides transparency to the participating processes. Therefore, in RPC, the caller process should not be aware of the existence of the remote callee process and the callee process also should not be aware of the presence of the remote caller process. To implement these transparencies, additional functions called stubs are created in both the client as well as the server side. These functions take care of the complexities of the presence of the remote machine for the client and the server processes.

Client process uses a local procedure call to the client stub when a certain function is required. The client stub contacts the RPC runtime or the local operating system to contact the remote system, which in turn, contacts the server stub.

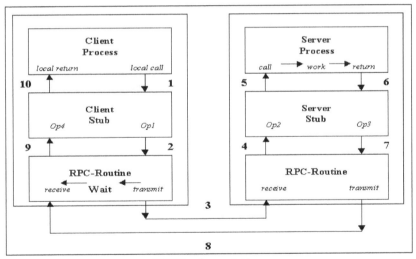

RPC Implementation.

The stubs play very important roles in RPC. These are essentially library functions that are executed using a local procedure call mechanism. There are a set of functionalities assigned to a stub. These are as follows:

- Accept a local procedure/function call from a client process running in the same machine.

- Transform such procedure/function call to a message that is understandable by the remote server process having the required function/procedure.

  ° This requires marshaling, which is changing the data format of the parameters to be passed to suit the server process.

- Interacting with the runtime system to ask this message to be sent to the stub running in the remote machine where this remote server is running.

- Block or wait for the remote machine to respond.

- Unpack the reply when one is received from the OD.

- Deliver it to the client process that is waiting.

Both the server and the client stubs execute all the steps.

RPC Steps

The steps involved in executing an RPC are given below. When client process wishes to get a function executed, it starts the following steps:

- The client procedure executes a local procedure call to the client stub.

- The client stub creates a suitable message after applying marshaling and calls the client's operating system.

- The local OS sends the message to the server's OS.

- The remote OS delivers the message to the server stub.

- The server stub unmarshals the parameters and executes a local call to the server.

- The server executes the function with the provided parameters and sends the result to the stub.

- The server stub packs it in a message and calls server's OS.

- The server's OS sends the message to the client's OS.

- The client's OS delivers the message to the client stub.

- The stub unmarshals the result and delivers the result to the client process.

This way, the client process can get a function executed in a remote server without having any knowledge of its existence using RPC.

XML-RPC

While RPC has various forms, this particular variant of RPC has seen much use. XM-LRPC is an RPC protocol, which uses XML (Extensible Markup Language) to encode its messages. Although, in general, the use of XML in an RPC is termed as XML-RPC, many of its implementations also use HTTP instead TCP or UDP in the transport layer. When a client wishes to execute a remote method using RPC, an HTTP request is sent to the server implementing the protocol. Rules of parameter passing and results are the same as the normal RPC.

RPC and Cloud

Cloud requires reliable and stable communication between various infrastructural resources in a data center and across data centers. Many cloud service providers like AWS and IaaS platforms like OpenNebula use some form of XML-RPC. However, using RPC at the SaaS level is difficult since RPC implementations are not necessarily compatible with other implementations thereby causing problem for SaaS environment.

Remote Method Invocation

Remote method invocation (RMI) strongly resembles remote procedure calls but in a world of distributed objects. With this approach, a calling object can invoke a method in a remote object. As with RPC, the underlying details are generally hidden from the user. The most popular is the Java RMI. Using Java RMI it is possible for one JVM (Java Virtual Machine) to use the methods belonging to another JVM.

Group Communication

Group communication is concerned with the delivery of messages to a set of recipients. While RPC and RMI are one-to-one communication mechanism, group communication is a multiparty communication paradigm supporting one-to-many communication. It relies on the abstraction of a group, which is represented in a distributed system by a group identifier. A process may be part of more than one group and must receive the communications of all the groups without any interruption. This is the job of the mechanism that implements group communication.

Processes in a distributed system use the underlying network to communicate. Unfortunately, network is an unreliable channel from two aspects: the first is that the networking system does not guarantee that a message sent in the form of a packet by a sender will always be delivered at the receiver's node. And even if there are mechanisms using which a guarantee can be obtained, it does not come with any promise of a time-bound within which such delivery will be completed.

In a network-based communication, a packet, which forms the basic unit of transport, may either be delayed or never be delivered. One may ask that if a packet is not delivered, then where do such packets go? There are many reasons for a network entity not to deliver a packet and that such undelivered packets are permanently lost. Use of certain mechanism such as reliable transport protocol TCP takes care of this by implementing a number of additional tasks like retransmitting a packet more than once, and hence guarantees that a packet sent by a sender will be received by a receiver.

However, TCP not only does not make any promise on the time of delivery, it actually implements slower methods to make good of its promise of guaranteed delivery. Therefore use of TCP injects latency in communication. UDP, on the other hand, is the other transport protocol that can be used, which delivers packets on the best effort basis. While the latency may be less in the use of UDP in communication, there is no guarantee about the delivery of packets. A distributed system such as Cloud must make a promise of reliability to its users and unfortunately, use of either TCP or UDP does not guarantee this. To understand the need of reliability and the kind of systems we deal with, first let us look at the various types of systems that are there.

Simple Primitive of Distributed Communication

We adopt a simple send and receive primitive in a request-reply protocol (RR protocol) for representing communication in a distributed environment, which means that when a sender process sends a message (request), it expects a reply from the receiver process. For example, say a client is asking a time server the current time. Here the client is the sender and sends the request and the time serve, after receiving the request and checking the current time, replies to the client. This whole process constitutes a RR protocol. Figure below shows the basic communication primitive of an RR protocol. In this model, the sender 'sends' a request to the receiver that travels though the communication channel, the Internet in our case, and gets delivered to the receiver, which 'receives' the message. Messages, at both the ends may be stored in the buffers provided, if required.

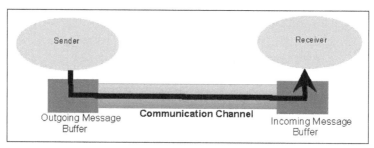

Send-Receive Primitives.

Two kinds of send and receive can be considered, viz., synchronous and asynchronous. A synchronous or blocking send requires that the sender process Sender Receiver Outgoing Message Buffer Incoming Message Buffer Communication Channel stops all other work and remains blocked till the receiver process's reply has been received by the sender. A synchronous or blocking receive requires a receiving process to remain waiting and not do any other work till it receives a message. A nonblocking send, on the other hand, allows a sender process to execute some other codes after sending a message and before receiving a reply. In cloud, both synchronous and asynchronous sends are used. Similarly, a nonblocking receive allows a receiver process to execute some other codes while expecting a request from a sender. While both synchronous and asynchronous receives are possible, blocking receives are generally used in distributed environment like cloud.

Let us ponder over the two types of send. When and why one would choose a blocking or non-blocking send? A blocking send is less costly to the communicating subsystem and is easier to render it reliable. A non-blocking sender, on the other hand, makes this mechanism more complex, adding overhead to the execution of reliability. For example, if a sender process is blocked until it has received a reply from the receiver, the size of the outgoing buffer fixed since at any time it will hold only one message. This is not the case if the sender is non-blocking since it may send many messages before even any reply has arrived.

Reliable Communication in Distributed Systems

In a distributed system, communication is dependent on the network and for reliability the ideal choice of transport protocol is TCP. However, TCP injects unnecessary delay into the system and a distributed system has to complete the actions as soon as possible to ensure transparency.

This requirement is even higher in a cloud environment. When a user submits a job through a virtual machine in cloud, she/he has no idea where the computing node is located and how the computation is being done. However, the user expects to obtain the required results within a specific time and the provider has to ensure this. Unnecessary delays in communication would pose a hindrance to this process. Therefore, using TCP poses a certain difficulty to the cloud provider. Having said that, reliability is a very important need for the CSPs since promise of reliability to the users must be upheld. Therefore sacrificing reliability for latency is not the solution. Here, we will look into why network is unreliable and the corresponding problems these cause to a reliable communication and then we will investigate mechanisms that will allow a distributed system like cloud to be reliable while avoiding the unnecessary delays as far as possible.

Reliable Communication in the Presence of Failures

The major challenges of reliability in communication are:

- Failures of the nodes.

- Failures of the network components.

- Delays (largely injected by the networking).

While there are various mechanisms that can be implemented in a distributed environment to ensure reliability in communication in the face of possible failures, delays in the networks cannot be distinguished from a failure by the either the sender or the receiver. Hence, in most cases, a delay is treated like a failure and the measures for failures are implemented in either case. This, in turn, causes additional problems in the communication mechanism.

Two important mechanisms to handle failures are timeout and retransmission. After a message is sent, the corresponding reply will arrive only after a finite amount of time. Thus to receive the reply in an ideal world having no failures, the sender has to wait for a designated amount of time. Before a message is sent out to the receiver through the Internet, the sender calculates the possible amount of time it would have to wait, called a timeout time. Timeout time consists of three components: time taken by the network to transport a request from the sender and transport back the reply from the receiver (called the round-trip time or RTT), the time it approximately takes the receiver to create the reply and an additional time for any expected delay during transmission.

The sender then sends the message and is set to wait for the receipt of the reply before the elapse of the timeout time it has calculated for the specific receiver. If the reply doesn't arrive at the sender's end even by the end of this duration, the sender has to assume that there is a possible failure and the sender has to take an appropriate action. A possible, and most frequently used, appropriate action here is retransmission. The sender simply sends the same message once more to the receiver hoping that the second time the failure (or whatever has caused the problem the first time) will not occur again and the receiver's reply will be received. Thus timeout and retransmission are two mechanisms used to fight failures in communication.

Example of Reliable Communication

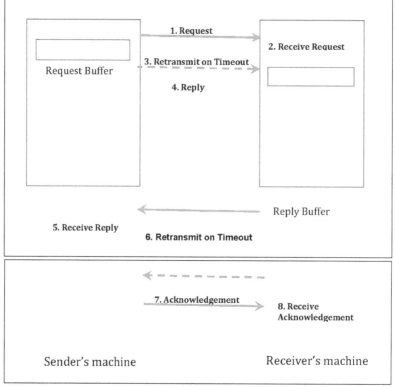

RRA Protocol.

Let us take an example to show how service providers in large distributed systems can implement mechanisms that ensure that the communication is rendered reliable. We describe a simple mechanism called the request-reply-acknowledgment (RRA) protocol using which a distributed communication between processes that exchange requests and replies is made reliable. RRA in this example uses both blocking send and blocking receive. When a process sends a request, reliability demands that the request is acknowledged. In an RRA protocol, receipt of the request. Hence there is no need to use a separate acknowledgment of the request. The sender, on receiving the reply, must send an explicit acknowledgment since here there is no other way of acknowledging the receipt of the reply. Figure above shows the protocol.

Algorithm: A Blocking RRA Protocol

- Sending a request: When a process, during its normal computation, needs to send a request to another process, it creates the request. The request is copied in a buffer called the request buffer available in the sender's machine and then the request is sent to the destination process in the form of one or more packets over the networks. The timeout time is calculated, a timer is set accordingly and the sender process blocks and waits. The wait of the sender process can be terminated by either the arrival of the reply or the end of the time set in the timer.

- Receiving a request: Typically, a destination process would be one of the servers in the system. On receiving the request message, the destination process unblocks, analyzes the request and prepares a reply. The reply is copied in a buffer called the reply buffer available in the destination machine and then sent to the sender process. The timeout time is calculated, a timer is set accordingly and the destination process blocks and waits for an acknowledgement. The wait of the destination process can be terminated by either the arrival of an acknowledgement or the end of the time set in the timer.

- Timeout at sender: When a time set in a timer ends in the sender process, an interrupt is generated and the sender process is unblocked. The sender process retransmits the same request available in the request buffer.

- Sending a reply: When the receiver process receives a request, it unblocks, prepares a reply in answer to the request, stores the reply in the reply buffer and sends the reply to the sender process. It then blocks on acknowledgement.

- Receiving a reply: When the sender process receives a reply, it unblocks, prepares an acknowledgment and releases the request buffer.

- Timeout at receiver: When a timeout occurs in the destination process it indicates to the receiver that no acknowledgement has been received, it retransmits the reply that is stored in the reply buffer and blocks.

- Sending an acknowledgement: The sender process sends the acknowledgement and continues with other execution.

- Receiving an acknowledgement: When the destination process receives an acknowledgment it releases the reply buffer and blocks for other requests that may arrive.

Problem in Reliable Communication

Timeout and retransmission solves the problems of failures and long delays in distributed communication. However, these mechanisms also inject an additional problem. We will understand this problem here. Let us assume that a process P_1 has sent a message M_1 and didn't receive the reply R_1 within the timeout time T_1 and retransmits. Some of the possible reasons for this retransmission are: (1) The request message is lost (2) the reply message is lost (3) there is a partition in the networking before the request has been delivered to the receiver (4) there is a partition in the networking after the request has been delivered to the receiver but before the reply has been delivered to the sender (5) the receiver has failed (6) there is a congestion and hence long delay in delivering the request or reply or both the messages. If the cause is 1, 3 or 5 above, the retransmission doesn't cause any problem.

However, if the reason is 2, 4 or 6, the retransmission creates a duplicate message in the system. For example, let us consider the reply message is delayed due to congestion. This means that the reply R_1 is on the way and will be delivered after T_1. However, the sender P_1 has retransmitted the request message once more already. Hence the receiver would receive the same message twice thereby generating a duplicate message. If adequate measure is not taken, a duplicate may be treated as a new message, causing serious problems in certain applications. Hence the system must take additional precautions. Hence a distributed system communication must protect the participating systems from both failures as well as duplications that arise.

Reliability in One-to-One Communication

Here we formally describe reliability in one-to-one communication in a distributed system. The term reliable communication is defined in terms of validity and integrity as follows:

- Validity: Any message in the outgoing message buffer is eventually delivered to the incoming message buffer.

- Integrity: The message received is identical to one sent, and no messages are delivered twice.

The above two promises constitute a reliable communication in a distributed environment. However, the complexity in distributed communication is only partly due to the fact that the processes are distributed. The other cause and perhaps a larger share goes to the fact that a large part of these communication involves more than two processes. This is called a group communication. Let us understand the distinctions in groups that exist in a distributed environment.

Reliability in Group Communication

In group communication a message sent by a sender is to be received by a group of receiving processes. Here the sender may not be aware of the identities of all the receivers. Group communication is harder in terms of identifying a problem in the communication protocol in the presence of failures and hence providing reliability is of high concern. Let us look at the types of groups available. There are various considerations that need to be made in case of group communication. We consider three distinctions, viz. closed versus open groups, overlapping versus nonoverlapping groups and synchronous versus asynchronous groups.

Closed and Open Groups

Typically groups are formed with processes having some common concerns. Here the issue is that once such a group is formed, whether all communication would occur amongst members of the group or communication is allowed to occur with other processes that are not members of the group. When, in a group, a process, which is not part of the group, is not able to communicate with the members of the group, it is called a closed group. On the other hand, if, in a group, a process external to the group is allowed to communicate with the members of a group, it is called an open group. An example of distinction can be found in mailing lists.

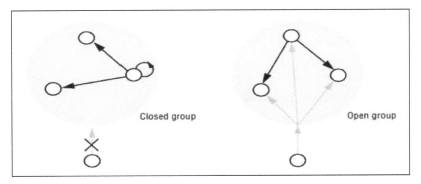

Closed group   Open group

Typically, a mailing list is formed with some members assigned to the list. It is possible to have such a mailing list where outsiders are not able to send a mail to the members of the group. On the other hand, there are such mailing lists where the members may receive mails sent to the group by outsiders. In either case, mails sent to the group will never be received by an outsider not part of the group. Figure above shows the two types. For applications where there is no involvement with the outside world, closed groups may be used. Closed groups of processes are useful, for example, for cooperating servers to send messages to one another that only they should receive.

Overlapping and Non-Overlapping Groups

There are many applications, which need their participating processes to be actively involved in multiple groups. For example, if there is a process that calculates the average of integers, many applications would wish to include this functionality and hence this particular process may be included in multiple groups. This is an example of overlapping groups. On the other hand, there are many applications, which need their participating processes to remain as part of only that group. This will constitute a nonoverlapping group. However, in real-life systems, largely groups are overlapping.

Synchronous and Asynchronous Systems

This distinction is not on the type of group but on the type of systems in a group and arises from the time factor. Time is a problem in a distributed environment in the sense that it is difficult to decide the time taken for process execution, message delivery or clock drift. Hence a system can be categorized based on the two opposing considerations with one that makes a commitment on the time and the other that does not make any commitment on the time. These two are called synchronous and asynchronous systems. A synchronous system can be defined to be have the lower and upper bounds of the execution time of each step, time bounds on the delivery of all the messages sent and received and a bound on the amount of drift of the system's local clock.

While a commitment is being made on the time, only upper and lower bounds of such commitment is required. Hence it is possible to obey such constraints and hence in environments like cloud synchronous systems are available. Asynchronous distributed systems, on the other hand, are those that do not set any time bounds on process execution, message transmission and drift of the local clock. For distributed systems, such as the Internet, it is easier not to assume any time boundaries and execute on a best effort basis.

Group Communication Mechanisms

There are three methods that can be used to send and receive messages over the networks. These are:

- Unicast: This is a typical mode used in one-to-one communication where a message is sent from one sender process to one receiver process.

- Multicast: This is used in one-to-many communication where a message is sent from one sender to a group of receiving processes.

- Broadcast: This is used in one-to-many communication where a message from one sender is sent to all processes available in the whole network.

If we make a comparative study of the above for a suitable candidate to be used in group communication, it becomes obvious that multicast communication is the most viable option. However, multicasting is a mechanism that may not be available in the underlying network and it is possible to simulate multicasting using either unicasting or broadcasting.

Multicast Communication

Multicast communication is the first choice in a distributed environment when it comes to send a message to a group. A multicast communication is very useful to the distributed environment. The most important of these would perhaps be the fault tolerance through replication of servers. It is possible to ensure fault tolerance in a distributed environment with replicated services consisting of a group of servers and using multicasting it is possible to send all communications to all the members of the group. This would improve the performance of the environment through replicated data and computation. Since multicast is being used, each time some computation takes place somewhere among these servers changing some data, the new value is multicast to the processes having the replicas for update.

Most distributed and cloud systems as well as many cloud-based applications use multicast communication. For example, applications such as online conferencing use multicasting to exchange audio, video, and/or text data among processes. Almost all the data in a cloud environment is replicated and hence all storage systems or databases use multicasting to maintain consistency of data. Online scoreboards such as ESPN, French Open, FIFA World Cup use multicast communication. Real-time systems such as air traffic control system also use multicast communication to ensure that all controllers receive the same updates in the same order.

When we use multicast communication, the group is called a multicast group in which each participating process would receive all the messages send to this group. Multicast groups are dynamic in the sense that a new process may join the group or an existing process may leave the group any point.

However, there are certain responsibilities of the mechanism. When a multicast message is sent by a process, the multicast mechanism is responsible for delivering the message correctly. Now, let us look at the meaning of correctness here. There are three factors in deciding correctness criteria in multicast communication:

- If a message, sent by a sender, is receive by some of the recipients but not all.

- A message sent is received by all the members, but the message is not correct.

- If a sender has sent a number of messages, these messages are all delivered correctly to all the members, but the order delivery of messages is not the same as the sender's order, i.e., wrong ordering of the messages delivered.

The factors in a multicast communication render the multicasting service incorrect. Essentially, the reasons are quite similar to those we identified for one-to-one communication, viz., some network hosts or link failure, communication delays and node failures.

The question here is while it is possible to identify and take corrective measure to ensure correctness in multicast used for group communication, is the cost involved in doing so justified? In fact, there are applications that can tolerate an occasional miss of a packet or even misordering of packets without causing a very serious problem. Video conferencing is an example. For a certain video is being delivered to multiple participants at the same time, if a few packets are not delivered or delivered in different orders in different locations, it really doesn't matter to the participants. However, there are certain other applications that cannot tolerate even one packet undelivered or delivered in the wrong order. For example a bank database being maintained in replicated environment and being constantly updated.

Multicast Communication in a Distributed Environment

There are three modes using which a group communication can be implemented, viz., unicast, multicast and broadcast. While unicasting is a one-to-one communication mechanism, it can also be used for a group communication. However, it becomes very costly and time consuming. On the other hand, broadcasting can be used for group communication where all the nodes in the network will receive a message sent by a sender to the members of a group. This is also not suitable since sending a message to all the nodes unnecessarily increases the traffic and hence congestion in the network. Therefore, multicasting is the best possible mode that can be used in group communication.

Reliable Multicast Communication

In computer networks parlance, multicast communication is a mechanism to implement one-to-many or many-to-many communication. Typically, a group communication is a mode of communication where data is required to be sent to a predefined group of processes. Multicasting is one, and perhaps the most suitable, mode of implementation of group communication. A reliable multicast is a multicast system, which guarantees that each message is eventually delivered to each process in the multicast group in uncorrupted form.

In this definition, we notice three important terms. The first is "eventually delivers". This expresses two aspects. While the mechanism (1) does not guarantee with respect to time as to when the message will be delivered after it has been dispatched, (2) there is guarantee that it will be delivered to the recipient. So reliability is there in the form of assured delivery but no assurance in terms of the length of time the recipient would have to wait. The second term to notice is "each process in the multicast group". This guarantees that if a message sent to the group is delivered to one of the recipient of the group; all the other members are definitely going to receive the same message. The third point to notice is that "in uncorrupted form." This point says that the message delivered will not be corrupt. Thus a sender is assured of the correct delivery of all its messages to all the recipients without any guarantee of the time when these messages will be delivered. Reliable multicast may be defined in terms of integrity, validity and agreement, the first two being the same as we have defined reliability in one-to-one communication. A multicast is reliable if it satisfies the following properties:

- Integrity: A correct process P delivers a message m at most once.

- Validity: If a correct process multicasts message m, then the multicast system will eventually deliver m.

- Agreement: If a correct process delivers message m, then all other correct processes in group will eventually deliver m.

The integrity property is similar to that for reliable one-to-one communication. The validity property ensures the basic delivery while the agreement condition is related the property of 'all or nothing'. These two properties together ensure that if a sent message is delivered to one member of the group, the system will deliver that message to all other members of the group no matter what.

Who Provides Reliability in Multicast Communication?

Reliable multicast can be provided by the service provider. This means that the service provider may use an underlying mechanism to implement reliable multicast. In cloud, this will be the cloud service provider or the CSP. The applications or the users may use this reliable multicast communication to get the benefit for any group activities. On the other hand, the service provider may offer an unreliable multicast to the applications and the interested application program writers add the necessary code in the application to make the multicast they use reliable.

Correctness in Multicast Communication

There are three criteria for correctness:

- All nodes of the group should receive the message.

- The complete message should be received by all.

- Messages should be delivered in order.

From the reliable multicasting we decipher that the first two requirements of correctness is fulfilled by reliable communication, viz., all nodes in the group should receive the message and the complete (uncorrupted) message should be received by all the members of the group. However, the third requirement of correctness says that the messages should be delivered in order.

Ordered Multicast Communication

A reliable multicast takes care of all possible failure in the environment and guarantees that a message sent is a message delivered to all alive and correct nodes. However, the order of various messages delivered to different processes belonging to the group is not taken care by the reliable multicast. The problem in ordering arises due to the fact that the network does not behave in a First In First Out (FIFO) manner. This means that there is no guarantee that a group of IP packets sent over the internetwork would necessarily be delivered to a recipient in the order in which they were sent. This problem gets multiplied when there are more than one recipients. It is perfectly possible that even when there is a single sender sending some IP packets to a group, some members of the group would receive these packets in an order different both from that of the sender and other receivers. This problem gets more complicated when we consider the possibility of the presence of more than one sender.

Unordered Multicast

An unordered multicast offers no guarantees in terms of the order of the delivered messages. If a process sends two messages, first m_1 followed by m_2, concurrently to a group of processes using an unordered multicast, the sender has no assurances about the relative order in which these two messages would be delivered.

Let us look at the example as shown in figure below. Process P_1 sends five messages, m_1 to m_5, in sequence to four other processes P_2 to P_5 in the group. The messages are delivered in different orders to each of the processes.

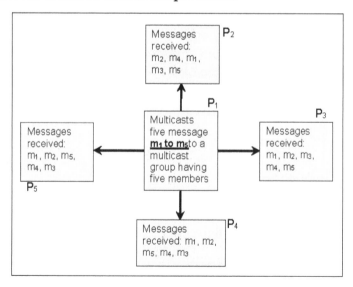

FIFO Ordering

Multicasts from a sender are received by all receivers in the order they are sent. In other words, if process P sends messages m_i and m_j, in that order, then each process in the multicast group will be delivered the messages m_i and m_j in that order.

FIFO is also called the 'sender order' and is the weakest of all the ordering available. This ordering requires that if two messages, m_1 and m_2, are sent by one sender, then these messages will be delivered to all the recipients in that order, i.e., m_1 followed by m_2. However, if the messages are sent by different senders, they may be delivered in any order, i.e., m_1 followed by m_2 for some recipients while m_2 followed by m_1 for others. Process P_1 sends five messages, m_1 to m_5, in sequence to four other processes P_2 to P_5 in the group. The messages are delivered in the same order to all the recipients since that is the order of the sender process.

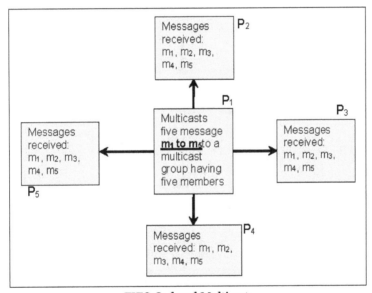

FIFO Ordered Multicast.

However, FIFO multicast does not place any restriction on the delivery order for messages sent by different processes. The following example shows this. Two processes P_1 and P_2 are sending two messages each to the group. The messages by P_1 are m_{11} and m_{12} and the messages by P_2 are m_{21} and m_{22} respectively. These messages may be delivered in various correct orders. Figure below shows the correct orders.

Causal Ordering

Let us now look at the next ordering, called the causal ordering that is stronger than the FIFO ordering. This ordering places additional restrictions on the delivery system. Multicasts whose send events are causally related, must be received in the same causality-obeying order at all receivers, i.e., if message m_i causes (results in) the occurrence of message m_j, then mi will be delivered to each recipient process prior to m_j. This ordering ensures that if the send(m_0) → send(m_1), then m_0 will be delivered before m_1 at all destinations they have in common.

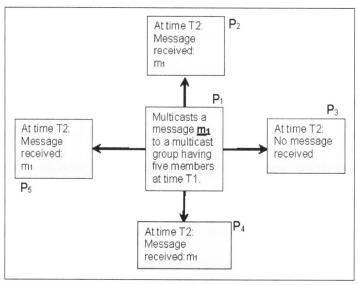

At time T2: | P_2
Message received: m_1

P_1
Multicasts a message m_1 to a multicast group having five members at time T1.

P_3
At time T2: No message received

At time T2: Message received: m_1
P_5

At time T2: | P_4
Message received: m_1

Causally Ordered Multicast.

Process P_1 sends a message, m_1 to four other processes P_2 to P_5 in the group at time T_1. At time T_2, the message is delivered to all the recipients except P_3 (it will receive m_1 later due to delay). At time T_3, P_2 sends a message m_2. At any time T_4 (> T_3), the message m_2 may be received by all the processes including P_3. The earlier message m_1 may be delivered to P_3 later on. This is acceptable to both unordered as well as FIFO ordered multicast messaging. However, if m_1 and m_2 are causally related, it will cause a problem. Let us understand this. Continuing with our earlier example, let the message m_1 from P_1 be this:

   m_1: "I think our office should be closed on Saturdays also".

If P_2 sends another independent message m_2 as follows:

   m_2: "What is the status of the project?"

P_3 who receives m_2 prepares for the project and later when it receives m_1, it may think of his opinion. However, if P_2 would send the following message m_2 in reply to P_1's message:

   m_2: "But that is not a fair demand".

P_3, on receiving m_2 before m_1 will be thoroughly surprised. A causally ordered multicast will not let this happen. Since m_2, in the second case, has been generated in reply to m_1, m_1 and m_2 are causally related. Hence, if m_2 has to be delivered to P_3 (because it is part of the multicast group), m_1 has to be delivered before m_2. However, in the first half of the example, this restriction is not there and hence m_1 and m_2 may be delivered in different orders to different recipients.

To extend our example, if process P_3 wishes to support P_2 and sends message m_3 "I support P_2 completely", all receivers must first receive m_1 followed by m_2, to comprehend the exchange of opinion. However, if P_3's message only refers P_1's message and is independent of P_2's message, that after m_1 and m_2, process P_3 wishes to support P_1 and sends message m_3 "I support P_1", then the causal relations are:

m_1 - m_2 and m_1 - m_3.

without having any relationship between m_2 and m_3. So the delivery of these message may have any of the following orders as per causal ordering:

m_1- m_2- m_3

m_1- m_3- m_2.

However, the followings are incorrect order:

m_2- m_1- m_3.

m_3- m_1- m_2.

Total Ordering

Also known as "Atomic Order", this does not pay attention to order of multicast sending. First let us define the ordering formally: In an atomic-order multicast system, all messages are guaranteed to be delivered to each participant in the exact same order. The point to note here is that the delivery order does not have to be FIFO or causal, but must be identical for each process. For example, if three messages are sent by three processes as follows:

- P_1 sends m_1.

- P_2 sends m_2.

- P_3 sends m_3.

An atomic system will guarantee that the messages will be delivered to all processes in only one of the six orders irrespective of any internal ordering these may have like FIFO or Causal.

- m_1-m_2- m_3.

- $m_1 - m_3 - m_2$.

- $m_2 - m_1 - m_3$.

- $m_2 - m_3 - m_1$.

- $m_3 - m_1 - m_2$.

- $m_3 - m_2 - m_1$.

An atomic system guarantees that messages sent by the same process are delivered in the original or the sender's order.

Interprocess Communication in Distributed Systems

Interprocess Communication is a process of exchanging the data between two or more independent process in a distributed environment is called as Interprocess communication. Interprocess communication on the internet provides both Datagram and stream communication. Examples of Interprocess Communication:

- N number of applications can communicate with the X server through network protocols.

- Servers like Apache spawn child processes to handle requests.

- Pipes are a form of IPC: Grep foo file | sort.

Functions of Interprocess Communication

- Synchronization: Exchange of data is done synchronously which means it has a single clock pulse.

- Message Passing: When processes wish to exchange information. Message passing takes several forms such as: pipes, FIFO, Shared Memory, and Message Queues.

Characteristics of Interprocess Communication

There are mainly five characteristics of inter-process communication in a distributed environment/system:

- Synchronous System Calls: In the synchronous system calls both sender and receiver use blocking system calls to transmit the data which means the sender will wait until the acknowledgment is received from the receiver and receiver waits until the message arrives.

- Asynchronous System Calls: In the asynchronous system calls, both sender and receiver use non-blocking system calls to transmit the data which means the sender doesn't wait from the receiver acknowledgment.

- Message Destination: A local port is a message destination within a computer, specified as an integer. A port has exactly one receiver but many senders. Processes may use multiple ports from which to receive messages. Any process that knows the number of a port can send the message to it.

- Reliability: It is defined as validity and integrity.

- Integrity: Messages must arrive without corruption and duplication to the destination.

- Validity: Point to point message services are defined as reliable, if the messages are guaranteed to be delivered without being lost is called validity.

- Ordering: It is the process of delivering messages to the receiver in a particular order. Some applications require messages to be delivered in the sender order i.e. the order in which they were transmitted by the sender.

References

- Distributed-systems: confluent.io, Retrieved 09, July 2020
- What-is-distributed-computing, digitalguide: ionos.com, Retrieved 27, February 2020

Parallel Computing

The process of breaking down larger problems into smaller operations which can be worked upon simultaneously by multiple processors is known as parallel computing. Some of the major types of parallelism are bit-level parallelism, instruction-level parallelism and task parallelism. This chapter has been carefully written to provide an easy understanding of these facets of parallel computing.

Parallel computing is a type of computation in which many calculations or the execution of processes are carried out simultaneously. Large problems can often be divided into smaller ones, which can then be solved at the same time. There are several different forms of parallel computing: bit-level, instruction-level, data, and task parallelism. Parallelism has been employed for many years, mainly in high-performance computing, but interest in it has grown lately due to the physical constraints preventing frequency scaling. As power consumption (and consequently heat generation) by computers has become a concern in recent years, parallel computing has become the dominant paradigm in computer architecture, mainly in the form of multi-core processors.

IBM's Blue Gene/P massively parallel supercomputer.

Parallel computing is closely related to concurrent computing—they are frequently used together, and often conflated, though the two are distinct: it is possible to have parallelism without concurrency (such as bit-level parallelism), and concurrency without parallelism (such as multitasking by time-sharing on a single-core CPU). In parallel computing, a computational task is typically broken down in several, often many, very similar subtasks that can be processed independently and whose results are combined afterwards, upon completion. In contrast, in concurrent computing, the various processes often do not address related tasks; when they do, as is typical in distributed computing, the separate tasks may have a varied nature and often require some inter-process communication during execution.

Parallel computers can be roughly classified according to the level at which the hardware supports parallelism, with multi-core and multi-processor computers having multiple processing elements within a single machine, while clusters, MPPs, and grids use multiple computers to work on the same task. Specialized parallel computer architectures are sometimes used alongside traditional processors, for accelerating specific tasks.

In some cases parallelism is transparent to the programmer, such as in bit-level or instruction-level parallelism, but explicitly parallel algorithms, particularly those that use concurrency, are more difficult to write than sequential ones, because concurrency introduces several new classes of potential software bugs, of which race conditions are the most common. Communication and synchronization between the different subtasks are typically some of the greatest obstacles to getting good parallel program performance.

A theoretical upper bound on the speed-up of a single program as a result of parallelization is given by Amdahl's law.

Background

Traditionally, computer software has been written for serial computation. To solve a problem, an algorithm is constructed and implemented as a serial stream of instructions. These instructions are executed on a central processing unit on one computer. Only one instruction may execute at a time—after that instruction is finished, the next one is executed.

Parallel computing, on the other hand, uses multiple processing elements simultaneously to solve a problem. This is accomplished by breaking the problem into independent parts so that each processing element can execute its part of the algorithm simultaneously with the others. The processing elements can be diverse and include resources such as a single computer with multiple processors, several networked computers, specialized hardware, or any combination of the above.

Frequency scaling was the dominant reason for improvements in computer performance from the mid-1980s until 2004. The runtime of a program is equal to the number of instructions multiplied by the average time per instruction. Maintaining everything else constant, increasing the clock frequency decreases the average time it takes to execute an instruction. An increase in frequency thus decreases runtime for all compute-bound programs.

However, power consumption P by a chip is given by the equation $P = C \times V^2 \times F$, where C is the capacitance being switched per clock cycle (proportional to the number of transistors whose inputs change), V is voltage, and F is the processor frequency (cycles per second). Increases in frequency increase the amount of power used in a processor. Increasing processor power consumption led ultimately to Intel's May 8, 2004 cancellation of its Tejas and Jayhawk processors, which is generally cited as the end of frequency scaling as the dominant computer architecture paradigm.

Moore's law is the empirical observation that the number of transistors in a microprocessor doubles every 18 to 24 months. Despite power consumption issues, and repeated predictions of its end, Moore's law is still in effect. With the end of frequency scaling, these additional transistors (which are no longer used for frequency scaling) can be used to add extra hardware for parallel computing.

Amdahl's Law and Gustafson's Law

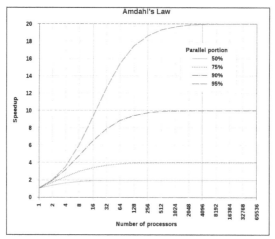

A graphical representation of Amdahl's law. The speedup of a program from parallelization is limited by how much of the program can be parallelized. For example, if 90% of the program can be parallelized, the theoretical maximum speedup using parallel computing would be 10 times no matter how many prozcessors are used.

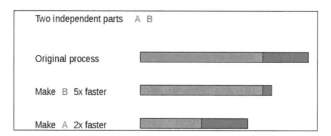

Assume that a task has two independent parts, A and B. Part B takes roughly 25% of the time of the whole computation. By working very hard, one may be able to make this part 5 times faster, but this only reduces the time for the whole computation by a little. In contrast, one may need to perform less work to make part A be twice as fast. This will make the computation much faster than by optimizing part B, even though part B's speedup is greater by ratio, (5 times versus 2 times).

Optimally, the speedup from parallelization would be linear—doubling the number of processing elements should halve the runtime, and doubling it a second time should again halve the runtime. However, very few parallel algorithms achieve optimal speedup. Most of them have a near-linear speedup for small numbers of processing elements, which flattens out into a constant value for large numbers of processing elements.

The potential speedup of an algorithm on a parallel computing platform is given by Amdahl's law

$$S_{latency}(s) = \frac{1}{1 - p + \dfrac{p}{s}},$$

where

$S_{latency}$ is the potential speedup in latency of the execution of the whole task;

s is the speedup in latency of the execution of the parallelizable part of the task;

p is the percentage of the execution time of the whole task concerning the parallelizable part of the task *before parallelization.*

Since $S_{latency} < 1/(1 - p)$, it shows that a small part of the program which cannot be parallelized will limit the overall speedup available from parallelization. A program solving a large mathematical or engineering problem will typically consist of several parallelizable parts and several non-parallelizable (serial) parts. If the non-parallelizable part of a program accounts for 10% of the runtime ($p = 0.9$), we can get no more than a 10 times speedup, regardless of how many processors are added. This puts an upper limit on the usefulness of adding more parallel execution units. "When a task cannot be partitioned because of sequential constraints, the application of more effort has no effect on the schedule. The bearing of a child takes nine months, no matter how many women are assigned."

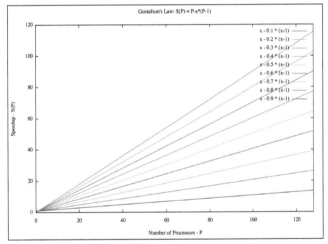

A graphical representation of Gustafson's law.

Amdahl's law only applies to cases where the problem size is fixed. In practice, as more computing resources become available, they tend to get used on larger problems (larger datasets), and the time spent in the parallelizable part often grows much faster than the inherently serial work. In this case, Gustafson's law gives a less pessimistic and more realistic assessment of parallel performance:

$$S_{latency}(s) = 1 - p + sp.$$

Both Amdahl's law and Gustafson's law assume that the running time of the serial part of the program is independent of the number of processors. Amdahl's law assumes that the entire problem is of fixed size so that the total amount of work to be done in parallel is also *independent of the number of processors*, whereas Gustafson's law assumes that the total amount of work to be done in parallel *varies linearly with the number of processors.*

Dependencies

Understanding data dependencies is fundamental in implementing parallel algorithms. No program can run more quickly than the longest chain of dependent calculations (known as the critical path), since calculations that depend upon prior calculations in the chain must be executed in order. However, most algorithms do not consist of just a long chain of dependent calculations; there are usually opportunities to execute independent calculations in parallel.

Let P_i and P_j be two program segments. Bernstein's conditions describe when the two are independent and can be executed in parallel. For P_j, let I_j be all of the input variables and O_i the output variables, and likewise for P_j. P_i and P_j are independent if they satisfy.

$$I_j \cap O_i = \emptyset,$$
$$I_i \cap O_j = \emptyset,$$
$$O_i \cap O_j = \emptyset.$$

Violation of the first condition introduces a flow dependency, corresponding to the first segment producing a result used by the second segment. The second condition represents an anti-dependency, when the second segment produces a variable needed by the first segment. The third and final condition represents an output dependency: when two segments write to the same location, the result comes from the logically last executed segment.

Consider the following functions, which demonstrate several kinds of dependencies:

    1: function Dep(a, b)

    2: c := a * b

    3: d := 3 * c

    4: end function

In this example, instruction 3 cannot be executed before (or even in parallel with) instruction 2, because instruction 3 uses a result from instruction 2. It violates condition 1, and thus introduces a flow dependency.

    1: function NoDep(a, b)

    2: c := a * b

    3: d := 3 * b

    4: e := a + b

    5: end function

In this example, there are no dependencies between the instructions, so they can all be run in parallel.

Bernstein's conditions do not allow memory to be shared between different processes. For that, some means of enforcing an ordering between accesses is necessary, such as semaphores, barriers or some other synchronization method.

Race Conditions, Mutual Exclusion, Synchronization, and Parallel Slowdown

Subtasks in a parallel program are often called threads. Some parallel computer architectures use smaller, lightweight versions of threads known as fibers, while others use bigger versions known as processes. However, "threads" is generally accepted as a generic term for subtasks. Threads will often need to update some variable that is shared between them. The instructions between the two programs may be interleaved in any order. For example, consider the following program:

Thread A	Thread B
1A: Read variable V	1B: Read variable V
2A: Add 1 to variable V	2B: Add 1 to variable V
3A: Write back to variable V	3B: Write back to variable V

If instruction 1B is executed between 1A and 3A, or if instruction 1A is executed between 1B and 3B, the program will produce incorrect data. This is known as a race condition. The programmer must use a lock to provide mutual exclusion. A lock is a programming language construct that allows one thread to take control of a variable and prevent other threads from reading or writing it, until that variable is unlocked. The thread holding the lock is free to execute its critical section (the section of a program that requires exclusive access to some variable), and to unlock the data when it is finished. Therefore, to guarantee correct program execution, the above program can be rewritten to use locks:

Thread A	Thread B
1A: Lock variable V	1B: Lock variable V
2A: Read variable V	2B: Read variable V
3A: Add 1 to variable V	3B: Add 1 to variable V
4A: Write back to variable V	4B: Write back to variable V
5A: Unlock variable V	5B: Unlock variable V

One thread will successfully lock variable V, while the other thread will be locked out—unable to proceed until V is unlocked again. This guarantees correct execution of the program. Locks, while necessary to ensure correct program execution, can greatly slow a program.

Locking multiple variables using non-atomic locks introduces the possibility of program deadlock. An atomic lock locks multiple variables all at once. If it cannot lock all of them, it does not lock any of them. If two threads each need to lock the same two variables using non-atomic locks, it is possible that one thread will lock one of them and the second thread will lock the second variable. In such a case, neither thread can complete, and deadlock results.

Many parallel programs require that their subtasks act in synchrony. This requires the use of a barrier. Barriers are typically implemented using a software lock. One class of algorithms, known as lock-free and wait-free algorithms, altogether avoids the use of locks and barriers. However, this approach is generally difficult to implement and requires correctly designed data structures.

Not all parallelization results in speed-up. Generally, as a task is split up into more and more threads, those threads spend an ever-increasing portion of their time communicating with each other. Eventually, the overhead from communication dominates the time spent solving the problem, and further parallelization (that is, splitting the workload over even more threads) increases rather than decreases the amount of time required to finish. This is known as parallel slowdown.

Fine-grained, Coarse-grained, and Embarrassing Parallelism

Applications are often classified according to how often their subtasks need to synchronize or communicate with each other. An application exhibits fine-grained parallelism if its subtasks must communicate many times per second; it exhibits coarse-grained parallelism if they do not communicate many times per second, and it exhibits embarrassing parallelism if they rarely or never have to communicate. Embarrassingly parallel applications are considered the easiest to parallelize.

Consistency Models

Parallel programming languages and parallel computers must have a consistency model (also known as a memory model). The consistency model defines rules for how operations on computer memory occur and how results are produced.

One of the first consistency models was Leslie Lamport's sequential consistency model. Sequential consistency is the property of a parallel program that its parallel execution produces the same results as a sequential program. Specifically, a program is sequentially consistent if "... the results of any execution is the same as if the operations of all the processors were executed in some sequential order, and the operations of each individual processor appear in this sequence in the order specified by its program".

Software transactional memory is a common type of consistency model. Software transactional memory borrows from database theory the concept of atomic transactions and applies them to memory accesses.

Mathematically, these models can be represented in several ways. Petri nets, which were introduced in Carl Adam Petri's 1962 doctoral thesis, were an early attempt to codify the rules of consistency models. Dataflow theory later built upon these, and Dataflow architectures were created to physically implement the ideas of dataflow theory. Beginning in the late 1970s, process calculi such as Calculus of Communicating Systems and Communicating Sequential Processes were developed to permit algebraic reasoning about systems composed of interacting components. More recent additions to the process calculus family, such as the π-calculus, have added the capability for reasoning about dynamic topologies. Logics such as Lamport's TLA+, and mathematical models such as traces and Actor event diagrams, have also been developed to describe the behavior of concurrent systems.

Flynn's Taxonomy

Michael J. Flynn created one of the earliest classification systems for parallel (and sequential) computers and programs, now known as Flynn's taxonomy. Flynn classified programs and computers by whether they were operating using a single set or multiple sets of instructions, and whether or not those instructions were using a single set or multiple sets of data.

The single-instruction-single-data (SISD) classification is equivalent to an entirely sequential program. The single-instruction-multiple-data (SIMD) classification is analogous to doing the same operation repeatedly over a large data set. This is commonly done in signal processing applications. Multiple-instruction-single-data (MISD) is a rarely used classification. While computer architectures to deal with this were devised (such as systolic arrays), few applications that fit this class materialized. Multiple-instruction-multiple-data (MIMD) programs are by far the most common type of parallel programs.

According to David A. Patterson and John L. Hennessy, "Some machines are hybrids of these categories, of course, but this classic model has survived because it is simple, easy to understand, and gives a good first approximation. It is also—perhaps because of its understandability—the most widely used scheme."

Types of Parallelism

Bit-level Parallelism

From the advent of very-large-scale integration (VLSI) computer-chip fabrication technology in the 1970s until about 1986, speed-up in computer architecture was driven by doubling computer word size—the amount of information the processor can manipulate per cycle. Increasing the word size reduces the number of instructions the processor must execute to perform an operation on variables whose sizes are greater than the length of the word. For example, where an 8-bit processor must add two 16-bit integers, the processor must first add the 8 lower-order bits from each integer using the standard addition instruction, then add the 8 higher-order bits using an add-with-carry instruction and the carry bit from the lower order addition; thus, an 8-bit processor requires two instructions to complete a single operation, where a 16-bit processor would be able to complete the operation with a single instruction.

Historically, 4-bit microprocessors were replaced with 8-bit, then 16-bit, then 32-bit microprocessors. This trend generally came to an end with the introduction of 32-bit processors, which has been a standard in general-purpose computing for two decades. Not until the early twothousands, with the advent of x86-64 architectures, did 64-bit processors become commonplace.

Instruction-level Parallelism

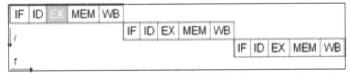

A canonical processor without pipeline. It takes five clock cycles to complete one instruction and thus the processor can issue subscalar performance (IPC = 0.2 < 1).

A canonical five-stage pipelined processor. In the best case scenario, it takes one clock cycle to complete one instruction and thus the processor can issue scalar performance (IPC = 1).

A computer program is, in essence, a stream of instructions executed by a processor. Without instruction-level parallelism, a processor can only issue less than one instruction per clock cycle (IPC < 1). These processors are known as *subscalar* processors. These instructions can be re-ordered and combined into groups which are then executed in parallel without changing the result of the program. This is known as instruction-level parallelism. Advances in instruction-level parallelism dominated computer architecture from the mid-1980s until the mid-1990s.

All modern processors have multi-stage instruction pipelines. Each stage in the pipeline corresponds to a different action the processor performs on that instruction in that stage; a processor with an N-stage pipeline can have up to N different instructions at different stages of completion and thus can issue one instruction per clock cycle (IPC = 1). These processors are known as *scalar* processors. The canonical example of a pipelined processor is a RISC processor, with five stages: instruction fetch (IF), instruction decode (ID), execute (EX), memory access (MEM), and register write back (WB). The Pentium 4 processor had a 35-stage pipeline.

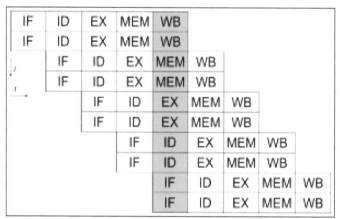

A canonical five-stage pipelined superscalar processor. In the best case scenario, it takes one clock cycle to complete two instructions and thus the processor can issue superscalar performance (IPC = 2 > 1).

Most modern processors also have multiple execution units. They usually combine this feature with pipelining and thus can issue more than one instruction per clock cycle (IPC > 1). These processors are known as *superscalar* processors. Instructions can be grouped together only if there is no data dependency between them. Scoreboarding and the Tomasulo algorithm (which is similar to scoreboarding but makes use of register renaming) are two of the most common techniques for implementing out-of-order execution and instruction-level parallelism.

Task Parallelism

Task parallelisms is the characteristic of a parallel program that "entirely different calculations can be performed on either the same or different sets of data". This contrasts with data parallelism, where the same calculation is performed on the same or different sets of data. Task parallelism involves the decomposition of a task into sub-tasks and then allocating each sub-task to a processor for execution. The processors would then execute these sub-tasks simultaneously and often cooperatively. Task parallelism does not usually scale with the size of a problem.

Hardware

Memory and Communication

Main memory in a parallel computer is either shared memory (shared between all processing elements in a single address space), or distributed memory (in which each processing element has its own local address space). Distributed memory refers to the fact that the memory is logically distributed, but often implies that it is physically distributed as well. Distributed shared memory and memory virtualization combine the two approaches, where the processing element has its own local memory and access to the memory on non-local processors. Accesses to local memory are typically faster than accesses to non-local memory.

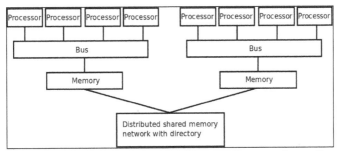

A logical view of a non-uniform memory access (NUMA) architecture. Processors in one directory can access that directory's memory with less latency than they can access memory in the other directory's memory.

Computer architectures in which each element of main memory can be accessed with equal latency and bandwidth are known as uniform memory access (UMA) systems. Typically, that can be achieved only by a shared memory system, in which the memory is not physically distributed. A system that does not have this property is known as a non-uniform memory access (NUMA) architecture. Distributed memory systems have non-uniform memory access.

Computer systems make use of caches—small and fast memories located close to the processor which store temporary copies of memory values (nearby in both the physical and logical sense). Parallel computer systems have difficulties with caches that may store the same value in more than one location, with the possibility of incorrect program execution. These computers require a cache coherency system, which keeps track of cached values and strategically purges them, thus ensuring correct program execution. Bus snooping is one of the most common methods for keeping track of which values are being accessed (and thus should be purged). Designing large, high-performance cache coherence systems is a very difficult problem in computer architecture. As a result, shared memory computer architectures do not scale as well as distributed memory systems do.

Processor–processor and processor–memory communication can be implemented in hardware in several ways, including via shared (either multiported or multiplexed) memory, a crossbar switch, a shared bus or an interconnect network of a myriad of topologies including star, ring, tree, hypercube, fat hypercube (a hypercube with more than one processor at a node), or n-dimensional mesh.

Parallel computers based on interconnected networks need to have some kind of routing to enable the passing of messages between nodes that are not directly connected. The medium used for communication between the processors is likely to be hierarchical in large multiprocessor machines.

Classes of Parallel Computers

Parallel computers can be roughly classified according to the level at which the hardware supports parallelism. This classification is broadly analogous to the distance between basic computing nodes. These are not mutually exclusive; for example, clusters of symmetric multiprocessors are relatively common.

Multi-core Computing

A multi-core processor is a processor that includes multiple processing units (called "cores") on the same chip. This processor differs from a superscalar processor, which includes multiple execution units and can issue multiple instructions per clock cycle from one instruction stream (thread); in contrast, a multi-core processor can issue multiple instructions per clock cycle from multiple instruction streams. IBM's Cell microprocessor, designed for use in the Sony PlayStation 3, is a prominent multi-core processor. Each core in a multi-core processor can potentially be superscalar as well—that is, on every clock cycle, each core can issue multiple instructions from one thread.

Simultaneous multithreading (of which Intel's Hyper-Threading is the best known) was an early form of pseudo-multi-coreism. A processor capable of simultaneous multithreading includes multiple execution units in the same processing unit—that is it has a superscalar architecture—and can issue multiple instructions per clock cycle from *multiple* threads. Temporal multithreading on the other hand includes a single execution unit in the same processing unit and can issue one instruction at a time from *multiple* threads.

Symmetric Multiprocessing

A symmetric multiprocessor (SMP) is a computer system with multiple identical processors that share memory and connect via a bus. Bus contention prevents bus architectures from scaling. As a result, SMPs generally do not comprise more than 32 processors. Because of the small size of the processors and the significant reduction in the requirements for bus bandwidth achieved by large caches, such symmetric multiprocessors are extremely cost-effective, provided that a sufficient amount of memory bandwidth exists.

Distributed Computing

A distributed computer (also known as a distributed memory multiprocessor) is a distributed memory computer system in which the processing elements are connected by a network. Distributed computers are highly scalable.

Cluster Computing

A cluster is a group of loosely coupled computers that work together closely, so that in some respects they can be regarded as a single computer. Clusters are composed of multiple standalone machines connected by a network. While machines in a cluster do not have to be symmetric, load balancing is more difficult if they are not. The most common type of cluster is the Beowulf cluster, which is a cluster implemented on multiple identical commercial off-the-shelf computers connected with a TCP/IP Ethernet local area network. Beowulf technology was originally developed by Thomas Sterling and Donald Becker. The vast majority of the TOP500 supercomputers are clusters.

A Beowulf cluster.

Because grid computing systems (described below) can easily handle embarrassingly parallel problems, modern clusters are typically designed to handle more difficult problems—problems that require nodes to share intermediate results with each other more often. This requires a high bandwidth and, more importantly, a low-latency interconnection network. Many historic and current supercomputers use customized high-performance network hardware specifically designed for cluster computing, such as the Cray Gemini network. As of 2014, most current supercomputers use some off-the-shelf standard network hardware, often Myrinet, InfiniBand, or Gigabit Ethernet.

Massively Parallel Computing

A cabinet from IBM's Blue Gene/L massively parallel supercomputer.

A massively parallel processor (MPP) is a single computer with many networked processors. MPPs have many of the same characteristics as clusters, but MPPs have specialized interconnect networks (whereas clusters use commodity hardware for networking). MPPs also tend to be larger than clusters, typically having "far more" than 100 processors. In an MPP, "each CPU contains its own memory and copy of the operating system and application. Each subsystem communicates with the others via a high-speed interconnect."

IBM's Blue Gene/L, the fifth fastest supercomputer in the world according to the June 2009 TOP500 ranking, is an MPP.

Grid Computing

Grid computing is the most distributed form of parallel computing. It makes use of computers communicating over the Internet to work on a given problem. Because of the low bandwidth and extremely high latency available on the Internet, distributed computing typically deals only with embarrassingly parallel problems. Many distributed computing applications have been created, of which SETI@home and Folding@home are the best-known examples.

Most grid computing applications use middleware (software that sits between the operating system and the application to manage network resources and standardize the software interface). The most common distributed computing middleware is the Berkeley Open Infrastructure for Network Computing (BOINC). Often, distributed computing software makes use of "spare cycles", performing computations at times when a computer is idling.

Specialized Parallel Computers

Within parallel computing, there are specialized parallel devices that remain niche areas of interest. While not domain-specific, they tend to be applicable to only a few classes of parallel problems.

Reconfigurable Computing with Field-programmable Gate Arrays

Reconfigurable computing is the use of a field-programmable gate array (FPGA) as a co-processor to a general-purpose computer. An FPGA is, in essence, a computer chip that can rewire itself for a given task.

FPGAs can be programmed with hardware description languages such as VHDL or Verilog. However, programming in these languages can be tedious. Several vendors have created C to HDL languages that attempt to emulate the syntax and semantics of the C programming language, with which most programmers are familiar. The best known C to HDL languages are Mitrion-C, Impulse C, DIME-C, and Handel-C. Specific subsets of SystemC based on C++ can also be used for this purpose.

AMD's decision to open its HyperTransport technology to third-party vendors has become the enabling technology for high-performance reconfigurable computing. According to Michael R. D'Amour, Chief Operating Officer of DRC Computer Corporation, "when we first walked into AMD, they called us 'the socket stealers.' Now they call us their partners."

General-purpose Computing on Graphics Processing Units (GPGPU)

General-purpose computing on graphics processing units (GPGPU) is a fairly recent trend in computer engineering research. GPUs are co-processors that have been heavily optimized for computer graphics processing. Computer graphics processing is a field dominated by data parallel operations—particularly linear algebra matrix operations.

Nvidia's Tesla GPGPU card.

In the early days, GPGPU programs used the normal graphics APIs for executing programs. However, several new programming languages and platforms have been built to do general purpose computation on GPUs with both Nvidia and AMD releasing programming environments with CUDA and Stream SDK respectively. Other GPU programming languages include BrookGPU, PeakStream, and RapidMind. Nvidia has also released specific products for computation in their Tesla series. The technology consortium Khronos Group has released the OpenCL specification, which is a framework for writing programs that execute across platforms consisting of CPUs and GPUs. AMD, Apple, Intel, Nvidia and others are supporting OpenCL.

Application-specific Integrated Circuits

Several application-specific integrated circuit (ASIC) approaches have been devised for dealing with parallel applications.

Because an ASIC is (by definition) specific to a given application, it can be fully optimized for that application. As a result, for a given application, an ASIC tends to outperform a general-purpose computer. However, ASICs are created by UV photolithography. This process requires a mask set, which can be extremely expensive. A mask set can cost over a million US dollars. (The smaller the transistors required for the chip, the more expensive the mask will be.) Meanwhile, performance increases in general-purpose computing over time (as described by Moore's law) tend to wipe out these gains in only one or two chip generations. High initial cost, and the tendency to be overtaken by Moore's-law-driven general-purpose computing, has rendered ASICs unfeasible for most parallel computing applications. However, some have been built. One example is the PFLOPS RIKEN MDGRAPE-3 machine which uses custom ASICs for molecular dynamics simulation.

Vector Processors

The Cray-1 is a vector processor.

A vector processor is a CPU or computer system that can execute the same instruction on large sets of data. Vector processors have high-level operations that work on linear arrays of numbers or vectors. An example vector operation is $A = B \times C$, where A, B, and C are each 64-element vectors of 64-bit floating-point numbers. They are closely related to Flynn's SIMD classification.

Cray computers became famous for their vector-processing computers in the 1970s and 1980s. However, vector processors—both as CPUs and as full computer systems—have generally disappeared. Modern processor instruction sets do include some vector processing instructions, such as with Freescale Semiconductor's AltiVec and Intel's Streaming SIMD Extensions (SSE).

Software

Parallel Programming Languages

Concurrent programming languages, libraries, APIs, and parallel programming models (such as algorithmic skeletons) have been created for programming parallel computers. These can generally be divided into classes based on the assumptions they make about the underlying memory architecture—shared memory, distributed memory, or shared distributed memory. Shared memory programming languages communicate by manipulating shared memory variables. Distributed memory uses message passing. POSIX Threads and OpenMP are two of the most widely used shared memory APIs, whereas Message Passing Interface (MPI) is the most widely used message-passing system API. One concept used in programming parallel programs is the future concept, where one part of a program promises to deliver a required datum to another part of a program at some future time.

CAPS entreprise and Pathscale are also coordinating their effort to make hybrid multi-core parallel programming (HMPP) directives an open standard called OpenHMPP. The OpenHMPP directive-based programming model offers a syntax to efficiently offload computations on hardware accelerators and to optimize data movement to/from the hardware memory. OpenHMPP directives describe remote procedure call (RPC) on an accelerator device (e.g. GPU) or more generally a set of cores. The directives annotate C or Fortran codes to describe two sets of functionalities: the offloading of procedures (denoted codelets) onto a remote device and the optimization of data transfers between the CPU main memory and the accelerator memory.

The rise of consumer GPUs has led to support for compute kernels, either in graphics APIs (referred to as compute shaders), in dedicated APIs (such as OpenCL), or in other language extensions.

Automatic Parallelization

Automatic parallelization of a sequential program by a compiler is the holy grail of parallel computing. Despite decades of work by compiler researchers, automatic parallelization has had only limited success.

Mainstream parallel programming languages remain either explicitly parallel or (at best) partially implicit, in which a programmer gives the compiler directives for parallelization. A few fully implicit parallel programming languages exist—SISAL, Parallel Haskell, SequenceL, System C (for FPGAs), Mitrion-C, VHDL, and Verilog.

Application Checkpointing

As a computer system grows in complexity, the mean time between failures usually decreases. Application checkpointing is a technique whereby the computer system takes a "snapshot" of the application—a record of all current resource allocations and variable states, akin to a core dump—; this information can be used to restore the program if the computer should fail. Application checkpointing means that the program has to restart from only its last checkpoint rather than the beginning. While checkpointing provides benefits in a variety of situations, it is especially useful in highly parallel systems with a large number of processors used in high performance computing.

Algorithmic Methods

As parallel computers become larger and faster, it becomes feasible to solve problems that previously took too long to run. Parallel computing is used in a wide range of fields, from bioinformatics (protein folding and sequence analysis) to economics (mathematical finance). Common types of problems found in parallel computing applications are:

- dense linear algebra;
- sparse linear algebra;
- spectral methods (such as Cooley–Tukey fast Fourier transform);
- N-body problems (such as Barnes–Hut simulation);
- structured grid problems (such as Lattice Boltzmann methods);
- unstructured grid problems (such as found in finite element analysis);
- Monte Carlo method;
- combinational logic (such as brute-force cryptographic techniques);
- graph traversal (such as sorting algorithms);
- dynamic programming;
- branch and bound methods;
- graphical models (such as detecting hidden Markov models and constructing Bayesian networks);
- finite-state machine simulation.

Fault-tolerance

Parallel computing can also be applied to the design of fault-tolerant computer systems, particularly via lockstep systems performing the same operation in parallel. This provides redundancy in case one component should fail, and also allows automatic error detection and error correction if the results differ. These methods can be used to help prevent single event upsets caused by transient errors. Although additional measures may be required in embedded or specialized systems, this method can provide a cost effective approach to achieve n-modular redundancy in commercial off-the-shelf systems.

History

ILLIAC IV, "the most infamous of supercomputers".

The origins of true (MIMD) parallelism go back to Luigi Federico Menabrea and his *Sketch of the Analytic Engine Invented by Charles Babbage.*

In April 1958, S. Gill (Ferranti) discussed parallel programming and the need for branching and waiting. Also in 1958, IBM researchers John Cocke and Daniel Slotnick discussed the use of parallelism in numerical calculations for the first time. Burroughs Corporation introduced the D825 in 1962, a four-processor computer that accessed up to 16 memory modules through a crossbar switch. In 1967, Amdahl and Slotnick published a debate about the feasibility of parallel processing at American Federation of Information Processing Societies Conference. It was during this debate that Amdahl's law was coined to define the limit of speed-up due to parallelism.

In 1969, company Honeywell introduced its first Multics system, a symmetric multiprocessor system capable of running up to eight processors in parallel. C.mmp, a 1970s multi-processor project at Carnegie Mellon University, was among the first multiprocessors with more than a few processors. The first bus-connected multiprocessor with snooping caches was the Synapse N+1 in 1984."

SIMD parallel computers can be traced back to the 1970s. The motivation behind early SIMD computers was to amortize the gate delay of the processor's control unit over multiple instructions. In 1964, Slotnick had proposed building a massively parallel computer for the Lawrence Livermore National Laboratory. His design was funded by the US Air Force, which was the earliest SIMD parallel-computing effort, ILLIAC IV. The key to its design was a fairly high parallelism, with up to 256 processors, which allowed the machine to work on large datasets in what would later be known as vector processing. However, ILLIAC IV was called "the most infamous of supercomputers", because the project was only one fourth completed, but took 11 years and cost almost four times the original estimate. When it was finally ready to run its first real application in 1976, it was outperformed by existing commercial supercomputers such as the Cray-1.

Consistency Model

In computer science, Consistency models are used in distributed systems like distributed shared memory systems or distributed data stores (such as a filesystems, databases, optimistic replication systems or Web caching). The system is said to support a given model if operations on memory follow specific rules. The data consistency model specifies a contract between programmer and system, wherein the system guarantees that if the programmer follows the rules, memory will be consistent and the results of memory operations will be predictable. This is different from Cache coherence, an issue that occurs in systems that are cached or cache-less is consistency of data with respect to all processors. This is not handled by Coherence as coherence deals with maintaining a global order in which writes only to a single location or a single variable are seen by all processors. Consistency deals with the ordering of operations to multiple locations with respect to all processors.

High level languages, such as C++ and Java, partially maintain the contract by translating memory operations into low-level operations in a way that preserves memory semantics. To hold to the contract, compilers may reorder some memory instructions, and library calls such as pthread_mutex_lock() encapsulate required synchronization.

Verifying sequential consistency through model checking is undecidable in general, even for finite-state cache-coherence protocols.

Consistency models define rules for the apparent order and visibility of updates, and it is a continuum with tradeoffs.

Example

Assume that the following case occurs:

- The row X is replicated on nodes M and N.

- The client A writes row X to node N.

- After a period of time t, client B reads row X from node M.

The consistency model has to determine whether client B sees the write from client A or not.

Types

There are two methods to define and categorize consistency models; issue and view.

Issue: Issue method describes the restrictions that define how a process can issue operations.

View: View method which defines the order of operations visible to processes.

For example, a consistency model can define that a process is not allowed to issue an operation until all previously issued operations are completed. Different consistency models enforce different conditions. One consistency model can be considered stronger than another if it requires all conditions of that model and more. In other words, a model with fewer constraints is considered a weaker consistency model.

These models define how the hardware needs to be laid out and at high-level, how the programmer must code. The chosen model also affects how the compiler can re-order instructions. Generally, if control dependencies between instructions and if writes to same location are ordered, then the compiler can reorder as required. However, with the models described below, some may allow Writes before Loads to be reordered while some may not.

Strict Consistency

Strict consistency is the strongest consistency model. Under this model, a write to a variable by any processor needs to be seen instantaneously by all processors. The Strict model diagram and non-Strict model diagrams describe the time constraint – instantaneous. It can be better understood as though a global clock is present in which every write should be reflected in all processor caches by the end of that clock period. The next operation must happen only in the next clock period.

P_1: $W(x)1$	P_1: $W(x)1$
P_2: $R(x)1$	P_2: $R(x)0$ $R(x)1$
Strict Model	Non-strict Model

This is the most rigid model and is impossible to implement without forgoing performance. In this model, the programmer's expected result will be received every time. It is deterministic. A distributed system with many nodes will take some time to copy information written to one node to all the other nodes responsible for replicating that information. That time can't be zero because it takes time for information to propagate through space, and there is a limit to how fast information can travel through space: the speed of light. Therefore, strict consistency is impossible. The best one can do is design a system where the time-to-replicate approaches the theoretical minimum.

Sequential Consistency

The sequential consistency model is a weaker memory model than strict consistency. A write to a variable does not have to be seen instantaneously, however, writes to variables by different processors have to be seen in the same order by all processors. As defined by Lamport(1979), Sequential Consistency is met if "the result of any execution is the same as if the operations of all the processors were executed in some sequential order, and the operations of each individual processor appear in this sequence in the order specified by its program."

Program order within each processor and sequential ordering of operations between processors should be maintained. In order to preserve sequential order of execution between processors, all operations must appear to execute instantaneously or atomically with respect to every other processor. These operations need only "appear" to be completed because it is physically impossible to send information instantaneously. For instance, once a bus line is posted with information, It is guaranteed that all processors will see the information at the same instant. Thus, passing the information to the bus line completes the execution with respect to all processors and has appeared to have been executed. Cache-less architectures or cached architectures with interconnect networks that are not instantaneous can contain a slow path between processors and memories. These slow paths can result in sequential inconsistency, because some memories receive the broadcast data faster than others.

Sequential consistency can produce non-deterministic results. This is because the sequence of sequential operations between processors can be different during different runs of the program. All memory operations need to happen in the program order.

Linearizability (also known as atomic consistency) can be defined as sequential consistency with the real-time constraint.

Causal Consistency

Causal consistency is a weakening model of sequential consistency by categorizing events into those causally related and those that are not. It defines that only write operations that are causally related need to be seen in the same order by all processes.

This model relaxes Sequential consistency on concurrent writes by a processor and on writes that are not causally related. Two writes can become causally related if one write to a variable is dependent on a previous write to any variable if the processor doing the second write has just read the first write. The two writes could have been done by the same processor or by different processors.

As in sequential consistency, reads do not need to reflect changes instantaneously, however, they need to reflect all changes to a variable sequentially.

$$P1: W_1(x)3$$
$$P2: W_2(x)5 \ R_1(x)3$$

W_1 is not causally related to W_2. R1 would be Sequentially Inconsistent but is Causally consistent.

$P1$:W(x)1		W(x)3	
$P2$:R(x)1	W(x)2		
$P3$:R(x)1		R(x)3	R(x)2
$P4$:R(x)1		R(x)2	R(x)3

W(x)1 and W(x) 2 are causally related due to the read made by P2 to x before W(x)2.

Processor Consistency

In order for consistency in data to be maintained and to attain scalable processor systems where every processor has its own memory, the Processor consistency model was derived. All processors need to be consistent in the order in which they see writes done by one processor and in the way they see writes by different processors to the same location (coherence is maintained). However, they do not need to be consistent when the writes are by different processors to different locations.

Every write operation can be divided into several sub-writes to all memories. A read from one such memory can happen before the write to this memory completes. Therefore, the data read can be stale. Thus, a processor under PC can execute a younger load when an older store needs to be stalled. Read before Write, Read after Read and Write before Write ordering is still preserved in this model.

The processor consistency model is similar to PRAM consistency model with a stronger condition that defines all writes to the same memory location must be seen in the same sequential order by all other processes. Process consistency is weaker than sequential consistency but stronger than PRAM consistency model.

The Stanford DASH multiprocessor system implements a variation of processor consistency which is incomparable (neither weaker nor stronger) to Goodmans definitions. All processors need to be consistent in the order in which they see writes by one processor and in the way they see writes by different processors to the same location. However, they do not need to be consistent when the writes are by different processors to different locations.

PRAM Consistency (Also known as FIFO Consistency)

PRAM consistency (Pipelined RAM) was presented by Lipton and Sandberg in 1988 as one of the first described consistency models. Due to its informal definition, there are in fact at least two subtle different implementations, one by Ahamad et al. and one by Mosberger.

In PRAM consistency, all processes view the operations of a single process in the same order that they were issued by that process, while operations issued by different processes can be viewed in different order from different processes. PRAM consistency is weaker than processor consistency. PRAM relaxes the need to maintain coherence to a location across all its processors. Here, reads to any variable can be executed before writes in a processor. Read before Write, Read after Read and Write before Write ordering is still preserved in this model.

P1:	W(x)1				
P2:		R(x)1	W(x)2		
P3:				R(x)1	R(x)2
P4:				R(x)2	R(x)1

Cache Consistency

Cache consistency requires that all write operations to the same memory location are performed in some sequential order. Cache consistency is weaker than process consistency and incomparable with PRAM consistency.

Slow Consistency

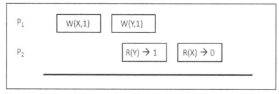

Slow Memory

In slow consistency, if a process reads a value previously written to a memory location, it cannot subsequently read any earlier value from that location. Writes performed by a process are immediately visible to that process. Slow consistency is a weaker model than PRAM and cache consistency.

Example: Slow memory diagram depicts a slow consistency example. The first process writes 1 to the memory location X and then it writes 1 to the memory location Y. The second process reads 1 from Y and it then reads 0 from X even though X was written before Y.

Hutto, Phillip W., and Mustaque Ahamad (1990) illustrate that by appropriate programming, slow memory (consistency) can be expressive and efficient. They mention that slow memory has two valuable properties; locality and supporting reduction from atomic memory. They propose two algorithms to present the expressiveness of slow memory.

The following models require specific synchronization by programmers.

Weak Ordering

Program order and atomicity is maintained only on a group of operations and not on all reads and writes. This was derived from the understanding that certain memory operations – such as those conducted in a critical section - need not be seen by all processors – until after all operations in the critical section are completed for instance. It also exploits the fact that programs written to be executed on a multi-processor system contain the required synchronization to make sure that data races do not occur and SC outcomes are produced always. Thus, in weak ordering, operations other than synchronization operations can be classified as *data* operations.

P1	P2
X = 1;	fence
fence	while(!xready) {};
xready = 1;	fence
	y = 2;

Synchronization operations signal the processor to make sure it has completed and seen all previous operations done by all processors. In order to maintain Weak ordering, write operations prior to a synchronization operation must be globally performed before the synchronization operation. Operations present in after a synchronization operation should also be performed only after the synchronization operation completes. Therefore, accesses to synchronization variables is sequentially consistent and any read or write should be performed only after previous synchronization operations have completed. Coherence is not relaxed in this model. Once these requirements are met, all other "data" operations can be reordered.

There is high reliance on explicit synchronization in the program. For weak ordering models, the programmer must use atomic locking instructions such as test-and-set, fetch-and-op, store conditional, load linked or must label synchronization variables or use fences.

Release Consistency

This model relaxes the Weak consistency model by distinguishing the entrance synchronization operation from the exit synchronization operation. Under weak ordering, when a synchronization operation is to be seen, all operations in all processors need to be visible before the Synchronization operation is done and the processor proceeds. However, under Release consistency model, during the entry to a critical section, termed as "acquire", all operations with respect to the local memory variables need to be completed. During the exit, termed as "release", all changes made by the local processor should be propagated to all other processors. Coherence is still maintained.

The acquire operation is a load/read that is performed to access the critical section. A release operation is a store/write performed to allow other processors use the shared variables.

Among synchronization variables, sequential consistency or processor consistency can be maintained. Using SC, all competing synchronization variables should be processed in order. However, with PC, a pair of competing variables need to only follow this order. Younger Acquires can be allowed to happen before older Releases.

Entry Consistency

This is a variant of the Release Consistency model. It also requires the use of Acquire and Release instructions to explicitly state an entry or exit to a critical section. However, under Entry Consistency, every shared variable is assigned a synchronization variable specific to it. This way, only when the Acquire is to variable x, all operations related to x need to be completed with respect to that processor. This allows concurrent operations of different critical sections of different shared variables to occur. Concurrency cannot be seen for critical operations on the same shared variable. Such a consistency model will be useful when different matrix elements can be processed at the same time.

General Consistency

In general consistency, all the copies of a memory location are eventually identical after all processes' writes are completed.

Local Consistency

In local consistency, each process performs its own operations in the order defined by its program. There is no constraint on the ordering in which the write operations of other processes appear to be performed. Local consistency is the weakest consistency model in shared memory systems.

Some other consistency models are as follows:

- Causal+ Consistency
- Delta consistency
- Eventual consistency
- Fork consistency
- One-copy serializability
- Serializability
- Vector-field consistency
- Weak consistency
- Strong consistency

Several other consistency models have been conceived to express restrictions with respect to ordering or visibility of operations, or to deal with specific fault assumptions.

Relaxed Memory Consistency Models

Some different consistency models can be defined by relaxing one or more requirements in sequential consistency called relaxed consistency models. These consistency models do not provide memory consistency at the hardware level. In fact, the programmers are responsible for implementing the memory consistency by applying synchronization techniques. The above models are classified based on four criteria and are detailed further.

There are four comparisons to define the relaxed consistency:

- Relaxation: One way to categorize the relaxed consistency is to define which sequential consistency requirements are relaxed. We can have less strict models by relaxing either program order or write atomicity requirements defined by Adve and Gharachorloo, 1996. Program order guarantees that each process issues a memory request ordered by its program and write atomicity defines that memory requests are serviced based on the order of a single FIFO queue. In relaxing program order, any or all the ordering of operation pairs, write-after-write, read-after-write, or read/write-after-read, can be relaxed. In the relaxed write atomicity model, a process can view its own writes before any other processors.

- Synchronizing vs. Non-Synchronizing: A synchronizing model can be defined by dividing the memory accesses into two groups and assigning different consistency restrictions to each group considering that one group can have a weak consistency model while the other one needs a more restrictive consistency model. In contrast, a non-synchronizing Model assigns the same consistency model to the memory access types.

- Issue vs. View-Based: Issue method provides sequential consistency simulation by defining the restrictions for processes to issue memory operations. Whereas, view method describes the visibility restrictions on the events order for processes.

- Relative Model Strength: Some consistency models are more restrictive than others. In other words, strict consistency models enforce more constraints as consistency requirements. The strength of a model can be defined by the program order or atomicity relaxations and the strength of models can also be compared. Some models are directly related if they apply same relaxations or more. On the other hand, the models that relax different requirements are not directly related.

Sequential consistency has two requirements, program order and write atomicity. Different relaxed consistency models can be obtained by relaxing these requirements. This is done so that, along with relaxed constraints, the performance increases, but the programmer is responsible for implementing the memory consistency by applying synchronisation techniques and must have a good understanding of the hardware.

Potential relaxations:

- Write to Read program order.

- Write to Write program order.

- Read to Read and Read to Write program orders.

Relaxation Models

The following models are some models of relaxed consistency:

Relaxed Write to Read

An approach to improving the performance at the hardware level is by relaxing the PO of a write followed by a read which effectively hides the latency of write operations. The optimisation this type of relaxation relies on is that it allows the subsequent reads to be in a relaxed order with respect to the previous writes from he processor. Because of this relaxation some programs like XXX may fail to give SC results because of this relaxation. Whereas, programs like YYY are still expected to give consistent results because of the enforcement of the remaining program order constraints.

Three models fall under this category. IBM 370 model is the strictest model. A Read can be complete before an earlier write to a different address, but it is prohibited from returning the value of the write unless all the processors have seen the write. The SPARC V8 total store ordering model (TSO) model partially relaxes the IBM 370 Model, it allows a read to return the value of its own processor's write with respect to other writes to the same location i.e. it returns the value of its own write before others see it. Similar to the previous model, this cannot return the value of write unless all the processors have seen the write. The processor consistency model (PC) is the most relaxed of the three models and relaxes both the constraints such that a read can complete before an earlier write even before it is made visible to other processors.

In Example A, the result is possible only in IBM 370 because Read(A) is not issued until the write(A) in that processor is completed. On the other hand, this result is possible in TSO and PC because they allow the reads of the flags before the writes of the flags in a single processor.

In Example B the result is possible only with PC as it allows P2 to return the value of a write even before it is visible to P3. This won't be possible in the other two models.

To ensure sequential consistency in the above models, safety nets or fences are used to manually enforce the constraint. The IBM370 model has some specialised *serialisation instructions* which are manually placed between operations. These instructions can consist of memory instructions such or non-memory instructions such as branches. On the other hand, the TSO and PC models do not provide safety nets, but the programmers can still use read-modify-write operations to make it appear like the program order is still maintained between a write and a following read. In case of TSO, PO appears to be maintained if the R or W which is already a part of a R-modify-W is replaced by a R-modify-W, this requires the W in the R-modify-W is a 'dummy' that returns the read value. Similarly for PC, PO seems to be maintained if the read is replaced by a write or is already a part of R-modify-W.

However, compiler optimisations cannot be done after exercising this relaxation alone. Compiler optimisations require the full flexibility of reordering any two operations in the PO, so the ability to reorder a write with respect to a read is not sufficiently helpful in this case.

```
Example A.

Initially, A=flag1=flag2=0

P1                      P2

flag1=1                 flag2=1

A=1                     A=2

reg1=A                  reg3=A

reg2=flag2              reg4=flag1


Result: reg1=1 ; reg3=2, reg2=reg4=0

Example B. Initially, A=B=0

P1              P2              P3

A=1

                if(A==1)

                B=1             if(B==1)

                                reg1=A


Result: B=1, reg1=0
```

Relaxed Write to Read and Write to Write

Some models relax the program order even further by relaxing even the ordering constraints between writes to different locations. The SPARC V8 Partial Store Ordering model (PSO) is the only example of such a model. The ability to pipeline and overlap writes to different locations from the same processor is the key hardware optimisation enabled by PSO. PSO is similar to TSO in terms of atomicity requirements, in that, it allows a processor to read the value of its own write and preventing other processors from reading another processor's write before the write is visible to all other processors. Program order between two writes is maintained by PSO using an explicit STBAR instruction. The STBAR is inserted in a write buffer in implementations with FIFO write buffers. A counter is used to determine when all the writes before the STBAR instruction have been completed, which triggers a write to the memory system to increment the counter. A write acknowledgement decrements the counter, and when the counter becomes 0, it signifies that all the previous writes are completed.

In the examples A and B, PSO allows both these non-sequentially consistent results. The safety net that PSO provides is similar to TSO's, it imposes program order from a write to a read and enforces write atomicity.

Similar to the previous models, the relaxations allowed by PSO are not sufficiently flexible to be useful for compiler optimisation, which requires a much more flexible optimisation.

Relaxing Read and Read to Write Program Orders

In some models, all operations to different locations are relaxed. A read or write may be reordered with respect a different read or write in a different location. The *weak ordering* may be classified under this category and two types of Release consistency models (RCsc and RCpc) also come under this model. Three commercial architectures are also proposed under this category of relaxation: the Digital Alpha, SPARC V9 relaxed memory order (RMO), and IBM PowerPC models. All these models allow reordering of reads to the same location, except the Digital Alpha. These models violate sequential in examples A and B. An additional relaxation allowed in these models that is absent ninth previous models is that memory operations following a read operation can be overlapped and reordered with respect to the read. All these models, expect the RCpc and PowerPC allow a read to return the value of another processor's early write. From a programmer's perspective all these models must maintain the illusion of write atomicity even though they allow the processor to read its own write early.

These models can be classified into two categories based on the type of safety net provided. Here, the necessity for carefully written programs is seen. The nature of the synchronization helps to categorize between Weak Ordering, RCsc and RCpc models. Where as, The Alpha, RMO and PowerPC models provide fence instructions so that program order can be imposed between different memory operations.

Weak Ordering

An example of a model that relaxes most of the above constraints (except reading others' write early) is Weak Ordering. It classifies memory operations into two categories: *Data operations* and *Synchronization operations*. To enforce program order, a programmer needs to find at least one synchronisation operation in a program. The assumption under which this works is that, reordering memory operations to data regions between synchronisation operations does not affect the outcome of the program. They just act as the safety net for enforcing program order. The way this works is that a counter tracks the number of data operations and until this counter becomes zero, the synchronisation operation isn't issued. Furthermore, no more data operations are issued unless all the previous synchronisation's are completed. Memory operations in between two synchronisation variables can be overlapped and reordered without affecting the correctness of the program. This model ensures that write atomicity is always maintained, therefore no additional safety net is required for Weak Ordering.

Release Consistency (RCsc/RCpc)

More classification is made to memory operations depending on when they occur. Operations are divided into ordinary and special. Special operations are further divided into sync or sync operations. Syncs correspond to synchronisation operations and syncs correspond to data operations or other special operations that aren't used for synchronisation. Sync operations are further divided into acquire or release operations. An acquire is effectively a read memory operation used to obtain access to a certain set of shared locations. Release, on the other hand, is a write operation that is performed for granting permission to access the shared locations.

There are two types of Release consistency, RCsc (Release consistency with Sequential consistency) and RCpc (Release consistency with processor consistency). The first type, RCsc maintains SC among special operations, while RCpc maintains PC among such operations.

For RCsc the constraints are: Acquire->All, All->Release,Special->Special.

For RCpc the write to read program order is relaxed: Acquire->All, All->Release, Special->Special(expect when special write is followed by special read)

NOTE: the above notation A->B, implies that if the operation A precedes B in the program order, then program order is enforced.

Alpha, RMO, and PowerPC

These three commercial architectures exhibit explicit fence instructions as their safety nets. The Alpha model provides two types of fence instructions, Memory barrier(MB) and Write memory barrier(WMB). The MB operation can be used to maintain program order of any memory operation before the MB with a memory operation after the barrier. Similarly, the WMB maintains program order only among writes. The SPARC V9 RMO model provides a MEMBAR instruction which can be customised to order previous reads and writes with respect to future read and write operations. There is no need for using read-modify-writes to achieve this order because the MEMBAR instruction can be used to order a write with respect to a succeeding read. The PowerPC model uses a single fence instruction called the SYNC instruction. It is similar to the MB instruction, but with a little exception that reads can occur out of program order even if a SYNC is placed between two reads to the same location. This model also differs from Alpha and RMO in terms of Atomicity. It allows write to be seen earlier than a read's completion. A combination of read modify write operations may be required to make an illusion of write atomicity.

Transactional Memory Models

Transactional Memory model is the combination of cache coherency and memory consistency models as a communication model for shared memory systems supported by software or hardware; a transactional memory model provides both memory consistency and cache coherency. A transaction is a sequence of operations executed by a process that transforms data from one consistent state to another. A transaction either commits when there is no conflict or aborts. In commits, all changes are visible to all other processes when a transaction is completed, while aborts discard all changes. Compared to relaxed consistency models, a transactional model is easier to use and can provide the higher performance than a sequential consistency model.

Consistency and Replication

Tanenbaum et al., 2007 defines two main reasons for replicating; reliability and performance. Reliability can be achieved in a replicated file system by switching to another replica in the case of the current replica failure. The replication also protects data from being corrupted by providing multiple copies of data on different replicas. It also improves the performance by dividing the work. While replication can improve performance and reliability, it can cause consistency problems between multiple copies of data. The multiple copies are consistent if a read operation returns the same value from all copies and a write operation as a single atomic operation (transaction) updates all copies before any other operation takes place. Tanenbaum, Andrew, & Maarten Van Steen, 2007 refer to this type of consistency as tight consistency provided by synchronous replication. However, applying global synchronizations to keep all copies consistent is costly. One way to decrease the cost of global synchronization and improve the performance can be weakening the consistency restrictions.

Data-centric Consistency Models

Tanenbaum et al., 2007 defines the consistency model as a contract between the software (processes) and memory implementation (data store). This model guarantees that if the software follows certain rules, the memory works correctly. Since, in a system without a global clock, defining the last operation writes is difficult, some restrictions can be applied on the values that can be returned by a read operation.

Consistent Ordering of Operations

Some consistency models such as sequential and also causal consistency models deal with the order of operations on shared replicated data in order to provide consistency. In this models, all replicas must agree on a consistent global ordering of updates.

Sequential Consistency

The goal of data-centric consistency models is to provide a consistent view on a data store where processes may carry out concurrent updates. One important data-centric consistency model is sequential consistency defined by Lamport (1979). Tanenbaum et al., 2007 defines sequential consistency under following condition:

"The result of any execution is the same as if the (read and write) operations by all processes on the data store were executed in some sequential order and the operations of each individual process appear in this sequence in the order specified by its program."

Adve and Gharachorloo, 1996 define two requirements to implement the sequential consistency; program order and write atomicity.

- Program order: Program order guarantees that each process issues a memory request ordered by its program.

- Write atomicity: Write atomicity defines that memory requests are serviced based on the order of a single FIFO queue.

In sequential consistency, there is no notion of time or most recent write operations. There are some operations interleaving that is same for all processes. A process can see the write operations of all processes but it can just see its own read operations.

Linearizability (Atomic memory) can be defined as a sequential consistency with real time constraint by considering a begin time and end time for each operation. An execution is linearizable if each operation taking place in linearizable order by placing a point between its begin time and its end time and guarantees sequential consistency.

Causal Consistency

The causal consistency defined by Hutto and Ahamad, 1990 is a weaker consistency model than sequential consistency by making the distinction between causally related operations and those that are not related. For example, if an event b takes effect from an earlier event a, the causal consistency guarantees that all processes see event b after event a.

Tanenbaum et al., 2007 defines that a data store is considered causal consistent under the following condition:

"Writes that are potentially causally related must be seen by all processes in the same order. Concurrent writes may be seen in a different order on different machines."

Grouping Operations

In grouping operation, accesses to the synchronization variables are sequentially consistent. A process is allowed to access a synchronization variable that all previous writes have been completed. In other words, accesses to synchronization variables are not permitted until all operations on the synchronization variables are completely performed.

Continuous Consistency

The continuous consistency is defined later in the consistency protocol section.

Client-centric Consistency Models

In distributed systems, maintaining sequential consistency in order to control the concurrent operations is essential. In some special data stores without simultaneous updates, client-centric consistency models can deal with inconsistencies in a less costly way. The following models are some client-centric consistency models:

Eventual Consistency

An eventual consistency is a weak consistency model in the system with the lack of simultaneous updates. It defines that if no update takes a very long time, all replicas eventually become consistent.

Monotonic Read Consistency

Tanenbaum et al., 2007 defines monotonic read consistency as follows:

"If a process reads the value of a data item x, any successive read operation on x by that process will always return that same value or a more recent value."

Monotonic read consistency guarantees that after a process reads a value of data item x at time t, it will never see the older value of that data item.

Monotonic Write Consistency

Monotonic write consistency condition is defined by Tanenbaum et al., 2007.

"A write operation by a process on a data item X is completed before any successive write operation on X by the same process."

Read-your-writes Consistency

A value written by a process on a data item X will be always available to a successive read operation performed by the same process on data item X.

Writes-follows-reads Consistency

In Writes-follow-reads consistency, updates are propagated after performing the previous read operations. Tanenbaum et al., 2007 defines the following condition for Writes-follow-reads consistency:

"A write operation by a process on a data item x following a previous read operation on x by the same process is guaranteed to take place on the same or a more recent value of x that was read."

Consistency Protocols

The implementation of a consistency model is defined by a consistency protocol. Tanenbaum et al., 2007 illustrates some consistency protocols for data-centric models.

Continuous Consistency

Continuous consistency introduced by Yu and Vahdat (2000). In this model, consistency semantic of an application is described by using conits in the application. Since the consistency requirements can differ based on application semantics, Yu and Vahdat (2000) believe that a predefined uniform consistency model may not be an appropriate approach. The application should specify the consistency requirements that satisfy the application semantic. In this model, an application specifies each consistency requirements as a conits (abbreviation of consistency units). A conit can be a physical or logical consistency and is used to measure the consistency. Tanenbaum et al., 2007 describes the notion of a conit by giving an example. There are three inconsistencies that can be tolerated by applications.

- Deviation in numerical values Numerical deviation bounds the difference between the conit value and relative value of last update. A weight can be assigned to the writes which defines the importance of the writes in a specific application. The total weights of unseen writes for a conit can be defined as a numerical deviation in an application. There are two different types of numerical deviation; absolute and relative numerical deviation.

- Deviation in ordering Ordering deviation is the discrepancy between the local order of writes in a replica and their relative ordering in the eventual final image.

- Deviation in staleness between replicas Staleness deviation defines the validity of the oldest write by bounding the difference between the current time and the time of oldest write on a conit not seen locally. Each server has a local queue of uncertain write that is required an actual order to be determined and applied on a conit. The maximal length of uncertain writes queue is the bound of ordering deviation. When the number of writes exceeds the limit, instead of accepting new submitted write, the server will attempt to commit uncertain writes by communicating with other servers based on the order that writes should be executed.

If all three deviation bounds set to zero, the continuous consistency model is the strong consistency.

Primary-based Protocols

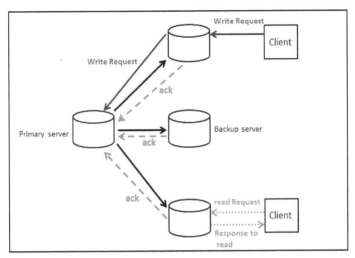

Primary-backup protocol.

Primary-based protocols can be considered as a class of consistency protocols that are simpler to implement. For instance, sequential ordering is a popular consistency model when consistent ordering of operations is considered. The sequential ordering can be determined as primary-based protocol. In these protocols, there is an associated primary for each data item in a data store to coordinate write operations on that data item.

Remote-write Protocols

In the simplest primary-based protocol that supports replication, also known as primary-backup protocol, write operations are forwarded to a single server and read operations can be performed locally.

Example: Tanenbaum et al., 2007 gives an example of a primary-backup protocol. The diagram of primary-backup protocol shows an example of this protocol. When a client requests a write, the write request is forwarded to a primary server. The primary server sends request to backups to perform the update. The server then receives the update acknowledgement from all backups and sends the acknowledgement of completion of writes to the client. Any client can read the last available update locally. The trade-off of this protocol is that a client who sends the update request might have to wait so long to get the acknowledgement in order to continue. This problem can be solved by performing the updates locally, and then ask other backups perform their updates. The non-blocking primary-backup protocol does not guarantee the consistency of update on all backup servers. However, it improves the performance. In the primary-backup protocol, all processes will see the same order of write operations since this protocol orders all incoming writes based on a globally unique time. Blocking protocols guarantee that processes view the result of the last write operation.

Local-write Protocols

In primary-based local-write protocols, primary copy moves between processes willing to perform an update. To update a data item, a process first moves it to its location. As a result, in this approach, successive write operations can be performed locally while each process can read their local copy of data items. After the primary finishes its update, the update is forwarded to other replicas and all perform the update locally. This non-blocking approach can lead to an improvement. The diagram of the local-write protocol depicts the local-write approach in primary-based protocols. A process requests a write operation in a data item x. The current server is considered as the new primary for a data item x. The write operation is performed and when the request is finished, the primary sends an update request to other backup servers. Each backup sends an acknowledgment to the primary after finishing the update operation.

Replicated-write Protocols

In Replicated-write protocols, unlike the primary-based protocol, all updates are carried out to all replicas.

Active Replication

In active replication, there is a process associated to each replica to perform the write operation. In other words, updates are sent to each replica in the form of an operation in order to be executed. All updates need to be performed in the same order in all replicas. As a result, a totally-ordered multicast mechanism is required. There is a scalability issue in implementing such a multicasting mechanism in large distributed systems. There is another approach in which each operation is sent to a central coordinator (sequencer). The coordinator first assigns a sequence number to each operation and then forwards the operation to all replicas. Second approach cannot also solve the scalability problem.

Quorum-based Protocols

Voting can be another approach in replicated-write protocols. In this approach, a client requests and receives permission from multiple servers in order to read and write a replicated data. As an example, suppose in a distributed file system, a file is replicated on N servers. To update a file, a client must send a request to at least $N/2+1$ in order to make their agreement to perform an update. After the agreement, changes are applied on the file and a new version number is assigned to the updated file. Similarly, for reading replicated file, a client sends a request to $N/2+1$ servers in order to receive the associated version number from those servers. Read operation is completed if all received version numbers are the most recent version.

Cache-coherence Protocols

In a replicated file system, a cache-coherence protocol provides the cache consistency while caches are generally controlled by clients. In many approaches, cache consistency is provided by the underlying hardware. Some other approaches in middleware-based distributed systems apply software-based solutions to provide the cache consistency. Cache consistency models can differ in their coherence detection strategies that define when inconsistencies occur. There are two approaches to detect the inconsistency; static and dynamic solutions. In the static solution, a compiler determines which variables can cause the cache inconsistency. So, the compiler enforces an instruction in order to avoid the inconsistency problem. In the dynamic solution, the server checks for inconsistencies at run time to control the consistency of the cached data that has changed after it was cached. The coherence enforcement strategy is another cache-coherence protocol. It defines that *how* to provide the consistency in caches by using the copies located on the server. One way to keep the data consistent is to never cache the shared data. A server can keep the data and apply some consistency protocol such as primary-based protocols to ensure the consistency of shared data. In this solution, only private data can be cached by clients. In the case that shared data are cached, there are two approaches in order to enforce the cache coherence. In first approach, when a shared data is updated, the server forwards invalidation to all caches. In second approach, an update is propagated. Most caching systems apply these two approaches or dynamically choose between them.

Ocean Current Simulation

- Regular structure, scientific computing, important for weather forecast.
- Want to simulate the eddy current along the walls of ocean basin over a period of time:
  - Discretize the 3-D basin into 2-D horizontal grids.
  - Discretize each 2-D grid into points.
  - One time step involves solving the equation of motion for each grid point.
  - Enough concurrency within and across grids.
  - After each time step synchronize the processors.

Galaxy Simulation

- Simulate the interaction of many stars evolving over time.
- Want to compute force between every pair of stars for each time step:
  - Essentially $O(n^2)$ computations (massive parallelism).
- Hierarchical methods take advantage of square law:
  - If a group of stars is far enough it is possible to approximate the group entirely by a single star at the center of mass.
  - Essentially four subparts in each step: divide the galaxy into zones until further division does not improve accuracy, compute center of mass for each zone, compute force, update star position based on force.
- Lot of concurrency across stars.

Ray Tracing

- Want to render a scene using ray tracing.

- Generate rays through pixels in the image plane.

- The rays bounce from objects following reflection/refraction laws:

  o New rays get generated: tree of rays from a root ray.

- Need to correctly simulate paths of all rays.

- The outcome is color and opacity of the objects in the scene: thus you render a scene.

- Concurrency across ray trees and subtrees.

Writing a Parallel Program

- Start from a sequential description.

- Identify work that can be done in parallel.

- Partition work and/or data among threads or processes:

  o Decomposition and assignment.

- Add necessary communication and synchronization:

  o Orchestration.

- Map threads to processors (Mapping).

- How good is the parallel program?

- Measure speedup = sequential execution time/parallel execution time = number of processors ideally.

Some Definitions

- Task:

  o Arbitrary piece of sequential work.

  o Concurrency is only across tasks.

  o Fine-grained task vs. coarse-grained task: controls granularity of parallelism (spectrum of grain: one instruction to the whole sequential program).

- Process/thread:

  o Logical entity that performs a task.

  o Communication and synchronization happen between threads.

- Processors:

  o Physical entity on which one or more processes execute.

Decomposition of Iterative Equation Solver

- Find concurrent tasks and divide the program into tasks:

  - Level or grain of concurrency needs to be decided here.

  - Too many tasks: may lead to too much of overhead communicating and synchronizing between tasks.

  - Too few tasks: may lead to idle processors.

  - Goal: Just enough tasks to keep the processors busy.

- Number of tasks may vary dynamically:

  - New tasks may get created as the computation proceeds: new rays in ray tracing.

  - Number of available tasks at any point in time is an upper bound on the achievable speedup.

Static Assignment

- Given a decomposition it is possible to assign tasks statically:

  - For example, some computation on an array of size N can be decomposed statically by assigning a range of indices to each process: for k processes P_0 operates on indices 0 to $(N/k)-1$, P_1 operates on N/k to $(2N/k)-1$,..., P_{k-1} operates on $(k-1)N/k$ to N-1.

  - For regular computations this works great: simple and low-overhead.

- What if the nature computation depends on the index?

  - For certain index ranges you do some heavy-weight computation while for others you do something simple.

  - Is there a problem?

Dynamic Assignment

- Static assignment may lead to load imbalance depending on how irregular the application is.

- Dynamic decomposition/assignment solves this issue by allowing a process to dynamically choose any available task whenever it is done with its previous task.

  - Normally in this case you decompose the program in such a way that the number of available tasks is larger than the number of processes.

  - Same example: divide the array into portions each with 10 indices; so you have N/10 tasks.

  - An idle process grabs the next available task.

- o Provides better load balance since longer tasks can execute concurrently with the smaller ones.

- Dynamic assignment comes with its own overhead:

  - o Now you need to maintain a shared count of the number of available tasks.

  - o The update of this variable must be protected by a lock.

  - o Need to be careful so that this lock contention does not outweigh the benefits of dynamic decomposition.

- More complicated applications where a task may not just operate on an index range, but could manipulate a subtree or a complex data structure:

  - o Normally a dynamic task queue is maintained where each task is probably a pointer to the data.

  - o The task queue gets populated as new tasks are discovered.

Decomposition Types

- Decomposition by data:

  - o The most commonly found decomposition technique.

  - o The data set is partitioned into several subsets and each subset is assigned to a process.

  - o The type of computation may or may not be identical on each subset.

  - o Very easy to program and manage.

- Computational decomposition:

  - o Not so popular: tricky to program and manage.

  - o All processes operate on the same data, but probably carry out different kinds of computation.

  - o More common in systolic arrays, pipelined graphics processor units (GPUs) etc.

Orchestration

- Involves structuring communication and synchronization among processes, organizing data structures to improve locality, and scheduling tasks:

  - o This step normally depends on the programming model and the underlying architecture.

- Goal is to:

  - o Reduce communication and synchronization costs.

- o Maximize locality of data reference.

- o Schedule tasks to maximize concurrency: do not schedule dependent tasks in parallel.

- o Reduce overhead of parallelization and concurrency management (e.g., management of the task queue, overhead of initiating a task etc.)

Mapping

- At this point you have a parallel program:

  - o Just need to decide which and how many processes go to each processor of the parallel machine.

- Could be specified by the program:

  - o Pin particular processes to a particular processor for the whole life of the program; the processes cannot migrate to other processors.

- Could be controlled entirely by the OS:

  - o Schedule processes on idle processors.

  - o Various scheduling algorithms are possible e.g., round robin: process#k goes to processor#k.

  - o NUMA-aware OS normally takes into account multiprocessor-specific metrics in scheduling.

- How many processes per processor? Most common is one-to-one.

An Example

- Iterative equation solver:

  - o Main kernel in Ocean simulation.

  - o Update each 2-D grid point via Gauss-Seidel iterations.

  - o $A[i,j] = 0.2(A[i,j]+A[i,j+1]+A[i,j-1]+A[i+1,j]+A[i-1,j])$.

  - o Pad the n by n grid to (n+2) by (n+2) to avoid corner problems.

  - o Update only interior n by n grid.

  - o One iteration consists of updating all n2 points in-place and accumulating the difference from the previous value at each point.

  - o If the difference is less than a threshold, the solver is said to have converged to a stable grid equilibrium.

Sequential Program

```
int n;                                          begin Solve (A)
```

```
float **A, diff;                                    int i, j, done = 0;

                                                       float temp;

                                                       while (!done)

begin main()                                             diff = 0.0;

   read (n);   /* size of grid */                   for i = 0 to n-1

   Allocate (A);                                                    for
j = 0 to n-1

   Initialize (A);                                             temp =
A[i,j];

   Solve (A);                                              A[i,j]
= 0.2(A[i,j]+A[i,j+1]+A[i,j-1]+A[i-

end main                                              1,j]+A[i+1,j]);

                                                           diff
+= fabs (A[i,j] - temp);

                                                          end-
for

                                                        endfor

                                                           if
(diff/(n*n) < TOL) then done = 1;

                                                      endwhile
                                                    end Solve
```

Decomposition of Iterative Equation Solver

- Look for concurrency in loop iterations:
  - In this case iterations are really dependent.
  - Iteration (i, j) depends on iterations $(i, j-1)$ and $(i-1, j)$.

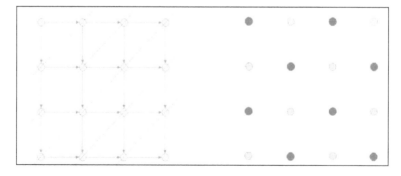

  - Each anti-diagonal can be computed in parallel.

- o Must synchronize after each anti-diagonal (or pt-to-pt).
- o Alternative: red-black ordering (different update pattern).
- Can update all red points first, synchronize globally with a barrier and then update all black points:
  - o May converge faster or slower compared to sequential program.
  - o Converged equilibrium may also be different if there are multiple solutions.
  - o Ocean simulation uses this decomposition.
- We will ignore the loop-carried dependence and go ahead with a straight-forward loop decomposition:
  - o Allow updates to all points in parallel.
  - o This is yet another different update order and may affect convergence.
  - o Update to a point may or may not see the new updates to the nearest neighbors (this parallel algorithm is non-deterministic).

```
while (!done)
    diff = 0.0;
    for_all i = 0 to n-1
        for_all j = 0 to n-1
            temp = A[i, j];
            A[i, j] = 0.2(A[i, j]+A[i, j+1]+A[i, j-1]+A[i-1, j]+A[i+1, j]);
            diff += fabs (A[i, j] - temp);
        end for_all
    end for_all
    if (diff/(n*n) < TOL) then done = 1;
end while
```

- Offers concurrency across elements: degree of concurrency is n^2.
- Make the j loop sequential to have row-wise decomposition: degree n concurrency.

Assignment

- Possible static assignment: block row decomposition:
  - o Process 0 gets rows 0 to $(n/p)-1$, process 1 gets rows n/p to $(2n/p)-1$ etc.
- Another static assignment: cyclic row decomposition.

- o   Process 0 gets rows 0, p, 2p,...; process 1 gets rows 1, p+1, 2p+1,....
- Dynamic assignment:
  - o   Grab next available row, work on that, grab a new row,...
- Static block row assignment minimizes nearest neighbor communication by assigning contiguous rows to the same process.

Shared memory version

```
/* include files */
MAIN_ENV;
int P, n;
void Solve ();
struct gm_t {
   LOCKDEC (diff_lock);
   BARDEC (barrier);
   float **A, diff;
} *gm;
int main (char **argv, int argc)
{
   int i;
   MAIN_INITENV;
   gm = (struct gm_t*) G_MALLOC (sizeof (struct gm_t));
   LOCKINIT (gm->diff_lock);
BARINIT (gm->barrier);
   n = atoi (argv);
   P = atoi (argv);
   gm->A = (float**) G_MALLOC ((n+2)*sizeof (float*));
   for (i = 0; i < n+2; i++) {
      gm->A[i] = (float*) G_MALLOC ((n+2)*sizeof (float));
   }
   Initialize (gm->A);
   for (i = 1; i < P; i++) {  /* starts at 1 */
      CREATE (Solve);
   }
   Solve ();
```

```
    WAIT_FOR_END (P-1);

    MAIN_END;

}

void Solve (void)

{

    int i, j, pid, done = 0;

    float temp, local_diff;

    GET_PID (pid);

    while (!done) {

        local_diff = 0.0;

        if (!pid) gm->diff = 0.0;

        BARRIER (gm->barrier, P);/*why?*/

        for (i = pid*(n/P); i < (pid+1)*(n/P); i++) {

            for (j = 0; j < n; j++) {

                temp = gm->A[i] [j];

            gm->A[i] [j] = 0.2*(gm->A[i] [j] + gm->A[i] [j-1] + gm->A[i] [j+1] +
gm->A[i+1] [j] + gm->A[i-1] [j]);

local_diff += fabs (gm->A[i] [j] - temp);

            }   /* end for */

        }     /* end for */

        LOCK (gm->diff_lock);

        gm->diff += local_diff;

        UNLOCK (gm->diff_lock);

        BARRIER (gm->barrier, P);

        if (gm->diff/(n*n) < TOL) done = 1;

        BARRIER (gm->barrier, P); /* why? */

    }   /* end while */

}
```

Mutual Exclusion

- Use LOCK/UNLOCK around critical sections:
  - Updates to shared variable diff must be sequential.
  - Heavily contended locks may degrade performance.

- o Try to minimize the use of critical sections: they are sequential anyway and will limit speedup.
- o This is the reason for using a local_diff instead of accessing gm->diff every time.
- o Also, minimize the size of critical section because the longer you hold the lock, longer will be the waiting time for other processors at lock acquire.

LOCK Optimization

- Suppose each processor updates a shared variable holding a global cost value, only if its local cost is less than the global cost: found frequently in minimization problems.

```
LOCK (gm->cost_lock);

if (my_cost < gm->cost) {

gm->cost = my_cost;

}

UNLOCK (gm->cost_lock);

/* May lead to heavy lock contention if everyone tries to update at the
same time */

if (my_cost < gm->cost) {

LOCK (gm->cost_lock);

if (my_cost < gm->cost)

{ /* make sure*/

gm->cost = my_cost;

}

UNLOCK (gm->cost_lock);

} /* this works because gm->cost is monotonically decreasing */
```

More Synchronization

- Global synchronization:
  - o Through barriers.
  - o Often used to separate computation phases.
- Point-to-point synchronization:
  - o A process directly notifies another about a certain event on which the latter was waiting.
  - o Producer-consumer communication pattern.
  - o Semaphores are used for concurrent programming on uniprocessor through P and V functions.

o Normally implemented through flags on shared memory multiprocessors (busy wait or spin).

P_0: A = 1; flag = 1;

P_1: while (!flag); use (A);

Message Passing

- What is different from shared memory?

  o No shared variable: expose communication through send/receive.

  o No lock or barrier primitive.

  o Must implement synchronization through send/receive.

- Grid solver example:

  o P_0 allocates and initializes matrix A in its local memory.

  o Then it sends the block rows, n, P to each processor i.e. P_1 waits to receive rows n/P to 2n/P-1 etc. (this is one-time).

  o Within the while loop the first thing that every processor does is to send its first and last rows to the upper and the lower processors (corner cases need to be handled).

  o Then each processor waits to receive the neighboring two rows from the upper and the lower processors.

- At the end of the loop each processor sends its local_diff to P_0 and P_0 sends back the done flag.

Major Changes

```
/* include files */
MAIN_ENV;
int P, n;
void Solve ();
struct gm_t {
    LOCKDEC (diff_lock);            Local
    BARDEC (barrier);              Alloc.
    float **A, diff;
} *gm;

int main (char **argv, int argc)
{
    int i; int P, n; float **A;
    MAIN_INITENV;
    gm = (struct gm_t*) G_MALLOC
    (sizeof (struct gm_t));
    LOCKINIT (gm->diff_lock);
```

```
BARINIT (gm->barrier);
n = atoi (argv[1]);
P = atoi (argv[2]);
gm->A = (float**) G_MALLOC
((n+2)*sizeof (float*));
for (i = 0; i < n+2; i++) {
    gm->A[i] = (float*) G_MALLOC
    ((n+2)*sizeof (float));
}
Initialize (gm->A);
for (i = 1; i < P; i++) { /* starts at 1 */
    CREATE (Solve);
}
Solve ();
WAIT_FOR_END (P-1);
MAIN_END;
}
```

```
void Solve (void)
{
  int i, j, pid, done = 0;
  float temp, local_diff;
  GET_PID (pid);
  while (!done) {          ── if (pid) Recv rows, n, P
    local_diff = 0.0;              Send up/down
    if (!pid) gm->diff = 0.0;   ── Recv up/down
    BARRIER (gm->barrier, P);/*why?*/
    for (i = pid*(n/P); i < (pid+1)*(n/P);
    I++) {
      for (j = 0; j < n; j++) {
        temp = gm->A[i] [j];
        gm->A[i] [j] = 0.2*(gm->A[i] [j] +
        gm->A[i] [j-1] + gm->A[i] [j+1] + gm-
        >A[i+1] [j] + gm->A[i-1] [j];
```

```
          local_diff += fabs (gm->A[i] [j] –
      temp);
      } /* end for */
    } /* end for */
    LOCK (gm->diff_lock);     Send local diff
    gm->diff += local_diff;     to P₀
    UNLOCK (gm->diff_lock);   Recv diff
    BARRIER (gm->barrier, P);
    if (gm->diff/(n*n) < TOL) done = 1;
    BARRIER (gm->barrier, P); /* why? */
  } /* end while */
}
```

Message Passing

- This algorithm is deterministic.

- May converge to a different solution compared to the shared memory version if there are multiple solutions: why?

  o There is a fixed specific point in the program (at the beginning of each iteration) when the neighboring rows are communicated.

  o This is not true for shared memory.

Message Passing Grid Solver

MPI-like Environment

- MPI stands for Message Passing Interface:

  o A C library that provides a set of message passing primitives (e.g., send, receive, broadcast etc.) to the user.

- PVM (Parallel Virtual Machine) is another well-known platform for message passing programming.

- Only need to know:

  o When you start an MPI program every thread runs the same main function.

  o We will assume that we pin one thread to one processor just as we did in shared memory.

- Instead of using the exact MPI syntax we will use some macros that call the MPI functions.

```
MAIN_ENV;
```

```
/* define message tags */
 #define ROW 99
#define DIFF 98
#define DONE 97
int main(int argc, char **argv)
{
    int pid, P, done, i, j, N;
    float tempdiff, local_diff, temp, **A;
    MAIN_INITENV;
    GET_PID(pid);
    GET_NUMPROCS(P);
    N = atoi(argv);
    tempdiff = 0.0;
    done = 0;
    A = (double **) malloc ((N/P+2) * sizeof(float *));
    for (i=0; i < N/P+2; i++) {
        A[i] = (float *) malloc (sizeof(float) * (N+2));
    }
    initialize(A);
while (!done) {
    local_diff = 0.0;
    /* MPI_CHAR means raw byte format */
    if (pid) {  /* send my first row up */
        SEND(&A, N*sizeof(float), MPI_CHAR, pid-1, ROW);
    }
    if (pid != P-1) {  /* recv last row */
        RECV(&A[N/P+1], N*sizeof(float), MPI_CHAR, pid+1, ROW);
    }
    if (pid != P-1) {  /* send last row down */
        SEND(&A[N/P], N*sizeof(float), MPI_CHAR, pid+1, ROW);
```

```
    }
    if (pid) {  /* recv first row from above */

       RECV(&A, N*sizeof(float), MPI_CHAR, pid-1, ROW);

    }

    for (i=1; i <= N/P; i++) for (j=1; j <= N; j++) {

          temp = A[i][j];

          A[i][j] = 0.2 * (A[i][j] + A[i][j-1] +            A[i-1][j] + A[i]
[j+1] + A[i+1][j]);

          local_diff += fabs(A[i][j] - temp);

          }
if (pid) {  /* tell P0 my diff */

     SEND(&local_diff, sizeof(float),    MPI_CHAR, 0, DIFF);

      RECV(&done, sizeof(int), MPI_CHAR, 0, DONE);

   }

   else {  /* recv from all and add up */

      for (i=1; i < P; i++) {

         RECV(&tempdiff, sizeof(float), MPI_CHAR, MPI_ANY_SOURCE, DIFF);

         local_diff += tempdiff;

      }

      if (local_diff/(N*N) < TOL) done=1;

      for (i=1; i < P; i++) {

         /* tell all if done */

         SEND(&done, sizeof(int), MPI_CHAR, i, DONE);

      }

   }

}  /* end while */

MAIN_END;

}  /* end main */
```

- Note the matching tags in SEND and RECV.
- Macros used in this program.

- o GET_PID

- o GET_NUMPROCS

- o SEND

- o RECV

- These will get expanded into specific MPI library calls.

- Syntax of SEND/RECV

  - o Starting address, how many elements, type of each element (we have used byte only), source/dest, message tag.

Bit-level Parallelism

Bit-level parallelism is a form of parallel computing based on increasing processor word size. Increasing the word size reduces the number of instructions the processor must execute in order to perform an operation on variables whose sizes are greater than the length of the word. (For example, consider a case where an 8-bit processor must add two 16-bit integers. The processor must first add the 8 lower-order bits from each integer, then add the 8 higher-order bits, requiring two instructions to complete a single operation. A 16-bit processor would be able to complete the operation with single instruction.)

Originally, all electronic computers were serial (single-bit) computers. The first electronic computer that was not a serial computer—the first bit-parallel computer—was the 16-bit Whirlwind from 1951.

From the advent of very-large-scale integration (VLSI) computer chip fabrication technology in the 1970s until about 1986, advancements in computer architecture were done by increasing bit-level parallelism, as 4-bit microprocessors were replaced by 8-bit, then 16-bit, then 32-bit microprocessors. This trend generally came to an end with the introduction of 32-bit processors, which have been a standard in general purpose computing for two decades. Only recently, with the advent of x86-64 architectures, have 64-bit processors become commonplace.

On 32-bit processors, external data bus width continues to increase. For example, DDR1 SDRAM transfers 128 bits per clock cycle. DDR2 SDRAM transfers a minimum of 256 bits per burst.

Instruction-level Parallelism

Instruction-level parallelism (ILP) is a measure of how many of the instructions in a computer program can be executed simultaneously.

There are two approaches to instruction level parallelism:

- Hardware

- Software

Atanasoff–Berry computer, the first computer with parallel processing.

Hardware level works upon dynamic parallelism whereas, the software level works on static parallelism. Dynamic parallelism means the processor decides at run time which instructions to execute in parallel, whereas static parallelism means the compiler decides which instructions to execute in parallel. The Pentium processor works on the dynamic sequence of parallel execution but the Itanium processor works on the static level parallelism.

Consider the following program:

1. $e = a + b$

2. $f = c + d$

3. $m = e * f$

Operation 3 depends on the results of operations 1 and 2, so it cannot be calculated until both of them are completed. However, operations 1 and 2 do not depend on any other operation, so they can be calculated simultaneously. If we assume that each operation can be completed in one unit of time then these three instructions can be completed in a total of two units of time, giving an ILP of 3/2.

A goal of compiler and processor designers is to identify and take advantage of as much ILP as possible. Ordinary programs are typically written under a sequential execution model where instructions execute one after the other and in the order specified by the programmer. ILP allows the compiler and the processor to overlap the execution of multiple instructions or even to change the order in which instructions are executed.

How much ILP exists in programs is very application specific. In certain fields, such as graphics and scientific computing the amount can be very large. However, workloads such as cryptography may exhibit much less parallelism.

Micro-architectural techniques that are used to exploit ILP include:

- Instruction pipelining where the execution of multiple instructions can be partially overlapped.

- Superscalar execution, VLIW, and the closely related explicitly parallel instruction computing concepts, in which multiple execution units are used to execute multiple instructions in parallel.

- Out-of-order execution where instructions execute in any order that does not violate data dependencies. Note that this technique is independent of both pipelining and superscalar. Current implementations of out-of-order execution dynamically (i.e., while the program is executing and without any help from the compiler) extract ILP from ordinary programs. An alternative is to extract this parallelism at compile time and somehow convey this information to the hardware. Due to the complexity of scaling the out-of-order execution technique, the industry has re-examined instruction sets which explicitly encode multiple independent operations per instruction.

- Register renaming which refers to a technique used to avoid unnecessary serialization of program operations imposed by the reuse of registers by those operations, used to enable out-of-order execution.

- Speculative execution which allow the execution of complete instructions or parts of instructions before being certain whether this execution should take place. A commonly used form of speculative execution is control flow speculation where instructions past a control flow instruction (e.g., a branch) are executed before the target of the control flow instruction is determined. Several other forms of speculative execution have been proposed and are in use including speculative execution driven by value prediction, memory dependence prediction and cache latency prediction.

- Branch prediction which is used to avoid stalling for control dependencies to be resolved. Branch prediction is used with speculative execution.

It is known that the ILP is exploited by both the compiler and hardware support but the compiler also provides inherit and implicit ILP in programs to hardware by compilation optimization. Some optimization techniques for extracting available ILP in programs would include scheduling, register allocation/renaming, and memory access optimization.

Dataflow architectures are another class of architectures where ILP is explicitly specified.

Some limits to ILP are compiler sophistication and hardware sophistication. To overcome these limits, new and different hardware techniques may be able to overcome limitations. However, unlikely such advances when coupled with realistic hardware will overcome these limits in the near future.

In recent years, ILP techniques have been used to provide performance improvements in spite of the growing disparity between processor operating frequencies and memory access times (early ILP designs such as the IBM System/360 Model 91 used ILP techniques to overcome the limitations imposed by a relatively small register file). Presently, a cache miss penalty to main memory costs several hundreds of CPU cycles. While in principle it is possible to use ILP to tolerate even such memory latencies the associated resource and power dissipation costs are disproportionate. Moreover, the complexity and often the latency of the underlying hardware structures results in reduced operating frequency further reducing any benefits. Hence, the aforementioned techniques prove inadequate to keep the CPU from stalling for the off-chip data. Instead, the industry is heading towards exploiting higher levels of parallelism that can be exploited through techniques such as multiprocessing and multithreading.

Task Parallelism

Task parallelism (also known as function parallelism and control parallelism) is a form of parallelization of computer code across multiple processors in parallel computing environments. Task parallelism focuses on distributing tasks—concurrently performed by processes or threads—across different processors. In contrast to data parallelism which involves running the same task on different components of data, task parallelism is distinguished by running many different tasks at the same time on the same data. A common type of task parallelism is pipelining which consists of moving a single set of data through a series of separate tasks where each task can execute independently of the others.

Description

In a multiprocessor system, task parallelism is achieved when each processor executes a different thread (or process) on the same or different data. The threads may execute the same or different code. In the general case, different execution threads communicate with one another as they work, but is not a requirement. Communication usually takes place by passing data from one thread to the next as part of a workflow.

As a simple example, if a system is running code on a 2-processor system (CPUs "a" & "b") in a parallel environment and we wish to do tasks "A" and "B", it is possible to tell CPU "a" to do task "A" and CPU "b" to do task "B" simultaneously, thereby reducing the run time of the execution. The tasks can be assigned using conditional statements as described below.

Task parallelism emphasizes the distributed (parallelized) nature of the processing (i.e. threads), as opposed to the data (data parallelism). Most real programs fall somewhere on a continuum between task parallelism and data parallelism.

Thread-level parallelism (TLP) is the parallelism inherent in an application that runs multiple threads at once. This type of parallelism is found largely in applications written for commercial servers such as databases. By running many threads at once, these applications are able to tolerate the high amounts of I/O and memory system latency their workloads can incur - while one thread is delayed waiting for a memory or disk access, other threads can do useful work.

The exploitation of thread-level parallelism has also begun to make inroads into the desktop market with the advent of multi-core microprocessors. This has occurred because, for various reasons, it has become increasingly impractical to increase either the clock speed or instructions per clock of a single core. If this trend continues, new applications will have to be designed to utilize multiple threads in order to benefit from the increase in potential computing power. This contrasts with previous microprocessor innovations in which existing code was automatically sped up by running it on a newer/faster computer.

Example

The pseudocode below illustrates task parallelism:

```
program:

...

if CPU="a" then

    do task "A"

else if CPU="b" then

    do task "B"

end if

...

end program
```

The goal of the program is to do some net total task ("A+B"). If we write the code as above and launch it on a 2-processor system, then the runtime environment will execute it as follows.

- In an SPMD system, both CPUs will execute the code.

- In a parallel environment, both will have access to the same data.

- The "if" clause differentiates between the CPUs. CPU "a" will read true on the "if" and CPU "b" will read true on the "else if", thus having their own task.

- Now, both CPU's execute separate code blocks simultaneously, performing different tasks simultaneously.

Code executed by CPU "a":

```
program:

...

do task "A"

...

end program
```

Code executed by CPU "b":

```
program:
```

```
...

do task "B"

...

end program
```

This concept can now be generalized to any number of processors.

Language Support

Task parallelism can be supported in general-purposes languages either built-in facilities or libraries. Notable examples include:

- C++ (Intel): Threading Building Blocks

- C++ (Open Source/Apache 2.0): RaftLib

- C, C++, Objective-C (Apple): Grand Central Dispatch

- D: tasks and fibers

- Go: goroutines

- Java: Java concurrency

- .NET: Task Parallel Library

Examples of fine-grained task-parallel languages can be found in the realm of Hardware Description Languages like Verilog and VHDL.

References

- Steinke, Robert C.; Gary J. Nutt (2004). "A unified theory of shared memory consistency.". Journal of the ACM (JACM). 51 (5): 800–849. doi:10.1145/1017460.1017464

- Hicks, Michael. "Concurrency Basics" (PDF). University of Maryland: Department of Com-puter Science. Retrieved 20, May 2020

- Quinn, Michael J. (2007). Parallel programming in C with MPI and openMP (Tata McGraw-Hill ed. ed.). New Delhi: Tata McGraw-Hill Pub. ISBN 0070582017

- Hutto, Phillip W.; Mustaque Ahamad. "Slow memory: Weakening consistency to enhance concurrency in distributed shared memories.". IEEE: 302–309. doi:10.1109/ICDCS.1990.89297

- David E. Culler, Jaswinder Pal Singh, Anoop Gupta. Parallel Computer Architecture - A Hardware/ Software Approach. Morgan Kaufmann Publishers, 1999. ISBN 1-55860-343-3, pg 15

- Paolo Viotti; Marko Vukolic (2016). "Consistency in Non-Transactional Distributed Stor-age Systems". ACM Computer Surveys. 49 (1): 19:1––19:34. doi:10.1145/2926965

- Sarita V. Adve; Kourosh Gharachorloo (December 1996). "Shared Memory Consistency Models: A Tutorial" (PDF). IEEE Computer. 29 (12): 66–76. doi:10.1109/2.546611. Retrieved 20, January 2020

Permissions

All chapters in this book are published with permission under the Creative Commons Attribution Share Alike License or equivalent. Every chapter published in this book has been scrutinized by our experts. Their significance has been extensively debated. The topics covered herein carry significant information for a comprehensive understanding. They may even be implemented as practical applications or may be referred to as a beginning point for further studies.

We would like to thank the editorial team for lending their expertise to make the book truly unique. They have played a crucial role in the development of this book. Without their invaluable contributions this book wouldn't have been possible. They have made vital efforts to compile up to date information on the varied aspects of this subject to make this book a valuable addition to the collection of many professionals and students.

This book was conceptualized with the vision of imparting up-to-date and integrated information in this field. To ensure the same, a matchless editorial board was set up. Every individual on the board went through rigorous rounds of assessment to prove their worth. After which they invested a large part of their time researching and compiling the most relevant data for our readers.

The editorial board has been involved in producing this book since its inception. They have spent rigorous hours researching and exploring the diverse topics which have resulted in the successful publishing of this book. They have passed on their knowledge of decades through this book. To expedite this challenging task, the publisher supported the team at every step. A small team of assistant editors was also appointed to further simplify the editing procedure and attain best results for the readers.

Apart from the editorial board, the designing team has also invested a significant amount of their time in understanding the subject and creating the most relevant covers. They scrutinized every image to scout for the most suitable representation of the subject and create an appropriate cover for the book.

The publishing team has been an ardent support to the editorial, designing and production team. Their endless efforts to recruit the best for this project, has resulted in the accomplishment of this book. They are a veteran in the field of academics and their pool of knowledge is as vast as their experience in printing. Their expertise and guidance has proved useful at every step. Their uncompromising quality standards have made this book an exceptional effort. Their encouragement from time to time has been an inspiration for everyone.

The publisher and the editorial board hope that this book will prove to be a valuable piece of knowledge for students, practitioners and scholars across the globe.

Index

A

Administer, 56

Advertising Revenue, 103-104

Agility, 19, 63, 69

Arrays, 118-121, 123-124, 190, 192, 214

Artificial Intelligence, 2, 147, 154

B

Bandwidth, 12, 14, 59, 61, 64, 71, 93, 96, 102, 119, 143-144, 187-190

C

C Programming, 190

Cache, 34, 116, 187, 195-196, 198, 205, 210-211, 227

Calculus, 184

Capacitance, 179

Capital Cost, 67

Compiler, 192, 196, 202-203, 210, 226-227

Composition, 52

Conditional Statements, 228

Conjunction, 89, 108, 149

Constant Value, 180

Convergence, 217

Cryptography, 75, 226

D

Data Bus, 225

Data Integrity, 56, 143

Data Structures, 183, 214

Database Management System, 147

Datum, 192

Direct Memory Access, 137

E

E-commerce, 140-143, 147, 154

E-learning, 154

Encoding, 46, 107, 129, 139

Encryption, 73-74, 92-93, 104-106, 128, 141

Error Correction, 193

Etymology, 126

Execution Unit, 188

F

Firewalls, 111-112, 115, 137, 150

Fourier Transform, 193

G

Graphical User Interface, 2

Grid Computing, 19, 39, 150-151, 189-190

H

Hypertext Transfer Protocol, 106

I

Information Systems, 94

Information Technology, 5, 19, 97, 126

Integer, 177, 225

Integrated Circuits, 2, 191

Intellectual Property, 62, 94

Internet Of Things, 87

Internet Protocol, 75, 118, 156-158

Interoperability, 42, 52, 56, 69, 111, 113, 123, 135, 139

Intranet, 148

Intranets, 118

J

Javascript, 45, 116

L

Law Enforcement, 105

Linear Algebra, 191, 193

M

Machine Language, 1-2

Mainframe, 14, 126

Market Analysis, 100

Memory Location, 198-200

Metadata, 47, 94-98, 101, 116

Microprocessor, 2, 179, 188, 229

Multicasting, 169-171, 210

Multimode Fiber, 133

Multiplexing, 29

N
National Security, 94
Natural Language Processing, 2

O
Operating Expenses, 91
Operating Systems, 11, 21, 28, 35, 55, 59-60, 84-85, 87-88, 107, 119-120, 124, 136-138, 147, 150

P
Parallel Processing, 2, 147, 194, 226
Procurement, 51
Proliferation, 14
Public Agencies, 94
Python, 101

R
Redundancy, 12, 58-59, 61, 63, 91, 128, 143-144, 193-194
Return On Investment, 67

S
Semantics, 109, 114-115, 190, 195, 208
Semiconductor, 192
Single-mode Fiber, 132
Social Networking, 3, 48-49
Source Code, 140
Startup Company, 144

Stock Market, 39
Stratosphere, 12
String, 101, 122
Supercomputers, 2-3, 99, 152, 154, 189, 194
Syntax, 45, 111, 114, 155, 158, 190, 192, 222, 225

T
Topology, 127-128, 130
Transmission Control Protocol, 157-158

U
Uniform Resource Identifier, 47

V
Vacuum Tubes, 1-2
Value Proposition, 57
Variables, 182-183, 192, 196, 199-200, 204, 207, 210, 225
Virtual Private Network, 76
Virtualization, 5, 13, 20-27, 30-32, 34-40, 54, 56, 59, 63, 66, 70, 83, 187

W
Web 2.0, 49
Web Application, 113
Web Browser, 81, 103
Web Page, 86
While Loop, 221
World Wide Web, 5, 108, 113, 116, 154

9 781639 891153